The Program Evaluation Standards, 2nd Edition

Dedicated to
RALPH W. TYLER

The Program Evaluation Standards

*How to Assess Evaluations
of Educational Programs*

2nd Edition

THE JOINT COMMITTEE ON STANDARDS
FOR EDUCATIONAL EVALUATION
James R. Sanders, Chair

Sponsored by

American Association of School Administrators
American Educational Research Association
American Evaluation Association
American Federation of Teachers
American Psychological Association
Association for Assessment in Counseling
Association for Supervision and Curriculum Development
Canadian Society for the Study of Education
Council of Chief State School Officers
Council on Postsecondary Accreditation
National Association of Elementary School Principals
National Association of Secondary School Principals
National Council on Measurement in Education
National Education Association
National School Boards Association

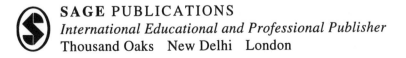

SAGE PUBLICATIONS
International Educational and Professional Publisher
Thousand Oaks   New Delhi   London

For information address:

SAGE Publications, Inc.
2455 Teller Road
Thousand Oaks, California 91320

SAGE Publications Ltd.
6 Bonhill Street
London EC2A 4PU
United Kingdom

SAGE Publications India Pvt. Ltd.
M-32 Market
Greater Kailash I
New Delhi 110 048 India

JCSEE PR-1994
Approved by the American
National Standards Institute as an
American National Standard.
Approval date: March 15, 1994.

Printed in the United States of America

Library of Congress Cataloging-in-Publication Data

Joint Committee on Standards for Educational Evaluation.
    The program evaluations standards: how to assess evaluations of
educational programs / the Joint Committee on Standards for
Educational Evaluation with James R. Sanders, chair.—2nd ed.
        p.   cm.
    "Sponsored by American Association of School Administration [i.e.
Administrators] . . . [et al.]."
    Rev. ed. of: Standards for evaluations of educational programs,
projects, and materials. 1981.
    Includes bibliographical references and index.
    ISBN 0-8039-5731-9 (cloth).—ISBN 0-8039-5732-7 (pbk.)
    1. Educational tests and measurements—United States.
2. Educational evaluations—United States.   I. Sanders, James R.
II. American Association of School Administrators.   III. Joint
Committee on Standards for Educational Evaluation. Standards for
evaluations of educational programs, projects, and materials.
IV. Title.
LB3051.J57   1994
379.1′54—dc20   94-1178

94 95 96 97 98   10 9 8 7 6 5 4 3 2 1

Sage Production Editor: Astrid Virding

❖ Contents ❖

THE STANDARDS

Functional ❖ Table of Contents ❖

Here the standards are reorganized in terms of the major tasks of a program evaluation. This helps the user of the evaluation to see that the Standards can be applied throughout the process of planning, conducting, and reporting the evaluation. It also illustrates that some standards typically are more applicable than others to certain evaluation tasks. However, it would be a mistake to apply only the identified standards for a given task without determining which other ones might also be relevant. All standards should be considered regarding their possible relevance to any given evaluation task.

Deciding Whether to Evaluate

Most relevant standards:

Defining the Evaluation Problem

Most relevant standards:

Designing the Evaluation

Most relevant standards:

Collecting Information

Most relevant standards:

Analyzing Information

Most relevant standards:

Reporting the Evaluation

Most relevant standards:

Budgeting the Evaluation

Most relevant standards:

Contracting for Evaluation

Most relevant standards:

Managing the Evaluation

Most relevant standards:

Staffing the Evaluation

Most relevant standards:

❖ The Joint Committee ❖

Chair

James R. Sanders

Committee Members

Ralph Alexander and Robert Baker, representing the American Psychological Association

Marsha Berger and Beth Bader, representing the American Federation of Teachers

Rolf Blank, representing the Council of Chief State School Officers

Oliver W. Cummings and Constance M. Filling, representing the American Evaluation Association

Esther E. Diamond, representing the Association for Assessment in Counseling

Joy Frechtling, representing the American Educational Research Association

Philip Hosford, representing the Association for Supervision and Curriculum Development

Thomas Houlihan and Henry Johnson, representing the American Association of School Administrators

Edgar A. Kelley and W. Eugene Werner, representing the National Association of Secondary School Principals

William Mays, Jr., representing the National Association of Elementary School Principals

Diana Pullin, an at-large member

Rodney Riffel, Sheila Simmons, and Gerald Bracey, representing the National Education Association

W. Todd Rogers, representing the Canadian Society for the Study of Education

Daniel L. Stufflebeam, an at-large member

Bruce Thompson and Ross E. Traub, representing the National Council on Measurement in Education

Jeffrey W. Wadelin and Thurston E. Manning, representing the Council on Postsecondary Accreditation

Barbara M. Wheeler, representing the National School Boards Association

❖ Acknowledgments ❖

Several organizations and many people contributed to the publication of the 1994 *Program Evaluation Standards* and its predecessor, the 1981 *Standards for Evaluations of Educational Programs, Projects, and Materials*. Financial and in-kind support for the 1994 volume was provided by the Sponsoring Organizations of the Joint Committee, the W. K. Kellogg Foundation, and the Western Michigan University Evaluation Center. Support for the 1981 volume was provided by the Sponsoring Organizations of the Joint Committee, The Evaluation Center, and grants from the Lilly Endowment, the National Institute of Education, the National Science Foundation, and the Weyerhaeuser Company Foundation. Individuals who contributed to the development of the 1981 and 1994 Standards are identified in the lists of support groups in the Appendix. It should be clear, however, that the Joint Committee on Standards for Educational Evaluation is solely responsible for the contents of this book.

The members of the Joint Committee and the various support groups are a powerful force for improving the practice of educational program evaluation and consequently improving educational practice. The Joint Committee owes a debt of gratitude to those who contributed to this work.

Royalties from the sales of this book will be used to promote effective use of the *Standards* and to support ongoing review and revision activities.

❖ Invitation to Users ❖

The Program Evaluation Standards is the result of a pioneer project started in 1975. The goal was to develop standards to help ensure useful, feasible, ethical, and sound evaluation of educational programs, projects, and materials. These standards must be used, reviewed, and improved in many fields as part of a continuing effort of many persons committed to advancing the practice of evaluation. We encourage those who use the *Standards* in many fields or settings to share their experiences in using the *Standards* with the Joint Committee. To help in this process, the committee has prepared a package of information consisting of a letter of acknowledgment, information about the review and update process, and a supply of feedback forms with directions for their use. This package may be ordered from the Joint Committee. Forms in the package request that the user

(a) describe roles and responsibilities—for example, those of the evaluator, client, and other audiences—that existed during the evaluation being reported;

(b) provide a summary of the evaluation, including an application of the standards;

(c) provide copies of reports from the evaluation;

(d) describe problems that arose in applying individual standards;

(e) describe conflicts found among the *Standards* and how they were resolved;

(f) describe flaws found in the *Standards* and suggest improvements or refinements; and

(g) identify important areas that should be, but are not, covered by the *Standards*.

The Joint Committee has also developed a citation form provided in the Introduction. Users of the *Standards* may wish to complete and attach it to evaluation RFPs, designs, contracts, reports, and the like to which the *Standards* were applied.

Address all inquiries to

> The Joint Committee on Standards for Educational Evaluation
> The Evaluation Center
> Western Michigan University
> Kalamazoo, Michigan 49008-5178

❖ Preface ❖

In 1974 a committee appointed by the American Educational Research Association, the American Psychological Association, and the National Council on Measurement in Education completed a revision of the 1966 edition of the *Standards for Educational and Psychological Tests and Manuals* published by the American Psychological Association. An issue of some importance at the time was the use of tests in evaluating educational programs. After considerable debate, the committee decided that including a section on evaluation in the *Test Standards* was not within the scope of its revision task, and it recommended that a new committee be created to address this topic. The three organizations accepted this recommendation and formed a new committee composed of three members from each organization. The committee met for the first time in spring 1975 and recommended to their organizations that they launch a project to develop standards, not only for using tests in evaluation but for educational evaluation generally. The three organizations accepted this recommendation. In addition, the new committee voted to expand its membership to include other organizations concerned with the quality of evaluation in education. Eventually, 12 organizations appointed members to the new Joint Committee on Standards for Educational Evaluation. The Joint Committee began its work in fall 1975.

It was not clear in the beginning that the effort to develop standards for educational evaluation would be successful. The 12 sponsoring organizations had not had a history of working together, and there were serious and fundamental differences in the points of view of committee members. For example, one member advocated banning the use of standardized tests, while others advocated their use. There were serious disagreements about topics that should be addressed by the new standards. Questions about whether institution or personnel evaluation should be included were debated, for example.

The Joint Committee worked together to resolve the issues that confronted it and decided to limit its initial effort to evaluations of educational programs, projects, and materials. This resulted in publication of *Standards for Evaluations of Educational Programs, Projects, and Materials* (McGraw-Hill, 1981). Evaluation of institutions was not included, given the work of accreditation agencies. Personnel evaluation was put aside for later, so as not to take on too much and because of concern over the potential political consequences of a fledgling committee tackling this emotion-laden topic. Subsequently, the Joint Committee published *The Personnel Evaluation Standards* (Sage, 1988).

The Joint Committee developed a systematic public process for establishing and testing the new standards before recommending their use. This process is described in the *Operating Procedures of the Joint Committee on Standards for Educational Evaluation*, which is available from The Evaluation Center at Western Michigan University. The process involves many experts in evaluation, users of evaluation, and others who are concerned about the quality of evaluation in education. These people are involved in a public standard-setting process as members of a Panel of Writers, Review Panels, Field Test sites, Public Hearings, a Validation Panel, the Joint Committee, and interested critics. Several hundred educators, social scientists, and lay citizens were involved in the development of the first program evaluation standards and also the personnel evaluation standards.

In 1981 the Joint Committee was incorporated as a continuing nonprofit organization dedicated to the development of evaluation standards, periodic review and revision of the standards, support and promotion of the use of the standards, and research and development related to the standards. In 1989 the Joint Committee's process for developing standards was accredited by the American National Standards Institute (ANSI). Standards approved by ANSI become American National standards, and as such become available worldwide.

In 1989 the Joint Committee decided the time had come to examine the *Standards for Evaluations of Educational Programs, Projects, and Materials*. This decision was based on a growing interest by evaluators in fields beyond school settings in applying the standards to program evaluations in their own fields. Further, the 1981 *Standards* did not include new developments in evaluation that had been introduced since the *Standards* were first published.

It was decided that the principles of the 1981 work could be applied to a new work broader in scope. The new *Program Evaluation Standards* is the result of an extensive review process. Original standards have been combined and others added. And, importantly, new illustrations featuring applications of the standards to education and training efforts in settings that include schools, universities, law, medicine, nursing, the military, business, government, and social service agencies have been added. A Validation

Panel whose composition reflected these expanded audiences was appointed to oversee the development of this document.

Taken as a set, the 30 standards provide a working philosophy for evaluation. They define the Joint Committee's conception of the principles that should guide and govern program evaluation efforts, and they offer practical suggestions for observing these principles.

The Joint Committee urges all who are involved in program evaluation to apply the standards, completely and diligently. Users are further encouraged to become involved in the refinement of these standards by assessing and reporting on the adequacy of the standards when they are applied in their own program evaluations or in training new evaluators.

The Standards are an effort to provide guidance to effective evaluation. The Standards alone cannot guarantee or ensure the quality of any evaluation. Sound evaluation will require the exercise of professional judgment in order to adequately apply the Standards to a particular evaluation setting. The Standards are intended to reflect best practice at the time the Standards were written. The Joint Committee recognizes that, as professional practice changes and the professional knowledge base concerning evaluation develops over time, the Standards themselves will need to be revised to address those new developments. However, the Joint Committee is confident that the Standards will continue to lead to useful, feasible, ethical, and sound program evaluations, and that these evaluations will, in turn, contribute significantly to the betterment of education in diverse settings.

❖ Introduction ❖

Education and training programs are evaluated in order to determine their quality and gain direction for improving them. In the absence of any clear definition of what constitutes a reasonable evaluation of educational programs, the Joint Committee compiled knowledge about program evaluation gained from professional literature and from years of experience by educators and evaluation specialists. This knowledge is organized and presented in this book as standards for the practice of educational program evaluation.

The Standards provide a guide for evaluating educational and training programs, projects, and materials in a variety of settings. They are intended both for users of evaluations and for evaluators. People who commission or conduct evaluations, or who use evaluation results to improve education and training in schools, universities, medical and health care fields, the military, business and industry, the government, and law, will find the Standards useful. They have been developed for use by teachers, administrators, school board members, trainers, evaluators, curriculum specialists, legislators, personnel administrators, counselors, community leaders, business and educational associations, parents, and others. The Standards guide the design, employment, and assessment of evaluations of educational programs, projects, and materials. Past experience indicates that other groups may find different uses for the Standards. The Joint Committee encourages innovative applications of the Standards, such as in teaching others about evaluation, and would appreciate learning about such applications as a part of its ongoing work.

Although some specialized terms have been used, attempts have been made to keep technical language to a minimum. Those terms most important to understanding the standards are defined in the introduction and in the text. In addition, a glossary of terms is provided.

1

A standard is a principle mutually agreed to by people engaged in a professional practice, that, if met, will enhance the quality and fairness of that professional practice, for example, evaluation.

This book contains a set of standards that speak to the responsible conduct and use of educational program, project, and materials evaluations. These Standards do not apply to the evaluation of professional personnel or individuals. For more information regarding personnel evaluations, the reader is encouraged to refer to *The Personnel Evaluation Standards* (1988). The Standards are not detailed technical standards, and they do not replace textbooks in technical areas such as qualitative and quantitative research design and analysis, measurement and data collection, data processing, and report writing. For example, when addressing the validity of inferences in an evaluation, the related standard states the principle that the instruments and procedures used should allow for valid interpretations, and it provides general guidelines for determining the validity of inferences. However, it does not present detailed validation procedures. Taken together, the Standards provide a framework for designing and assessing evaluations. The book thus complements textbooks, manuals, and handbooks concerned with evaluation instruments and methods.

The 30 standards are categorized into four groups corresponding to four attributes of sound and fair program evaluation—utility, feasibility, propriety, and accuracy. The 30 standards are listed on the inside front and back covers of this book. In the text that follows, each standard is accompanied by an overview of intent, guidelines for application, common errors, and one or more illustrations of the standard's application. As noted earlier, these illustrations come from a variety of educational settings.

Two Tables of Contents are presented at the beginning of this book. In the first, the standards are organized in terms of the four attributes listed above. The second, a Functional Table of Contents, contains the standards organized in terms of their contribution to major tasks of a program evaluation: deciding whether to evaluate, defining the evaluation problem, designing the evaluation, collecting information, analyzing information, reporting the evaluation, budgeting the evaluation, contracting for evaluation, managing the evaluation, and staffing the evaluation.

The Joint Committee acknowledges that standards are not all equally applicable in all evaluations. Professional judgment must be used to identify those that are most applicable in each situation. Users of the Standards should carefully consider the relevance of each standard in the particular context and then decide which ones should be accorded most importance. These decisions should be documented for later reference.

The remainder of this introduction addresses several topics that are important to understanding the content and use of the Standards:

1. Definitions
2. Domain of the Standards

3. Intended Audiences
4. Organization and Substance of the Standards
5. Format

Definitions

To guide the development of the standards, the Joint Committee defined certain key concepts. Because of their importance, these definitions are highlighted in the following box.

Evaluation: The systematic investigation of the worth or merit of an object. For the purpose of conciseness, in this book the term *program* will be used generically to refer to the object of evaluation. Objects covered by these standards include educational and training programs, projects, and materials. A metaevaluation is an evaluation of an evaluation.

Program: Educational activities that are provided on a continuing basis. Examples include a school district's reading program, a military or industrial training program, a medical education program, or a professional continuing education program.

Project: Educational activities that are provided for a defined period of time. Examples include a three-day workshop on instructional strategies, a two-year test development effort, or a three-year human resources development demonstration project. Projects that become institutionalized become programs.

Materials: Content-related educational materials, including books, program guides, software, hardware, films, tapes, and other tangible instructional and training products.

Evaluation standard: A principle mutually agreed to by people engaged in the professional practice of evaluation, that, if met, will enhance the quality and fairness of an evaluation.

Evaluator: Used broadly in this book to refer to anyone who conducts an evaluation.

Information: Numerical and nonnumerical presentations—including facts, narratives, graphs, pictures, maps, displays, statistics, and oral reports—that help illuminate issues, answer questions, and increase knowledge and understanding of a program or other object.

Client: The individual, group, or organization that commissions the evaluator(s), that is, the evaluation contractor.

Stakeholder: Individuals or groups that may be involved in or affected by a program evaluation.

Domain of the Standards

The Standards in this book are intended to guide the design, employment, and critique of evaluations of educational programs, projects, and materials. While the Standards present advice on how to judge the adequacy of evaluation activities, they do not present specific criteria for such judgments. The Standards are intended to stimulate and facilitate thoughtful dialogue among clients, evaluators, and other stakeholders, and, where the evaluation is conducted by an evaluation team, reflection within the team itself. In general, evaluators are advised to gather information that is (a) relevant to the questions posed by clients and other audiences and (b) sufficient for judging the effectiveness, costs, responsiveness to societal needs, feasibility, and worth of the program being evaluated.

In addition, the standards encourage the use of a variety of evaluation methods. These methods include, for example, surveys of various reference groups, archival searches, observation of educational and training practices, organizational profiles, case studies, advocacy teams to generate and assess competing plans, adversary and advocacy teams to expose the strengths and weaknesses of projects, assessment programs, simulation studies, time series studies, checklists, the delphi technique, focus group interviews, goal-free evaluation, secondary data analysis, and experimental and quasi-experimental designs.

The Standards also help evaluators identify and confront political reality. Political agendas and money are sources of power that may corrupt evaluation in any setting. Adherence to the Standards will help minimize the chances that evaluators or their clients will misuse their power.

Intended Audiences

As noted earlier, the Standards are for people who commission evaluations, conduct evaluations, and/or who use the results of evaluations. The Joint Committee holds the view that good evaluations require the involvement of many people with different perspectives. The Joint Committee believes that any particular evaluation task should not automatically or permanently be assigned to a person solely because that individual occupies a particular position in an organization or in society. It also believes that special tasks should be assigned to particular persons from time to time as an evaluation proceeds, and that these assignments will differ from place to place and from circumstance to circumstance. Each of these individuals should, of course, have the training and experience required to carry out the given tasks.

The Standards are intended to help people judge or comment on plans for evaluations, decide whether to conduct an evaluation, judge external agencies' bids to evaluate particular programs, decide whether to accept the findings and recommendations of evaluation reports, design and conduct their own evaluations, and play support roles in the evaluation process.

The Standards are intended to assist legislators and funding agencies to plan the evaluations of legislative programs, write requests for evaluation proposals, judge competing evaluation designs, and assess evaluation reports. They are intended to help directors of testing, researchers, and evaluators in diverse settings to assess the adequacy of their evaluation designs and reports and to make informed decisions about what improvements are needed in evaluation methodology. They are also intended to help evaluators, university professors, and staff developers provide training in the design, conduct, and assessment of evaluation. These examples are not exhaustive; they are presented to illustrate the range of individuals who will find the Standards useful.

Organization and Substance of the Standards

The Standards are organized around the four important attributes of an evaluation: *utility, feasibility, propriety,* and *accuracy.* The Joint Committee believes that these four attributes are necessary and sufficient for sound and fair evaluation.

Each standard helps define one of the four attributes. Experience has revealed, however, that a standard may be relevant to more than one attribute. For purposes of organization of this book, each standard is placed in the group that reflects its principal emphasis.

Utility Standards

Utility standards guide evaluations so that they will be informative, timely, and influential. They require evaluators to acquaint themselves with their audiences, define the audiences clearly, ascertain the audiences' information needs, plan evaluations to respond to these needs, and report the relevant information clearly and in a timely fashion.

The standards included in this category are Stakeholder Identification, Evaluator Credibility, Information Scope and Selection, Values Identification, Report Clarity, Report Timeliness and Dissemination, and Evaluation Impact. Overall, the utility standards define whether an evaluation serves the practical information needs of a given audience.

Feasibility Standards

Feasibility standards recognize that evaluations usually are conducted in a natural, as opposed to a laboratory, setting and consume valuable resources. Therefore evaluation designs must be operable in field settings, and evaluations must not consume more resources, materials, personnel, or time than necessary to address the evaluation questions.

The three standards in this category are Practical Procedures, Political Viability, and Cost Effectiveness. Taken together, the feasibility standards call for evaluations to be realistic, prudent, diplomatic, and economical.

Propriety Standards

Propriety standards reflect the fact that evaluations affect many people in a variety of ways. These standards are intended to facilitate protection of the rights of individuals affected by an evaluation. They promote sensitivity to and warn against unlawful, unscrupulous, unethical, and inept actions by those who conduct evaluations.

These standards require that individuals conducting evaluations learn about and obey laws concerning such matters as privacy, freedom of information, and the protection of human subjects. They charge those who conduct evaluations to respect the rights of others.

The eight standards in this category are Service Orientation, Formal Agreements, Rights of Human Subjects, Human Interactions, Complete and Fair Assessment, Disclosure of Findings, Conflict of Interest, and Fiscal Responsibility.

Accuracy Standards

Accuracy standards determine whether an evaluation has produced sound information. The evaluation of a program must be comprehensive; that is, the evaluators should have considered as many of the program's identifiable features as practical and should have gathered data on those particular features judged important for assessing the program's worth or merit. Moreover, the information must be technically adequate, and the judgments rendered must be linked logically to the data.

The 12 accuracy standards are Program Documentation, Context Analysis, Described Purposes and Procedures, Defensible Information Sources, Valid Information, Reliable Information, Systematic Information, Analysis of Quantitative Information, Analysis of Qualitative Information, Justified Conclusions, Impartial Reporting, and Metaevaluation. These standards are intended to ensure that an evaluation will reveal and convey accurate information about the program's merit and/or worth.

Format

The standards are presented in a uniform format to facilitate reading and to illuminate their interrelationships. The following format is used for each standard:

Descriptor: A descriptive title of the standard, for example, Context Analysis.

Standard: Presentation of the standard in the form of a "should" statement: For example, the Context Analysis standard (A2) is stated as follows: "The context in which the program exists should be examined in enough detail, so that its likely influences on the program can be identified."

Overview: A conceptual/introductory statement that gives definitions of key terms in the standard and a general rationale for its use.

Guidelines: A list of procedural suggestions intended to help evaluators and stakeholders meet the requirements of the standard: These guidelines are strategies for avoiding mistakes in applying the standard. The guidelines should not be considered exhaustive or mandatory; rather, they are procedures to consider and to follow when the evaluator judges them to be potentially helpful and feasible.

Common Errors: A list of difficulties that are associated with the standard: These difficulties include mistakes often made by evaluators who are inexperienced or unaware of the importance and intent of the standard, and mistakes that derive from overzealous applications of the standard.

Illustrative Case: One or two illustrations of how the standard might be applied, including the description of a setting, a situation in which the standard is or is not met, and a discussion of corrective actions, if needed, that should lead to the standard being met: The corrective actions that are discussed are only illustrative and are not intended to encompass all possible corrections. Most illustrative cases are based on actual evaluations.

❖ Applying the Standards ❖

The standards are guiding principles, not mechanical rules. They contain cautions and warnings against potential mistakes, identify practices generally agreed to be acceptable or unacceptable, and propose guidelines reflecting current best practice.

Regardless of the nature of the evaluation being conducted, those concerned with evaluation should reflect carefully on the Standards and how they apply to specific situations, especially the following key tasks in evaluation work:

1. Deciding whether to evaluate
2. Defining the evaluation problem
3. Designing the evaluation
4. Collecting information
5. Analyzing information
6. Reporting the evaluation
7. Budgeting the evaluation
8. Contracting for evaluation
9. Managing the evaluation
10. Staffing the evaluation
11. Developing evaluation policies

In addition, the Standards can be used to design a program for training evaluators. As a set, the Standards facilitate discussion about the following:

What is the purpose of the evaluation?

Is there an appropriate written agreement for the evaluation?

Is the program to be evaluated clearly identified?

How should one go about designing the program evaluation?

Are the criteria for judging the program's merit and worth clearly defined?

Is the program evaluation well designed?

Is the program evaluation adequately staffed?

How can the program evaluation design or process be improved?

How complete and defensible are the results of the program evaluation?

What are the strengths and weaknesses of the program evaluation's final report?

Did the evaluator adequately assist the stakeholders to use the findings?

What resulted from the program evaluation?

The applicability and/or importance of a standard on any one of the 11 key tasks varies depending upon the nature of the evaluation. For example, the standard that calls for a formal agreement to guide the evaluation applies more to large-scale, formal, summative evaluations and less to small-scale, internal, formative evaluations. In the former, a formal contract is often required; in the latter, a memorandum of agreement usually is sufficient. Nevertheless, to some degree this standard and all the others should be considered in all situations.

The relative importance of individual standards will differ from situation to situation. Often, increasing attempts to address one standard will detract from attempts to address others. For example, efforts to produce valid and reliable results may make it difficult to produce reports in time to influence crucial decisions. Or, the attempt to keep an evaluation within cost limits may conflict directly with meeting such standards as U3, Information Scope and Selection, and U6, Report Timeliness and Dissemination. Evaluators should recognize the need for trade-offs at times and deal with them as judiciously as possible. However, the Joint Committee believes that the propriety standards should be met under any circumstance.

In the end, whether a given standard has been addressed adequately in a particular situation is a matter of judgment. Precise decision rules regarding the satisfaction of a standard cannot be specified. Such rules would be arbitrary and not universally applicable; they would likely delude and mislead. Nevertheless, evaluators who cite the Standards should describe clearly how they used them, what judgments about addressing these Standards they made, and the evidence they used to support their judgments.

If an evaluation violates any standard judged to be important in a given situation, the evaluators should identify the standards not met and indicate why. Inability to address a standard adequately may not be just cause by itself to terminate an evaluation. However, if the violations seem likely to impair the evaluation on any of the four attributes of utility, feasibility, propriety, or accuracy, the evaluators should consider making necessary changes or consider terminating the evaluation.

In some cases, the best method for addressing a standard may require increased time and resources; in others, the most effective procedure may not be expensive. In the long run, the Joint Committee believes the decision to do only quality evaluations—even if this sometimes requires more resources—will be found cost beneficial by all who have a stake in the evaluations.

Last, the Standards must not stifle the creativity of evaluators or impede the development of innovative approaches to evaluation. The Standards should be used as a guide for assessing evaluation plans and reports, and not as a restrictive set of rules. They should be used as a means for exchanging information about the quality of an evaluation between evaluators, their clients, and other stakeholders. Further, use of the Standards should identify needed improvements in evaluation methodology.

The role of evaluation changes as programs evolve. In the early stages of program development, and through much of the developmental process, evaluation is interactive and improvement oriented, or formative. At the end of development, summative evaluation is often conducted by outside parties, and recommendations are made public as to whether to expand, alter, or drop the program.

A set of general steps may be followed in applying the Standards. These steps are as follows:

Step 1—Become acquainted with *The Program Evaluation Standards*.

Step 2—Clarify the purposes of the program evaluation.

Step 3—Clarify the context of the program evaluation.

Step 4—Apply each standard in light of the purposes and context (e.g., What should be done? What was done? What are strengths and weaknesses of the program evaluation?).

Step 5—Decide what to do with the results.

What is involved in implementing each of these steps is discussed below:

Step 1. Become Acquainted With The Program Evaluation Standards

The standards are presented in nontechnical language, in a common format for easy use, and illustrated with examples to show how they can be applied. It is important to read through the entire set of standards and then to discuss, where possible, the Standards with others in a workshop or small group setting. With practice, you will be able to regularly reference *The Program Evaluation Standards* as a manual for designing, improving, and assessing program evaluations.

Step 2. Clarify the Purposes of the Program Evaluation

There are many decisions that can be addressed by a program evaluation. What are the priority needs of the targeted program participants? What are the best approaches to address participant needs? Which components of the program should be kept or modified? Should all participants receive the same program? What, if any, follow-up activities should be pursued following the program? Should the program be disseminated?

It is important to be clear about the reasons(s) a program is being evaluated so that the purposes can be fulfilled. If there is no good reason for the evaluation, the whole process should be terminated before too much effort is wasted.

Step 3. Clarify the Context of the Program Evaluation

If one is *designing* a program evaluation, the following questions should be considered:

— Who wants it? Why? What will they do with the results? When do they need the results? How much has been budgeted for the evaluation?
— What is the program to be evaluated?
— What resources other than budget are available?
— What are the potential political issues?

Step 4. Apply Each Standard
in Consideration of the Purposes and Context

The standards can be applied, one by one, to guide the design of the program evaluation. Alternatively, the Functional Table of Contents may help in selecting the standards that are most critical in designing a particular component or activity within a program evaluation.

If one is *implementing* a program evaluation, the same questions listed above are pertinent but one would also want to ask questions driven by the evaluation design:

— Is the evaluation on schedule? Within budget?
— What flaws are turning up in the evaluation plan?
— Should we rethink the plan?
— Are there interim findings that should be reported?

Again, the standards can be applied, one by one, or the Functional Table of Contents may be used to evaluate the implementation of the evaluation. Is it going well? Are any midcourse corrections needed?

If the *evaluation has been completed* and a report is available, the evaluator will want to know what was done in the evaluation and what came out of it, as well as the evaluation's impact. Most of the time, information beyond the evaluation report itself will be needed to assess the entire program evaluation. Interviews with participants and recipients of the evaluation, for example, may be needed to supplement what is found in an evaluation report. Once again, the Standards can then be applied to assess the program evaluation. Is it believable? Can it be used as is? Is more information needed before the evaluation can be assessed fairly?

A form to facilitate application of standards to a program evaluation is provided later in this section. Following application of the standards, this form can be used to record decisions about how effectively standards are addressed by the evaluation design, by an ongoing program evaluation, or by a completed program evaluation by placing check marks in the appropriate columns.

Once the summary sheet is completed, one can list the strengths and weaknesses of the program evaluation. If more than one person applies the standards, agreements and disagreements about their findings can be discussed until an agreement is reached for each standard. Then the consensus judgments about the program evaluation can be summarized.

Step 5. Decide What to Do With the Results

Finally, one will want to discuss the results with the program staff, program evaluator, or others. Critical issues can be identified, recommendations for improving the evaluation can be made, plans for collecting further information can be formulated, or ways to enhance the evaluation capacity of an organization can be discussed. On this latter point, for example, a key issue might be inadequately trained evaluators or inadequate resources for evaluation. Recommendations to address these issues could strengthen the organization in which program evaluations are being conducted.

A Case Study Application

To facilitate an understanding of these Standards and to explain their applicability in a practical setting, a case study is presented here. The case sets forth the description of a typical situation confronting an evaluator. It is provided to illustrate the appropriate sequence of steps to follow in clarifying the purpose and describing, applying, and implementing the results of the evaluation. A discussion of the application of the Standards to the evaluation is then provided. As is the case in many evaluations, some of the standards are not applicable to the situation; these issues of applicability are also discussed in an effort to explain how professional judgment should be exercised in applying the Standards.

The Case

An external evaluation consultant was asked to evaluate the way in which professional development workshops, offered by a certain national organization, were being evaluated. The purpose of the metaevaluation was to identify strengths and deficiencies of the evaluation process used by the organization.

The consultant had studied and used *The Program Evaluation Standards* as part of her graduate training and was very familiar with their content and applicability to the task at hand.

Clarifying the Purpose of the Evaluation

The consultant asked the following questions and received the answers that are provided here.

Who wants this evaluation done? The workshop evaluator and the organization's executive director want the evaluation done so that they can verify the findings of the workshop evaluations. They are concerned that the evaluations may be missing some critical aspects of the workshops even though satisfaction data tend to be very favorable.

How soon do they need the evaluation? Within the next six months so that they can make changes for the next fiscal year.

How much has been budgeted for the evaluation? No more than $2,500.

Description of the Intended Evaluation Activities

From interviews with the workshop evaluator and executive director, the consultant was able to determine that the workshop evaluations included the following:

— feedback from a workshop program advisory committee
— workshop participant evaluations completed at each workshop

The consultant decided that, given budget and time constraints, the best approach to conducting the evaluation of the workshop program evaluation would be to list questions to be answered and to rely on document review (evaluation plans and reports) and interviews with program staff and a random sample of workshop participants as her main sources of information.

The questions to be addressed are listed as follows:

— What are the strengths and weaknesses of the workshop evaluations?
— What recommendations can be made based on the available evidence?

The consultant collected evaluation reports from the past two years and familiarized herself with each document. She also made appointments for one-hour interviews with the workshop evaluator and the executive director of the professional organization to get their views on the strengths and weaknesses of the workshop evaluations. She also asked how they used the evaluation results, and, given their situation, whether they would do things differently if they could redesign the evaluation. Last, she interviewed a 10% random sample of workshop participants to determine their perception of the workshop evaluations, particularly with respect to completeness. Then, armed with this information, she applied the Standards to what she knew about the evaluation processes that had been used.

Applying the Standards

The Program Evaluation Standards fall into four categories, reflecting four characteristics of good program evaluation. The consultant summarized her findings for each category as follows after considering the evidence related to each individual standard. She used the checklist at the end of this section to organize her analysis.

Utility Standards

She discovered from her interviews that staff members and participants who had a vested interest in the criteria used to judge the workshops had not been contacted for their views about the questions to be answered by the workshop evaluations. Consequently, they were left wondering why certain questions important to them were not being addressed. For example, there was no attempt to look at how workshop participants used the information, materials, and skills they acquired at the workshop. There was no workshop follow-up. This was a major flaw in the evaluation design due to not meeting the Stakeholder Identification Standard (U1).

The workshop evaluator had appropriate credentials for the evaluation assignment and was believed to be fair and competent by staff and administration of the organization. In these respects, the Evaluator Credibility Standard (U2) was addressed. However, the mistakes made in the evaluation detracted from the evaluator's credibility.

Due to the oversight of not addressing the needs of all audiences (U1), the Information Scope and Selection Standard (U3) was also not completely addressed. Follow-up information was important and missing from the evaluation reports. Otherwise, the scope of the evaluation appeared to address the major questions: Were needs met? Were participants satisfied? Were facilities adequate?

The Values Identification Standard (U4) was not met because the basis for judging the adequacy of workshops was not explicit. From the feedback provided by the workshop evaluator, it was often hard to see where judgments were coming from.

She found the evaluation reports to be clear (U5) and disseminated to the right audiences (U6). The workshop staff and the organization's administration were fully informed. Given that much of the feedback of the evaluations was positive, few changes had taken place in the workshop format and content over the past year. If follow-up data had been collected, perhaps the evaluations would have led to changes (U7).

Overall, this evaluation evidenced serious deficiencies pertaining to the Utility Standards. Some ideas about changing the scope of the evaluation did come from the analysis.

Feasibility Standards

The workshop evaluation procedures involved a simple feedback questionnaire given to participants as well as feedback from the program advisory committee. The evaluator also looked at workshop budgets and facilities. Short reports were written for each workshop. This evaluation process met standard (F1), Practical Procedures.

The Political Viability Standard (F2) was not met, in part because staff and participants had not been consulted when designing the evaluation. It would be easy to undermine the evaluation by asking, "Why were we not involved in the planning?" There is some vulnerability.

The Cost Effectiveness Standard (F3) was met in one sense because of the frugal procedures of the evaluation. For little cost, the organization received some useful information about how well the workshops were received. However, cost effectiveness would be improved if more attention was paid and investment made in consulting and addressing the information needs of all the stakeholders, as described above.

Propriety Standards

The Service Orientation Standard (P1) was not met because of the evaluator's failure to trace workshop effects to actual use or performance by participants. How would anyone know if participants benefited from the workshop?

There was no record of a formal agreement (P2) for the workshop evaluations. Probably a contract was not needed, but a memo of understanding in which the evaluator described what would be done was needed. The administrator/client could then have signed off or asked for changes. This is an important means for communication and should not have been overlooked.

Rights of Human Subjects (P3) was not an issue in this evaluation because there was no known threat to respondents. Data were presented in aggregate form only. Human Interactions (P4) were not a problem in that the evaluator was very personable to the staff.

Reports were sent to the workshop directors with a copy to the organization's executive director. Complete and Fair Assessment (P5) and Disclosure of Findings (P6) were not questioned by those who read the evaluator's reports. In an interview with the workshop evaluator, the consultant asked him whether there was any time when findings were masked or withheld. The answer was no. Both standards (P5) and (P6) appeared to have been met.

Conflict of Interest (P7) was not an issue in the workshop evaluations. The evaluator was not dependent on showing positive outcomes to keep his job, and he had no apparent vested interest in the results.

The standard on Fiscal Responsibility (P8) was not met because the evaluator failed to develop a budget and keep an accounting record for the workshop evaluations. Because the evaluations constituted a major expenditure of his time, accurate accounting was needed. This management practice is one that will need to be added.

Accuracy Standards

The consultant noted that each evaluation report had a short description of the workshop process, its content, and characteristics of the participants. She concluded that Standard A1, Program Documentation, was met in each instance. The Context Analysis Standard (A2) was not addressed in the workshop evaluation reports, although the evaluator said that he would have reported any unusual factors that appeared to affect the outcomes of a workshop. The consultant concluded that reporting such observations as appropriate would sufficiently meet the standard.

No evaluation reports described the evaluation procedure. When questioned about it, workshop staff and the organization's executive director said they knew what was done and did not feel a need for an evaluation procedures section in each report. The consultant concluded that the standard on Described Purposes and Procedures (A3) was not deemed applicable because the procedures were known, straightforward, and self-evident. "A rare case indeed," she thought.

For the questions that were addressed in the workshop evaluations, the participants and direct observations were appropriate sources of information. However, the advisory committee did not have one person on it who had experienced a workshop. At least one person from the advisory committee could have attended each workshop. Even having each committee member take part in at least one workshop would have been acceptable. But, when committee members have no workshop experience, the consultant concluded that they were not well enough informed. Therefore Standard A4, Defensible Information Sources, was only partially met.

Both of the Standards, Valid Information (A5) and Reliable Information (A6), were not explicitly addressed in any evaluation document. When asked about the validity and reliability of what was said in the reports, the evaluator was at a loss in responding. "Since I used questionnaires, observations, and interviews, do you mean I need to worry about validity and reliability?" he asked. The answer, of course, was yes. Validity of statements in the report could be shown by comparing the list of evaluation questions to data collected in the evaluation. Comprehensive coverage is one type of evidence about the validity of reports. Confirmation of reported findings by asking some participants to read and confirm reports is another type of validity evidence. Reliability evidence could be provided by comparing findings coming from different methods of data collection. Consistency of results would lead the reader to be more certain about the information that was reported. The consultant concluded that validity and reliability of findings were too important not to address, even if the evaluator only did so in a memo to the file or to the executive director.

Standards A7, A8, A9, and A11 were judged to be adequately addressed. Data processing was tightly controlled and routine. Appropriate data analysis procedures were used in each step of the evaluation and there was no evidence of bias in the way data were collected, analyzed, or reported.

While the reported conclusions were accompanied by the evidence used to draw the conclusions, one has to doubt the conclusions due to the failure to address the full range of relevant questions with valid and reliable information. The evaluator thus did not meet the Justified Conclusions Standard (A10).

Finally, the consultant concluded that the Metaevaluation Standard (A12) was being addressed through her assessment of the workshop evaluations. She felt that any evaluation that would affect an organization's practices should have this kind of review.

Using the Results

The consultant's conclusion was that the workshop program evaluation had some strengths but also that important changes needed to be recommended. The changes to be made included the following:

— Follow-up of participants is needed.
— The criteria for judging the workshops need to be made explicit.
— Staff and a representative sample of participants should review the evaluation process to be sure their questions are being addressed.
— The evaluator needs to prepare a memorandum of understanding to the executive director of the organization, in which the evaluation process and budget management plan are described.
— Evidence of validity and reliability of information is needed.
— Each advisory committee member should attend at least one workshop per year.

These recommendations, according to the consultant, were essential to increasing the quality and effectiveness of the workshop evaluations.

Our Charge to the Users of These Standards

Taken as a whole, the 30 standards provide a proposed working philosophy of evaluation. They define contemporary ideas of what principles

Checklist for Applying the Standards*

To interpret the information provided on this form, the reader needs to refer to the full text of the Standards as they appear in Joint Committee on Standards for Educational Evaluation, *The Program Evaluation Standards*.

The Standards were consulted and used as indicated in the table below (check as appropriate):

	The standard was addressed	*The standard was partially addressed*	*The standard was not addressed*	*The standard was not applicable*
U1 Stakeholder Identification				
U2 Evaluator Credibility				
U3 Information Scope and Selection				
U4 Values Identification				
U5 Report Clarity				
U6 Report Timeliness and Dissemination				
U7 Evaluation Impact				
F1 Practical Procedures				
F2 Political Viability				
F3 Cost Effectiveness				
P1 Service Orientation				
P2 Formal Agreements				
P3 Rights of Human Subjects				
P4 Human Interactions				

	The standard was addressed	The standard was partially addressed	The standard was not addressed	The standard was not applicable
P5 Complete and Fair Assessment				
P6 Disclosure of Findings				
P7 Conflict of Interest				
P8 Fiscal Responsibility				
A1 Program Documentation				
A2 Context Analysis				
A3 Described Purposes and Procedures				
A4 Defensible Information Sources				
A5 Valid Information				
A6 Reliable Information				
A7 Systematic Information				
A8 Analysis of Quantitative Information				
A9 Analysis of Qualitative Information				
A10 Justified Conclusions				
A11 Impartial Reporting				
A12 Metaevaluation				

*The publisher gives permission to photocopy this form.

should guide and govern evaluation efforts, and they offer practical suggestions for observing these principles.

The Joint Committee urges all who are involved with evaluation to begin applying the Standards in a conscientious and thoughtful manner. The Joint Committee further encourages users of the Standards to assess and report on the adequacy of the Standards and to involve themselves in improving them. Under these conditions, the committee is confident that the Standards will lead to sound, useful, ethical, and cost-effective evaluation that will contribute significantly to the improvement of educational programs in diverse settings.

It should be noted that in many evaluations systematic application and documentation of all of the standards may not be feasible. The Joint Committee has developed a checklist to assist in applying these standards. Shown below, the checklist provides a range of options for indicating the extent to which each standard was addressed. A process that could be used with this checklist includes the following steps:

A. On a separate sheet for each standard
    (1) list the strengths, weaknesses, and suggestions for improvement in terms of the overview, guidelines, and common errors identified for that standard;
    (2) based upon your professional judgment and using the list prepared in 1 above, decide upon the degree to which the standard is effectively addressed (addressed fully, addressed partially, not addressed, standard deemed not applicable).
B. Transfer the judgment for each standard to the checklist.
C. Based upon professional judgment, decide upon the degree to which the set of applicable standards is effectively addressed using the same scale as for the Standards.
D. Summarize improvements necessary to increase the quality and effectiveness of the evaluation.

Use of this checklist promotes effective evaluation practices and can serve as an audit of the evaluation process. This checklist can be used by a variety of stakeholders in the evaluation. However, there is a risk of oversimplifying the evaluation process by promoting a scorecard mentality through the use of a checklist. The Joint Committee warns users against superficial use of the checklist and recommends a procedure such as the one described above.

THE STANDARDS

Utility Standards

Summary of the Standards

U Utility Standards The utility standards are intended to ensure that an evaluation will serve the information needs of intended users. These standards are as follows:

> **U1 Stakeholder Identification** Persons involved in or affected by the evaluation should be identified, so that their needs can be addressed.

> **U2 Evaluator Credibility** The persons conducting the evaluation should be both trustworthy and competent to perform the evaluation, so that the evaluation findings achieve maximum credibility and acceptance.

> **U3 Information Scope and Selection** Information collected should be broadly selected to address pertinent questions about the program and be responsive to the needs and interests of clients and other specified stakeholders.

> **U4 Values Identification** The perspectives, procedures, and rationale used to interpret the findings should be carefully described, so that the bases for value judgments are clear.

U5 **Report Clarity** Evaluation reports should clearly describe the program being evaluated, including its context, and the purposes, procedures, and findings of the evaluation, so that essential information is provided and easily understood.

U6 **Report Timeliness and Dissemination** Significant interim findings and evaluation reports should be disseminated to intended users, so that they can be used in a timely fashion.

U7 **Evaluation Impact** Evaluations should be planned, conducted, and reported in ways that encourage follow-through by stakeholders, so that the likelihood that the evaluation will be used is increased.

U1 Stakeholder Identification

STANDARD Persons involved in or affected by the
evaluation should be identified, so that their needs
can be addressed.

Overview

Evaluations almost always involve multiple and diverse stakeholders. The
term *stakeholders* is commonly used to refer to those who should be
involved in or may be affected by a program evaluation. Stakeholders
include clients and others who will use the evaluation to make decisions,
such as school, university, and hospital boards, state boards of education,
and advisory committees; individual administrators; legislators; instructional and training staffs; and the large group of consumers who purchase
the goods and services being assessed. Furthermore, typical stakeholders
include the individuals and groups whose work is being studied, those who
will be affected by the results, community organizations, and the general
public.

It is crucial to identify potentially important stakeholders and, within
resource and time limitations, to involve them in the planning and conducting of the evaluation, especially striving to ascertain and accommodate their
information needs. In many evaluations, special efforts may be necessary to
promote the appropriate inclusion of less powerful groups or individuals as
stakeholders, such as racial, cultural, or language minority groups. If stakeholder identification is not done, the evaluation may become a misguided,
academic exercise, the results of which are ignored, criticized, or resisted
because they do not address anyone's particular questions. An evaluation
planned with stakeholders and conducted to meet their information needs is
likely to be attended to and receive a positive response.

❖ GUIDELINES

A. Identify persons in leadership roles first, as they can aid an evaluator to identify other stakeholders.

B. Contact representatives of identified stakeholder groups to learn how they view the evaluation's importance, how they would like to use its results, and what particular information would be useful. Where necessary, help them to develop realistic expectations that take into account the methodological, financial, and political constraints on the evaluation.

C. Use stakeholders to identify and contact other stakeholders.

D. Reach an understanding with the client concerning the relative importance of the potential stakeholders and the information they desire, and plan and implement the data collection and the reporting activities accordingly.

E. Throughout the evaluation, be alert to identifying additional stakeholders that should be served and, within the limits of time and resources, maintain some flexibility and capability to respond to their needs.

F. Involve clients and other stakeholders directly in designing and conducting the evaluation.

G. Be certain not to exclude any stakeholder because of gender, ethnicity, or language background.

❖ COMMON ERRORS

A. Allowing clients to inappropriately restrict the evaluator's contact with other involved or affected stakeholders

B. Implying that all stakeholder information needs will be addressed when, in reality, they cannot be

C. Assuming that persons in leadership or decision-making roles are the only, or most important, stakeholders

D. Overidentifying stakeholders, making it impossible to proceed

E. Failing to distinguish between clients and other stakeholders

F. Overlooking the needs and rights of stakeholders because of their gender, ethnicity, or language backgrounds

Illustrative Case 1—Description

A private evaluation firm was commissioned by a large state department of education to conduct an independent evaluation of a major early childhood education program. The program was first implemented in the state three years earlier in a small number of schools. As planned, additional schools were added in each of the next two years. Of concern to the state board was the increasing cost, which during the third year reached almost $24 million. The board requested the department to secure an external evaluation of the extent to which the new program was "worth the money it's costing."

The evaluators spent much of their planning time in conversations with the state superintendent of schools, the department administrator in charge of the early childhood education program, and each member of the state school board. Without exception, these individuals were concerned with the cognitive progress of the children in the program, with specific emphasis on mathematics and reading achievement. Accordingly, the evaluators focused the bulk of their data-gathering efforts on securing first-rate indicators of pupil performance in math and reading. They devised a series of high-quality, criterion-referenced tests for each of these areas and gathered much performance data from pupils who were in the program and pupils who were not.

After the evaluators released their report, it became apparent that the state legislature, which approved all fiscal allocations for such programs, was also interested in the report. Several key legislators, while attentive to the cognitive performance results, were far more concerned about the program's impact on student attitude toward school and student self-esteem. In addition, the legislators wanted a much more detailed elaboration of cost data than the report contained. Also, the report was criticized by early childhood interest groups, who viewed its contents as too narrow and therefore of limited usefulness.

Illustrative Case 1—Analysis

The evaluators, based on their conversations with their clients and immediate stakeholders, devised quality data collection instruments appropriate to the agreed-upon evaluation design/focus. However, beyond serving their client and other immediate stakeholders, the evaluators should have considered serving and accommodating a broader clientele and then discussed any expansions with their client. In planning their evaluation, they should have probed sufficiently to form some tentative conclusions about various groups' interests in the evaluation. They should have learned that key members of the legislature, such as the education committee of the state senate, and two strong advocacy groups favoring early childhood education—parents of participating children and paraprofessionals employed in the program—would be deeply interested in the results. They should have analyzed legislation and committee reports to understand the goals of the program's initiators.

With that knowledge, the evaluators could have informed the state board of education that other stakeholders were interested in the final report. They could have argued that the interests of the other stakeholders were legitimate, that their political action might be decisive in determining the consequences of the evaluation, and therefore that their questions should have been included in the evaluation design.

Illustrative Case 2—Description

For several years a government agency had been concerned about the success of one of its major funding programs through which money had been dispersed to community colleges for the training of unemployed individuals in marketable job skills. Given the size of the budget for this initiative, the government wanted to know how many graduates from college programs actually found jobs, how soon after graduation they were employed, and how long they kept their positions.

The colleges in which the training programs were conducted had developed specific objectives for these programs, many of which were related to general education competencies that prepared graduates for long-term encounters with the job market. The colleges were also well aware of factors that would influence placement rates, for example, rises and downturns in the economy, which had a direct effect upon job placement opportunities. In many fields, lack of job placements in the immediate term had nothing to do with the quality of the graduate and everything to do with the volatility of the job market. Furthermore, the colleges attempted to prepare graduates who would be flexible and adaptable and hence able to undertake various functions not directly related to their training.

Accordingly, the government commissioned a private agency to conduct an evaluation of job placement from college programs. The government did not release the names of the individual colleges or their program directors, and provided the private agency only with data related to job placement and current employment status of students. The evaluation team was unable to obtain specific information from the college personnel about the programs. The results indicated that graduates from college market training programs were no more successful in finding proper and meaningful employment than individuals who had not completed a formal college program, and that placement rates after a six-month period were equally unimpressive.

Based upon this evaluation, the government initiated major changes in policy, one aspect of which was the diversion of large amounts of money from the colleges to private sector agencies for "on-the-job" training.

Illustrative Case 2—Analysis

The evaluators, for whatever reasons, may have felt they could not aggressively pursue contacting the colleges involved in the program because the government did not initially provide this information to the evaluators. Failure to contact the colleges negatively affected the evaluation. As the colleges were not consulted by the evaluation team in the preparation of the evaluation strategy or in the interpretation of the results, many factors related to program objectives were never considered in the evaluation design. The results were then largely invalid with respect to the objectives of the training programs, as they measured only one small part of what the latter were intended to accomplish. But, far more serious were the actions taken as a result of the poorly designed evaluation exercise.

By consulting with the colleges, they could have sought information about the goals and objectives of each program, the nature of the instruction and training provided to students, and questions the colleges might have had that could have been addressed in the evaluation. By not doing so, the results of the evaluation were, at least from the point of view of the colleges, incomplete. Several factors related to job placement that should have been considered when interpreting and presenting results, and of which college officials were aware, were ignored by the government. Had they been considered, the action taken by the government either would not have occurred or would have been modified somewhat in light of the mitigating factors against immediate job placement.

Wider and intensive consultation with all affected parties in the preparation of the evaluation and its design no doubt would have resulted in a more responsive evaluation.

Supporting Documentation

Cousins, J. B., & Earl, L. M. (1992). The case for participatory evaluation. *Educational Evaluation and Policy Analysis, 14*(4), 397-418.

Greene, J. G. (1988). Stakeholder participation and utilization in program evaluation. *Evaluation Review, 12*(2), 96-116.

Nowakowski, J. (Ed.). (1987, Winter). The client perspective on evaluation [Entire issue]. *New Directions for Program Evaluation, 36.*

U2   Evaluator Credibility

STANDARD   The persons conducting the evaluation should be both trustworthy and competent to perform the evaluation, so that the evaluation findings achieve maximum credibility and acceptance.

Overview

Evaluators are credible to the extent that they exhibit the training, technical competence, substantive knowledge, experience, integrity, public relations skills, and other characteristics considered necessary by clients and other users of evaluation findings and reports. Because few individuals possess all of the characteristics needed for particular evaluations, it is often necessary that an evaluation be done by a team of persons who collectively possess these qualifications.

Evaluators should establish their credibility with the client and other users at the outset of the evaluation. If the confidence and trust of these audiences cannot be secured, the evaluators should seriously consider not proceeding. If they do go ahead when they are considered by their audiences to be unqualified or biased, they may find later that their findings and recommendations—however technically adequate—are ignored or rejected.

When conducting an evaluation, evaluators should maintain a pattern of consistent, open, and continuing communication and approachability with their clients and other stakeholders while still offering expertise and maintaining impartiality. They should also keep in mind that the fundamental test of their credibility will rest in an ability to defend the utility, practicality, integrity, and technical adequacy of their reports.

❖   GUIDELINES

A. Stay abreast of social and political forces associated with the evaluation, especially those linked to race, gender, socioeconomic status, and language and cultural differences (see A2, Context Analysis, and F2, Political Viability), and use this knowledge when designing and conducting the evaluation.

B. Ensure that both the work plan and the composition of the evaluation team are responsive to the concerns of key stakeholders (see U1, Stakeholder Identification, and U3, Information Scope and Selection).

C. Consider having the evaluation plan reviewed and the evaluation work audited by another evaluator whose credentials are acceptable to the client (A12, Metaevaluation).

D. Be clear in describing the evaluation plan to various stakeholders and demonstrate that the plan is realistic and technically sound.

E. Determine key audience needs for information on the progress of the evaluation and keep them informed about the progress of the evaluation through such means as newsletters, progress reports, telephone calls, memoranda, press releases, and meetings.

F. Include in evaluation proposals a statement describing the evaluator's qualifications relevant to the program being evaluated.

❖ COMMON ERRORS

A. Failing to establish the evaluator's credibility in both content and methodological areas

B. Pursuing an evaluation that is biased toward the values of one stakeholder perspective

C. Failing to disqualify oneself or any team member for lack of skills or experience required to do an evaluation

D. Failing to seek evaluators experienced in the setting of the evaluation (e.g., schools, industry, hospitals, government, military)

E. Failing to ensure that members of the evaluation team devote time and effort, as well as their reputations, to the evaluation

F. Overinvesting resources to achieve credibility and acceptance

G. Failing to establish personal integrity through past evaluations

H. Assuming that the evaluator's approach to evaluation is acceptable to the client

I. Turning over the evaluation to an inexperienced student assistant

Illustrative Case 1—Description

A law school instituted a program for tutoring minority students admitted to the school but who had not scored well on measures traditionally used to screen applicants. School representatives worked with the university's Teaching/Learning Center to develop programmed materials that the minority students could use to improve their basic communication and study skills.

Two professors of law, themselves minority group members, felt the materials were inappropriate because they did not take into account the cultural barriers constraining the learning of minority students. They therefore undertook an evaluation of the materials, focusing on the cultural barriers facing minority students. The evaluation report they produced was based mostly on anecdotal data drawn from interviews with a few students who volunteered to talk about their experiences in the Teaching/Learning Center and how the program helped them adjust to the cultural context of the law school.

The dean of the law school, upon receiving the professors' report, invited his department chairs and representatives of the Teaching/Learning Center to a meeting to discuss it. At the meeting, the chairs and center representatives politely but firmly rejected the professors' recommendations. It seemed clear to them that the evaluation had not been commissioned by anyone in a legitimate position to do so. Moreover, they felt that the evaluation results were biased by only including volunteers in the interview sample and by the limited focus on the Teaching/Learning Center's activities.

Illustrative Case 1—Analysis

The two professors clearly identified a deficiency in the programmed materials that might affect their utility for the minority students. This deficiency had not been taken into account by the designers of the materials and did need to be considered when assessing the materials' appropriateness for the minority students. However, the evaluators failed to address their credibility in the design and conduct of the evaluation. Prospects for acceptance and use of the evaluation would have been enhanced if the evaluators had taken steps to ensure their credibility and their competence to conduct the evaluation (also see U4, Values Identification). They should have sought the approval of the dean, their law school colleagues, and the developers of the materials before moving ahead. They should have recognized the need for evaluation expertise to supplement their own knowledge of minority affairs (such expertise was available in the university's Teaching/Learning Center and the School of Education). The expanded evaluation team probably would have planned and conducted the evaluation more rigorously, and the audiences would have been more receptive to considering and using the report. As an alternative to an expanded evaluation team, the professors could have asked their dean and the Teaching/Learning Center director to appoint a qualified evaluator to assess their evaluation plan and audit their evaluation report (see A12, Metaevaluation).

Illustrative Case 2—Description

Students in the medical fraternity at a large midwestern medical school voiced concern during a fraternity meeting that the honors-pass-fail grading system was promoting unhealthy competition to achieve the honors grade. The students formed a committee to evaluate the system and report their findings. The committee decided to create a questionnaire to distribute to the greater medical student body. The questionnaire was developed and distributed to all four classes of students. The results were compiled by the committee and a brief summary prepared. The results confirmed the committee's expectations that the broader student body felt that the grading system promoted unhealthy competition. The summary was sent to the faculty curriculum committee with a call to drop the honors grade because of the negative environment it created.

The faculty curriculum committee reviewed the report and expressed concern over three critical issues. The first issue was that the questions were worded in a way that would lead to the conclusion the students wished to reach. Thus the committee believed the questionnaire was too biased to provide valid results. The second issue was that the response rate to the questionnaire was low. It ranged between 15% and 40% across the four classes. Considering the low response rate, it was difficult to establish representativeness of the sample with the questionnaire results even if one were to accept the questions as valid. The third issue was that unhealthy competitiveness was only one of many concerns that should have been considered when the grading system was chosen. Another key concern was that the grading system needed to include the ability to provide some support for the more accomplished students who were attempting to get into the more competitive residencies after graduation. Yet another concern was the belief by faculty that students who excel need to have their achievement recognized in the grading system.

Although poorly designed and executed, the evaluation did act as a catalyst for a review of the grading system. The faculty committee felt that the grading system had been in place for a sufficient length of time that a review was warranted. It asked an evaluation specialist to develop an evaluation plan in consultation with the student committee. It also directed the evaluation specialist to work with the student committee to develop a new questionnaire that would be more balanced and develop administrative procedures likely to yield a higher response rate.

Illustrative Case 2—Analysis

The student committee had identified a problem voiced by their peers that they felt needed to be addressed. Unfortunately, they were not sufficiently equipped to conduct the type of evaluation that needed to be done. The questionnaire items were so leading that faculty basically discounted any results (see A5, Valid Information). The low response rate further justified the faculty's response. Rather than have a direct confrontation with the students, the faculty curriculum committee chose to involve a credible evaluation specialist to develop an evaluation plan and to work with the student committee.

Supporting Documentation

Love, A. J. (1991). *Internal evaluation.* Newbury Park, CA: Sage.

Mathison, S. (1991). What do we know about internal evaluation? *Evaluation and Program Planning, 14*(1), 159-165.

Torres, R. T. (1991). Improving the quality of internal evaluation: The evaluator as consultant-mediator. *Evaluation and Program Planning, 14*(1), 189-198.

U3   Information Scope and Selection

STANDARD   **Information collected should be broadly selected to address pertinent questions about the program and be responsive to the needs and interests of clients and other specified stakeholders.**

Overview

To have the appropriate scope of information, evaluations need to be relevant to decision makers' objectives, important to significant stakeholders, and sufficiently comprehensive to support a judgment of worth and merit. Most evaluations are of concern to multiple stakeholders, each of whom should have an opportunity to provide input to the evaluation design and have a claim for access to the results. But the evaluation should also strive to assess the program in terms of all important variables (e.g., effectiveness, harmful side effects, costs, responses to learner needs, meaningfulness of assumptions and values underlying the program, and feasibility) whether or not the stakeholders specifically ask for such information. It is important to examine and document the program to assure that the evaluation is appropriately delimited.

It usually will not be possible to gather all the information that is initially deemed important. However, not all information is equally important or essential to a sound evaluation. Once the potential body of information has been identified, it should be culled to eliminate what is minor and to emphasize the most important. This weeding-out procedure requires judgment. Evaluators should determine what the client considers significant but should also suggest significant areas the client may have overlooked, including areas identified by other stakeholders. The evaluator also should review pertinent literature, including previous evaluations, theoretical papers, research reports, and discussions with stakeholders to help identify and prioritize the questions to be addressed.

Care must also be taken to assure that mandated evaluation procedures do not drive practice—for example, the evaluation requirement that standardized tests be used. This requirement narrows the evaluation focus almost exclusively to test results. The result tends to be that the tests drive the curriculum.

Initial decisions may be made about classes of information, but ultimately a decision must be made about each single item of information. Gross judgments can be made during early conferences with the client; however, finer judgments are required when specific topics are chosen for measurement and data collection instruments and procedures are being selected or created. Prior to beginning data collection, the evaluator should share the evaluation plan, including identification of the information to be collected, with the client and other relevant stakeholders. This is done to ensure that the information to be collected addresses the important issues. The evaluator should also note that additional questions and unanticipated information may emerge during the evaluation, and that these may be incorporated into the evaluation process.

Evaluators, like other professionals, bring their own preferences to the task of carrying out an evaluation. Some, for example, are most concerned about cost effectiveness. Some are interested in cognitive outcomes to the exclusion of other outcomes. Despite their personal preferences, however, evaluators should strive to collect all relevant information and address all important questions about the program within the constraints of the budget (see U4, Values Identification).

❖ GUIDELINES

A. Understand client requirements for the evaluation (see U1, Stakeholder Identification).

B. Interview representatives of major stakeholders to gain an understanding of their different and perhaps conflicting points of view and of their need for information (see U1, Stakeholder Identification, and A3, Described Purposes and Procedures).

C. Avoid giving the impression that all questions will be answered.

D. Help stakeholders develop realistic expectations in light of available financial, time, and personnel resources.

E. Have the client rank potential audiences in order of importance and work with representatives of each stakeholder group to rank topics in order of importance to that audience (see U1, Stakeholder Identification).

F. Work with the client to collate the ordered topics from each audience, to remove items at the bottom of the list, and to add items that the evaluator believes to be important even though not requested.

G. Allow flexibility for adding questions and including unanticipated information that may arise during the evaluation.

H. Distribute the entire evaluation effort (data collection, analysis, interpretation, and reporting) over the final list of topics, placing the most effort on high-ranked items.

❖   COMMON ERRORS

A. Failing to consider the trade-offs between comprehensiveness and selectivity at every stage of the evaluation: developing the plan; setting the budget; and collecting, analyzing, interpreting, and reporting information

B. Failing to give voice to multiple stakeholder groups in the process of selecting priority evaluation questions

C. Neglecting to update information requirements through periodic contacts with the client and other stakeholders

D. Collecting information because it is convenient (e.g., because instruments already exist), rather than because it is necessary

E. Failing to delimit the scope of the evaluation, that is, failing to state the questions that will be answered and the purpose of the evaluation and failing to keep them in mind at every stage of the evaluation

F. Collecting information that is extraneous to the central purpose of the evaluation

G. Failing to clarify clients' needs

Illustrative Case—Description

A school superintendent decided to evaluate the curriculum and organization of the district's junior high schools (grades 7-9) and formed a panel of evaluators consisting of the elementary, junior high, and senior high school principals and a teacher at each level. They were requested to complete a written report for the superintendent within five weeks of commencing the evaluation.

The panel prepared the report for the superintendent based on their own knowledge and beliefs about the school system and its needs, supplemented by limited staff and student perceptions collected with a survey instrument. Included in the report were sections on academic achievement of local junior high school pupils, national trends in junior high school organization (stressing the advantages of the middle school concept), present and projected enrollments, gaps in the junior high school curriculum, and the physiological and social development of students in the junior high age group. The report recommended that the school system shift to a middle school organization, with grades 6, 7, and 8 in the middle schools, and grade 9 going to the senior high schools.

When the report was published, elementary and senior high parents were disturbed that specific concerns of theirs had not been addressed in the report. Elementary parents, especially, were upset about the prospect of the loss of the school leadership provided by sixth-grade students. They suggested, among other things, that many parents looked to sixth graders to escort their younger children safely to and from school. Senior high parents were alarmed at the potential overcrowding that would be brought about by the addition of grade-9 students.

Representatives of both parent groups complained to the school board. The board itself was irritated because the report did not assess the disadvantages and cost implications of the suggested reorganization and the advantages and disadvantages of other possible organizational changes. The board supported the parent groups and rejected the middle school concept.

Illustrative Case—Analysis

The panel addressed a wide range of pertinent topics, especially considering the short time available to conduct its evaluation. It discussed local and national trends in organization, enrollment, curriculum, and student development in the junior high age group. However, it did not adequately address some of the most important questions. It did not have a clear sense of the purpose of the evaluation.

This problem might have been avoided had the superintendent been asked for more time to check with key groups before designing the evaluation. Opinions should have been sought from teachers, students, parents, and school board members about the kinds of questions they wanted answered. Then cogent responses could have been provided, derived from information collected as part of an appropriately designed evaluation.

The panel could have systematically explored stakeholder views about the middle school concept. Based on reports from other school districts, the evaluators also could have provided comparisons of the advantages and disadvantages of the middle school concept with other forms of school organization.

The panel might have prepared two reports, assessing both the pros and the cons of a middle school for grades 6, 7, and 8. One report, written for parents and the general public, could have focused on the educational and fiscal advantages and disadvantages of their recommendations. The other, written for the superintendent and board (the decision makers), could have outlined the organizational, financial, and administrative ramifications, as well as the educational advantages and disadvantages, of their recommendations.

Supporting Documentation

Fitz-Gibbon, C. T., & Morris, L. L. (1987). *How to design a program evaluation.* In J. L. Herman (Ed.), *Program evaluation kit* (2nd ed.). Newbury Park, CA: Sage.

Guba, E. G. (Ed.). (1990). *The paradigm dialog*. Newbury Park, CA: Sage.

Nowakowski, J., Bunda, M. A., Working, R., Bernacki, G., & Harrington, P. (1985). *A handbook of educational variables*. Boston: Kluwer-Nijhoff.

Shadish, W. R., Jr., Cook, T. D., & Leviton, L. C. (1991). *Foundations of program evaluation: Theories of practice*. Newbury Park, CA: Sage.

Stecher, B. M., & Davis, W. A. (1987). How to focus an evaluation. In J. L. Herman (Ed.), *Program evaluation kit* (2nd ed.). Newbury Park, CA: Sage.

Worthen, B. R., & Sanders, J. R. (1987). *Educational evaluation: Alternative approaches and practical guidelines*. White Plains, NY: Longman.

U4   Values Identification

STANDARD   The perspectives, procedures, and
rationale used to interpret the findings should be
carefully described, so that the bases for value
judgments are clear.

Overview

Value is the root term in *evaluation*; and valuing—rating or scaling an object
for its usefulness, importance, or general worth—is the fundamental task in
evaluations. At the heart of this task is the need to interpret the information
obtained in an evaluation. Such information—whether quantitative or qualitative, process or product, formative or summative—will be of little interest
or use if it is not interpreted against some pertinent and defensible idea of
what has merit and what does not.

However, making an interpretation of the obtained information is a
complex and controversial undertaking. Among the issues involved are
deciding who will make the value judgments and determining what procedures they will use. Several possible responses to each of these issues are
identified in the guidelines below. But it seems doubtful that any particular
prescription for arriving at value judgments is consistently the best in all
evaluative contexts.

The point of this standard is that evaluators and their clients, along with
multiple stakeholders in that context, should thoughtfully determine the
approach to be followed in assigning values to the obtained information,
and they should reveal and justify their chosen approach.

❖   GUIDELINES

A. Consider alternative bases for interpreting findings: for example,
program objectives, procedural specifications, laws and regulations, institutional goals, democratic ideals, social norms, performance by a compari-

son group, assessed needs of a consumer group, expected performance of the sample group, professional standards, and reported judgments by various reference groups.

B. Consider who will make interpretations: for example, the evaluators, the client, the various stakeholders, a regulatory group, or some combination of these.

C. Consider alternative techniques that might be used to assign value meanings to collected information: for example, having different teams write advocacy reports, conducting a jury or administrative trial of the program being evaluated, or seeking convergence through a delphi study.

D. Report options, with the advantages and disadvantages of each, when there are different equally defensible value positions in an evaluation.

❖ COMMON ERRORS

A. Assuming that evaluations can be objective in the sense of being devoid of value judgment

B. Failing to determine what value perspectives (e.g., educational, social, economic, and scientific) the client and stakeholders perceive to be important in interpreting the findings of the evaluation

C. Designing the data collection and analysis procedures without considering what criteria, such as performance by a comparison group or performance in terms of a predetermined standard, will be needed to interpret the findings

D. Concentrating so heavily on clarifying values that insufficient time and effort are devoted to collecting and analyzing the information needed to make value judgments

E. Failing to acknowledge that decision rules often are arbitrary and therefore subject to debate

Illustrative Case 1—Description

The curriculum department of an urban school district reached the conclusion that the poor performance of black children on a battery of tests routinely administered within the system was related to the fact that instruction was based on standard English whereas the children in question spoke (and thought) in a nonstandard form of the language. Accordingly, the department decided to commission the development of new instructional materials based on the local nonstandard English that would, in effect, perform the same function for the black children that bilingual materials performed for speakers of other languages. The department set up a pilot project, Chapter I funded, in fifth- and sixth-grade language arts. If this pilot project was successful, similar developmental efforts would be initiated in other content areas.

The head of the curriculum department asked the district's evaluation unit to provide a team of formative evaluators to assist the development team in refining and improving the materials and procedures as they were being developed. While aware of the fact that multiple audiences were stakeholders in the proposed program, the evaluation team decided to focus only on the development team's questions because the evaluation team had been asked to do a formative evaluation. The evaluators decided to fulfill their mission in two ways: (a) by submitting each unit to a panel of experts who would assess it on such criteria as faithfulness to the vocabulary and idioms of the local language pattern, the modernity of its concepts, its internal consistency, and its integration into the year-long curriculum package as projected, and (b) by assessing each unit, comparing the performance of those children using the new materials with the performance of children using the conventional materials on an oral test of the material covered in the unit. Also, the "experimental" children were asked about their perceptions and reactions during an interview. The evaluation team would then make recommendations for refinements and improvements in each unit based on their findings.

When some four or five units had initially been developed and submitted to the formative evaluation procedure, the district superintendent, several board members, and the instructional supervisors began receiving letters and phone calls from parents and teachers who objected to the new approach. Some parents of black students felt their children were being reinforced in a socially dysfunctional language pattern that both stigmatized them and worked against their getting good jobs. Some parents of white children felt their children were being penalized—that the curriculum was being "watered down" because some of the students were slow learners. Some teachers objected because they did not feel competent to teach using nonstandard language and they did not want to invest the time and energy that would be necessary to learn the new ways. Finally, several teachers questioned the test norms that were being used as an inappropriate basis for interpreting the test scores.

The superintendent, responding to these pressures, placed the whole issue on the agenda of the next meeting of the district's school board. The board, after devoting most of three meetings to the problem, decided to abort the new curriculum and return to the former instructional pattern.

Illustrative Case 1—Analysis

While the evaluation team did solicit the assistance of experts in the field to assess the program, it made a serious error in assuming that the objectives of the curriculum department were the only values that needed to be taken into account in conducting the formative evaluation. The team should have realized that reference groups other than the curriculum department would surely render judgments in terms of their own values about whether the project goals were justified in the first place, whether some unanticipated side effects were occurring, and whether the project should be implemented if found worthy. Prior identification of such stakeholders, solicitation of their concerns and issues, and clarification of the values on which these concerns and issues were based would have been useful. Thus the fear of the parents of black children that their children would only be further disadvantaged might have been explicitly examined through systematic observation of the children's developing language skills or teacher feedback on classroom language patterns. The fear of parents of white children that their children were being penalized could have been similarly explored. The concern of teachers that more time and energy would be required in retraining than they were prepared to invest might have been investigated through a pilot training exercise. Systematic feedback of such information to parents and teachers would likely have allayed their fears or made it evident that they were justified; either of these outcomes would have led to a more rational and considered course of action than what occurred through the enforced decision of the board in response to political pressures. Even if the proposed curriculum was found to be worthwhile from one perspective (e.g., the curriculum department's) and without much worth from another (e.g., the parents of black children), so that a consensual decision could not be made, the board at least would have been aware of the reaction it was inviting and the risks it was taking in making any particular decision. Finally, the board would not have been forced to make a summative decision even before the formative evaluation data were collected and analyzed.

Illustrative Case 2—Description

A federally-funded wellness promotion project for older adults living in a rural area involved collaboration between a major medical research department at a university, a community-based service organization, and an educational institution serving specialized handicapped clientele. The stated goal of the project was to increase the knowledge of older adults about their access to the health care system. To increase this knowledge, eligible older adults, identified through a screening procedure, and members of the community service organization and educational institution attended training sessions in which available health care services were described and the process for referrals was outlined.

The availability of federal funding was contingent on the completion of an evaluation of the effectiveness of the screening procedure, the training provided, and the referral procedure at the end of 18 months. The project leaders commissioned a private evaluation agency in the health field to complete this evaluation.

The evaluators began their evaluation with an open planning session in which members of the medical research department, the community service organization, the older adult community, and the educational institution identified and discussed their needs. The medical researchers wanted to demonstrate a difference in quality of life, stating that this was the most valuable outcome of the project; the community service provider wanted to demonstrate an increase in service availability and use, stating that this was the factor on which continued funding would most likely hinge; and the specialized educational institution wanted to demonstrate its professional contribution to the community.

The evaluators considered these three different needs in light of available financial, time, and personnel resources for the evaluation. Although each organization's basic needs would be addressed, the evaluators considerably tailored and refined each organization's original suggestions to form a common set. An agreement was reached by the evaluators and representatives from the medical research department, the community service organization, and the educational institution that the training sessions would be evaluated to provide information on the usefulness of the content as well as the effectiveness of the training method. The screening process also would be evaluated to provide information on accessing health care services. The referral procedure would be evaluated to provide information on follow-up success. Following this agreement, a second open meeting was held to identify the criteria to be used to indicate success. Through continued negotiations, compromises, and refinement of the evaluation focus, agreement was reached.

Illustrative Case 2—Analysis

The evaluators avoided assuming there was only one set of values for this evaluation. During the in-depth discussion at the two open planning sessions, the evaluation team identified conflicting values and then, given the fiscal, personnel, and time restrictions of the evaluation, worked to determine a common set of values. Although each stakeholder group had to revise its initial value set, the compromises reached allowed each stakeholder group "to own" the evaluation plan, thereby contributing to the success of the evaluation.

Supporting Documentation

Campbell, D. T. (1988). *Methodology and epistemology for social science: Selected papers* (E. S. Overman, Ed.). Chicago: University of Chicago Press.

Guba, E. G. (Ed.). (1990). *The paradigm dialog.* Newbury Park, CA: Sage.

Guba, E. G., & Lincoln, Y. S. (1989). *Fourth generation evaluation.* Newbury Park, CA: Sage.

Madaus, G. F., Scriven, M., & Stufflebeam, D. L. (Eds.). (1983). *Evaluation models: Viewpoints on educational and human services evaluation.* Boston: Kluwer-Nijhoff.

Pitz, G. F., & McKillip, J. (1984). *Decision analysis for program evaluators*. Beverly Hills, CA: Sage.

Scriven, M. (1967). The methodology of evaluation. In R. E. Stake (Ed.), *Perspectives of curriculum evaluation* (American Educational Research Association monograph series on evaluation, No. 1). Chicago: Rand McNally.

U5   Report Clarity

> **STANDARD**   Evaluation reports should clearly
> describe the program being evaluated, including its
> context, and the purposes, procedures, and findings of
> the evaluation, so that essential information is
> provided and easily understood.

Overview

Reports can take many forms, including oral feedback, written memos, or
lengthy documents. Whatever the medium employed for reporting (e.g.,
written, oral, videotape, graphic, or some combination of media), clarity is
essential for audience understanding, report credibility, and application. In
order for an evaluation to be useful, it must be understood. Stakeholders
should readily understand the purposes of the evaluation, what was evaluated, how the evaluation was conducted, what information was obtained,
what conclusions were drawn, and what recommendations, if any, were
made. In this context, *clarity* refers to explicit and unencumbered narrative,
illustrations, and descriptions. In certain cases, reports may need to be
translated to be understandable to language minority groups.

❖   GUIDELINES

A. Carefully consider the appropriateness of the medium for reporting to
the intended audience.

B. Keep the presentation of reports as brief as possible, simple and direct,
and focused upon addressing the evaluation questions.

C. Consider the use of separate summary and technical reports, as well as
multiple media, targeting reports to client and other stakeholders.

D. Provide sufficient contextual, program, and evaluation information to constitute a firm foundation for conclusions and recommendations (see A2, Context Analysis).

E. Use examples to help the stakeholders relate the findings to practical situations.

F. Use technical language sparingly and help the stakeholders understand technical or unfamiliar terms (e.g., internal and external validity, reliability, standard deviation, categorical analysis, purposive sampling) by providing a glossary, separate summary and technical reports, and training opportunities for the stakeholders.

G. Support summary statements with clear discussions of related problems, objectives, questions, and, if appropriate, possible areas for future study (see U1, Stakeholder Identification, and U3, Information Scope and Selection).

H. Have the client and representatives of the intended audience(s) review report(s) for clarity, fairness, and understandability prior to their final release.

I. Make evaluation results available in the languages of all stakeholders through oral explanation or translation at meetings and through translation of reports into the languages of all stakeholders.

❖   COMMON ERRORS

A. Failing to consider the level of technical sophistication of stakeholders when deciding how to report information

B. Failing to take account of the audience's ability to understand technical terms or the English language

C. Failing to report various perceptions even if this introduces ambiguity (see U2, Evaluator Credibility, and A11, Impartial Reporting)

D. Sacrificing precision in an effort to achieve clarity

E. Failing to format reports so as to enhance their readability

F. Failing to explain how data were aggregated or disaggregated for reporting purposes

G. Overemphasizing methodology at the expense of findings

H. Failing to describe the program adequately, assuming that all stakeholders are already aware of the program specifics

Illustrative Case 1—Description

In response to a request to provide an evaluation of 10 specified areas within a large school system, the internal evaluation unit produced a 250-page report for the school board. However, after some preliminary reading, the board members requested that the report be simplified. The report they received was riddled with ill-defined technical jargon and ambiguities. It dealt in vague generalities with particular aspects of the program that required revision. It was imprecise regarding the exact nature of the changes needed to strengthen the 10 areas at different grade levels and with different kinds of students. Recommendations were so broad as to be almost truisms; for example, "Staff should devote more effort to the needs of individual students." The tables and figures could not be understood without frequent reference to preceding (and in some instances subsequent) sections of the text. The inclusion in the text of whole tests and related materials required the reader to skip numerous portions of the report in order to maintain continuity in the explanations of procedures and findings.

Illustrative Case 1—Analysis

The evaluator's report was thorough and contained accurate data. However, the evaluators should have focused on their audience's questions and responded directly and clearly. For example, the body of the evaluation report might have been divided into sections corresponding to the 10 specified areas that were investigated. Each section might have described an issue, its relevance to the area evaluated, the procedures for investigating the issue (including sample test items), the rationale for these procedures, the findings obtained, specific recommendations drawn from these findings, and an explicit rationale for the recommendations as related to the findings. This written information could have been further reported via oral presentations to the school board, specifically highlighting the 10 specific areas through the use of slides, transparencies, or videotape. The report might have been preceded by an executive summary and followed by a series of appendixes. The writing might have been more concise. Necessary technical terms could have been explained fully in the context of the evaluation report. Finally, a set of easily understood directions could have been provided for reading relevant portions of appended computer printouts.

Illustrative Case 2—Description

An instructional design team in a business setting requested that an evaluation be conducted of a new training program they had developed. They contracted with an evaluation consultant to conduct the evaluation and provide a written report containing recommendations for improvements to the training program. Two weeks after the evaluation had been conducted, the evaluator distributed to the instructional design team a report that was approximately one inch thick. The report was organized into sections beginning with the evaluation procedures and followed by findings and recommendations for each module in the training program, major conclusions and recommendations for the training overall, and finally a set of attachments. The word processing package used to type the report did not have many format features to enhance the report's appearance. In addition, the report contained a great deal of technical jargon.

Illustrative Case 2—Analysis

The evaluator should have organized the report so that all key conclusions and recommendations were provided at the beginning, perhaps in the form of an executive summary. Because the major conclusions and recommendations had been provided at the end of the report, the instructional design team had to wade through a great deal of detailed information to get to the information that was most important to them. In addition, some of the major conclusions and recommendations were hidden in the detail of the attachments, making it difficult for the instructional design team to find all of the important information. They became frustrated because their time was limited and they needed to be able to find the key points quickly. The sections of the report should have been reordered so that the major conclusions and recommendations came directly after the evaluation procedures at the front of the report.

The evaluator should have improved the visual presentation of the report and used terminology appropriate for the intended audience. He should have realized that, in order for a report to be used, it has to be read. Overall, the report was so long, so poorly organized, and so poorly displayed that its impact on the instructional design team was minimal. The evaluator should have explored, and discussed with the instructional design team, other methods for presenting the evaluation findings in addition to the written report, especially given the evaluator's limited access to word processing packages. The instructional design team might have been more receptive to a multimedia presentation using visual displays and graphs with the report itself, and oral and visual communication media to highlight and clarify the major conclusions and recommendations of the written report.

Supporting Documentation

Morris, L. L., Fitz-Gibbon, C. T., & Freeman, M. E. (1987). How to communicate evaluation findings. In J. L. Herman (Ed.), *Program evaluation kit* (2nd ed.). Newbury Park, CA: Sage.

Worthen, B. R., & Sanders, J. R. (1987). *Educational evaluation: Alternative approaches and practical guidelines*. White Plains, NY: Longman.

U6   Report Timeliness and Dissemination

> **STANDARD**   Significant interim findings and
> evaluation reports should be disseminated to intended
> users, so that they can be used in a timely fashion.

Overview

Evaluators should communicate evaluation findings to intended users at
times when the information can best be used (see P2, Formal Agreements).
An intended user is one entitled to be informed about the results of the
evaluation for such reasons as the following:

1. They are the client; that is, they commissioned the evaluation.
2. They are legally responsible for the program being evaluated.
3. They funded the programs being evaluated through taxes, gifts of money, or
   contributed time and effort.
4. They supplied a substantial amount of information for the evaluation.
5. They are stakeholders of other types; for example, developers of the program
   being evaluated, persons whose careers or professional status will be affected
   or who are quoted in the report, and parents, students, or representatives of
   the mass media.

It is essential that the evaluators, in cooperation with the client, exert special
effort to identify, reach, and inform all intended users. In carrying out this
function, the evaluators and their client will need to use reporting formats and
approaches appropriate for the different intended users (see U5, Report Clarity). In some cases, reports may need to be translated for language minority
groups, or dissemination may need to be tailored to fit cultural practices.

Because evaluators should share with their client both the authority and
the responsibility for dissemination, conflict can result over ultimate author-

ity and responsibility for this obligation. When this occurs, evaluators must bear in mind that they are responsible not only to the client but also to other intended users. Authority to fulfill this responsibility should be clearly specified in the formal agreement at the outset of the evaluation. If the client misrepresents important aspects of the evaluation or withholds its findings from an intended user, in violation of the formal agreement, the evaluator then must inform the client and subsequently take steps as necessary to inform the user.

❖ GUIDELINES

A. Have the client and representatives of the key stakeholder groups indicate what their primary objectives are, the reporting form and language desired, and the times when reports would be most useful (see U1, Stakeholder Identification; U3, Information Scope and Selection; and U5, Report Clarity).

B. Plan backward in time, starting with the targeted delivery dates for the reports, and make realistic projections of what must be done to meet deadlines, allowing sufficient time to address unanticipated problems and to meet requests for interim reports.

C. Negotiate an agreement with clients at the outset of the evaluation on a dissemination plan in which intended users are defined and their access to findings and recommendations is specified (see P2, Formal Agreements).

D. Establish a realistic time line in which dates for reports to intended users are specified.

E. Establish contingency plans in case the evaluation activities are delayed and cannot be returned to schedule.

F. When appropriate, arrange to have qualified persons who are independent of clients and evaluators audit the quality of the evaluation and its reports and communicate their findings to the intended users.

G. Reach an agreement with the client at the outset as to editorial control and who will release intermediate and final reports, reserving the right to release information in accordance with Standard P2, Formal Agreements.

H. Check draft reports as appropriate with representatives of the intended users for clarity and factual accuracy, taking steps to prevent premature release of findings.

I. In planning the dissemination of findings, consider a variety of methods such as executive summaries, printed reports, audiovisual presentations, hearings, meetings, conferences, interviews, panel discussions, and newspaper accounts (see U5, Report Clarity).

J. Be sensitive to social impediments to dissemination, such as religious holidays, cultural diversity in social behaviors, and language barriers.

❖   C O M M O N   E R R O R S

A. Directing the report to the client or sponsor while ignoring other intended users

B. Releasing findings before they are checked and any errors or misstatements corrected

C. Delaying release of findings for inappropriate reasons

D. Failing to estimate time lines adequately resulting in failure to deliver information in a timely fashion

E. Failing to take whatever steps are required to ensure that information about illegal practices, fraud, waste, or abuse uncovered in the course of the evaluation is released even at the risk of jeopardizing contractual agreements

F. Providing incomplete or inaccurate information in the interest of timely reporting

G. Failing to recognize stakeholders who do not have spokespersons

Illustrative Case 1—Description

An evaluator, at the request of a faculty committee comprising three teachers and the principal of a school, completed an evaluation of experimental outcomes-based materials designed by the committee to improve discipline. The materials had been piloted in three classrooms in the school. The report was highly favorable, suggesting few changes in the original materials, and recommending their use next year in all classes. The report was given to the principal three months behind schedule. Without discussion with the staff, the principal announced at the end of the school year that the entire faculty would implement the program the following year.

Strong protest came from the faculty committee responsible for the materials and that had commissioned the evaluation, the teachers in the pilot classes who had used the materials, and the remaining teachers on the staff. The teachers on the faculty committee were particularly concerned because they had not been provided with a copy of the evaluation report so they could assess the findings. The teachers who had used the materials contended they should have been the first to receive the report and hear the discussion because they had conducted the trial of the materials as well as provided much of the data on which the evaluation was based. The teachers who were destined to use the outcomes-based materials the second year complained that they were being asked to buy a "pig in a poke"—no one had shared or discussed the evaluation report with them until it was far too late for them to have any impact on the decision-making process.

Illustrative Case 1—Analysis

The evaluator erred in not meeting earlier (when planning the evaluation) with the faculty committee and principal to develop a dissemination plan and to identify right-to-know stakeholders. He then erred in not submitting the report on time. When the evaluation was completed, he should have provided copies of the draft report to the teachers on the faculty committee as well as the principal. He should also have requested their review and comment. He should have prepared a summary report for the entire staff. Finally, the evaluator should have recommended to the principal that the report and its findings be discussed with those teachers who had used the materials as well as those who might use them during the next school year. These discussions should have been held prior to any decision about the use of the outcomes-based materials in the next year.

Illustrative Case 2—Description

Due to increasing concern regarding health care personnel shortages, a college commissioned an external firm to assess the student attrition rates for its nursing and allied health education programs. The firm developed a novel methodology for the evaluation, which yielded predicted attrition rates for each program, based on characteristics of entering students admitted to that program for each of three preceding years. The predicted rate was derived from several variables, including high school grade point average, SAT scores, and student age at admission. The standard deviation for each predicted rate was also determined to indicate the expected variability around each point estimate.

The resulting data were shared with each program director in the form of a table that displayed the program's predicted attrition rate, the standard deviation of this predicted rate, and the actual program attrition rate for each of three preceding years. A letter explained the methodology for the study and a simple mathematical formula for interpreting the results.

Program directors were asked to provide comments in written form for inclusion with the final report. Nearly every program director submitted comments complaining that they did not understand the data or how to interpret them.

The form of the final report was a 100-page bound document with many pages of data tables and a large appendix containing unedited copies of all the written comments submitted by program directors as well as a two-page "executive" summary. The final report and two-page summary were distributed to the college administrators and members of the board of trustees at a joint meeting of the administration and board. Relying principally on the two-page summary, the board took formal action at this meeting that resulted in each program director being sent a letter stating that the evaluation had revealed a quality problem with their program and that a detailed quality improvement action plan was due from them in the president's office within five days. The program directors were outraged.

Illustrative Case 2—Analysis

The evaluators did provide an opportunity for stakeholders to provide feedback on preliminary results but failed to use the feedback to improve the report prior to dissemination. In addition, the evaluators made a number of report dissemination and timing errors. The process and content for report dissemination procedures should have been carefully planned at the outset of the project to ensure that the information needs of right-to-know stakeholders would be appropriately met. As stakeholders in the evaluation, program directors should have had more than a perfunctory review of findings.

The evaluators erred further in the way they reported findings to the administration and the board. It appears the evaluators elected to unveil the final report at a meeting and, perhaps recognizing that it could not be reviewed in its entirety, developed a two-page summary that became the primary source of information at this meeting. Failure to provide the full report prior to the meeting resulted in its not being reviewed in its entirety before follow-up actions were proposed. This is a serious time line failure. Had a thorough reading been possible prior to this meeting, the concerns of the program directors could have been revealed. These concerns might have alerted the decision makers to possible pitfalls in the evaluation. This in turn might have signaled the need for further consideration and dissemination of the evaluators' report and, perhaps, for additional information that provided some idea of the reasons that students left their programs (see U3, Information Scope and Selection). The report could also have been made more readable by analyzing the large appendix of unedited written comments (see A9, Analysis of Qualitative Information).

Supporting Documentation

Fetterman, D. M. (1984). *Ethnography in educational evaluation.* Beverly Hills, CA: Sage.

Greene, J. C. (1988). Communication of results and utilization in participatory program evaluation. *Evaluation and Program Planning, 11,* 341-351.

Mitchell, J. (1990). Policy evaluation for policy communities: Confronting the utilization problem. *Evaluation Practice, 11*(2), 109-114.

Smith, M. F. (1988). Evaluation utilization revisited. *New Directions for Program Evaluation: Evaluation Utilization, 39,* 7-19.

U7   Evaluation Impact

STANDARD   Evaluations should be planned, conducted, and reported in ways that encourage follow-through by stakeholders, so that the likelihood that the evaluation will be used is increased.

Overview

The *impact* of an evaluation refers to the influence it has on the decisions and follow-up actions of members of the audience. It also refers to the conceptual influence it has on stakeholders. Evaluators should help stakeholders use the evaluation findings in taking such beneficial actions as improving programs, selecting more cost-beneficial products or approaches, or stopping wasteful, unproductive efforts. Evaluators should also help stakeholders see programs in ways different than they might have viewed them previously.

Evaluators must not assume that improvements will occur automatically once the evaluation report is completed. In effect, evaluators may need to play the role of someone who plans, staffs, and conducts evaluation activities so as to assist the members of the audience in assessing and making constructive use of the results of an evaluation, or someone who helps stakeholders understand a program in new ways. Evaluators should not take on the role of the client, however.

❖   GUIDELINES

A. Demonstrate to key stakeholders at the beginning of the evaluation how the findings might be useful for their work.

B. Arrange for the involvement of stakeholders in determining the evaluation questions to be addressed and in assisting with the planning and, if appropriate, the conduct of the evaluation (see U1, Stakeholder Identification).

C. Be open, frank, and concrete in reporting to stakeholders, and be available and willing to assist in clarifying the reports (see U5, Report Clarity, and P6, Disclosure of Findings).

D. Periodically report interim results, noting especially how these may apply to different stakeholders (see U6, Report Timeliness and Dissemination).

E. Assess with stakeholders the merits of plausible alternative courses of action and discuss those in the final report.

F. Supplement written reports with ongoing oral communication (see U6, Report Timeliness and Dissemination).

G. Within limits of time, financial, and personnel resources, plan to help the stakeholders assess, interpret, and apply the evaluation findings following release of the final report.

❖ COMMON ERRORS

A. Exhibiting a lack of confidence in the stakeholders' abilities to make appropriate use of the evaluation findings, for example, by commenting publicly that stakeholders will only believe those parts of the evaluation that reinforce their current beliefs and practices

B. Becoming preoccupied with the theoretical value of the findings at the expense of their practical value

C. Failing to consider the values of the stakeholders when making recommendations (see U4, Values Identification)

D. Taking over the client's responsibilities for acting on evaluation findings

E. Assuming clients will read what you give to them

F. Failing to intervene if evaluation findings are seen to be misused or misinterpreted

G. Failing to target individual users

H. Believing that every evaluation job is complete once an evaluation report has been handed in or a presentation has been made

I. Forcing follow-through when evaluation results do not warrant it

Illustrative Case 1—Description

Through a state-supported project designed to increase parent involvement in an elementary school, a group of parents developed a guide and supplementary materials designed to assist parents of elementary school children to help their children improve their reading skills. The parent group decided that the guide and materials should be evaluated and probably revised before being put into general use. Accordingly, they asked the district's reading specialist to undertake the evaluation.

The evaluator assessed the guide and the materials in relation to appropriateness and completeness of content, format, readability, general ease of use, and effectiveness under trial conditions. She organized her final report in terms of these five components, preceded by a short introductory section in which she briefly described the guide and materials. In the concluding section of her report, she identified weaknesses and presented recommendations for rewriting the guide and adding a daily progress chart.

The parent group was pleased with the constructive posture of the evaluation report and invited the evaluator to meet with them to discuss its contents. The reading specialist readily agreed and attended the group's next meeting.

At the meeting, the reading specialist explained the evaluation report in great detail. She also distributed a new version of the guide and a sample progress report that she had prepared. The parent group was impressed with the follow-up work of the evaluator. They realized that they were not capable of completing the task they had set for themselves. They asked the evaluator to take over their role in the project and subsequently phased out their participation.

The reading specialist then finalized the guide and materials but, to her surprise and disappointment, found that the parents of students in the school did not adopt and use the materials.

Illustrative Case 1—Analysis

The evaluator chose relevant aspects of the guide/materials on which to base her assessment. Using these aspects, she designed a clear, comprehensive, constructive, and accessible report for the parent group. However, the evaluator erred by being overzealous in assisting the parents to use the results of the evaluation. While her willingness to provide some follow-through assistance was appropriate, she should not have taken over the parents' role in developing the guide and materials—especially because the purpose of the given project was to increase parent involvement. She might have at least delayed her direct participation in rewriting the materials and, instead, have volunteered to review subsequent drafts developed by the parents. Alternatively, she could have worked with the parents, assisting them with the further development of the guide and materials.

Illustrative Case 2—Description

The need to develop and implement a formative evaluation of a Performance-Based Training (PBT) program in an industrial setting was identified by the trainers within the program. Members of the Instructional Services Branch of the company were assisted by an evaluation consultant in doing the evaluation.

The evaluation consisted of monitoring trainee development and productivity both during and after the program. A checklist of baseline trainee instructional behaviors guided the observations by trainers. This checklist was jointly developed by the evaluator and the trainers through an analysis of the goals of the PBT program and its implementation. The trainers used different recording techniques to describe physical and/or verbal behaviors observed in the classroom and in the workplace.

During the program, the evaluator and trainers jointly analyzed the recordings for changes in the expected directions. When progress was not seen, the trainers and evaluator examined both trainee characteristics and the training that had been delivered. Adjustments were made and training was repeated whenever necessary. A follow-up evaluation report, focusing on continued improvement of the PBT program, was written based on postprogram performance of the trainees.

Illustrative Case 2—Analysis

The evaluation was successful for several reasons. To begin with, trainee behavior was the focus of all who were involved. Second, the evaluator and trainers shared common goals and language developed during the formative evaluation, thus enabling them to agree to all procedures to be followed. Third, progress during the program and performance after the program was monitored by trainers and the evaluator. This evaluation was planned and conducted in ways that encouraged follow-through by appropriate stakeholders.

Supporting Documentation

Alkin, M. C., Daillak, R., & White, P. (1979). *Using evaluation: Does evaluation make a difference?* Beverly Hills, CA: Sage.

Mitchell, J. (1990). Policy evaluation for policy communities: Confronting the utilization problem. *Evaluation Practice, 11*(2), 109-114.

Mowbray, C. T. (1988). Getting the system to respond to evaluation findings. *New Directions for Program Evaluation: Evaluation Utilization, 39*, 47-57.

Patton, M. Q. (1986). *Utilization-focused evaluation* (2nd ed.). Beverly Hills, CA: Sage.

Patton, M. Q. (1988). The evaluator's responsibility for utilization. *Evaluation Practice, 9*(2), 5-24.

Preskill, H. (1991, Spring). The cultural lens: Bringing utilization into focus. *New Directions in Program Evaluation, 49*, 5-13.

Smith, M. F. (1988). Evaluation utilization revisited. *New Directions for Program Evaluation: Evaluation Utilization, 39*, 7-19.

Stufflebeam, D. L., Foley, W. J., Gephart, W. J., Guba, E. G., Hammond, R. L., Merriman, H. O., & Provus, M. M. (1971). *Educational evaluation and decision making.* Itasca, IL: F. E. Peacock.

Winberg, A. (1991). Maximizing the contributions of internal evaluation units. *Evaluation and Program Planning, 14*(1), 167-172.

Feasibility Standards

Summary of the Standards

F Feasibility Standards   The feasibility standards are intended to ensure that an evaluation will be realistic, prudent, diplomatic, and frugal. The standards are as follows:

> **F1 Practical Procedures**   The evaluation procedures should be practical, to keep disruption to a minimum while needed information is obtained.

> **F2 Political Viability**   The evaluation should be planned and conducted with anticipation of the different positions of various interest groups, so that their cooperation may be obtained, and so that possible attempts by any of these groups to curtail evaluation operations or to bias or misapply the results can be averted or counteracted.

> **F3 Cost Effectiveness**   The evaluation should be efficient and produce information of sufficient value, so that the resources expended can be justified.

F1   Practical Procedures

> **STANDARD**   The evaluation procedures should be practical, to keep disruption to a minimum while needed information is obtained.

Overview

Evaluation procedures are the particular actions taken in the process of collecting and using information to judge the worth or merit of a program. These procedures include, but are not limited to, how contractual agreements with the client are reached; how data sources are chosen; which instruments are selected and how they are administered; how data and information are collected, recorded, stored, and retrieved; how data are analyzed; and how findings are reported. Evaluators should choose and implement procedures that minimize disruption and that are feasible and realistic given the availability of time, budget, staff, and participants.

If evaluators do not adhere to this standard, they may plan procedures that are theoretically sound but unworkable. Such a practice consumes resources without yielding valuable and/or usable results.

❖   GUIDELINES

A. Ensure the availability of qualified personnel to complete the evaluation as proposed, including the need to train any personnel who need it.

B. Choose procedures that can be carried out with reasonable effort and that are compatible with the skill level of personnel available for the study.

C. Select procedures in light of known time constraints and the availability of participants or respondents.

D. Whenever appropriate, make evaluation activities a part of routine events.

E. Develop alternative procedures in anticipation of potential problems and retain sufficient flexibility in the plan and budget so that unanticipated problems can be addressed as they occur.

F. Check with the clients about the viability of the schedule for completing the evaluation and the practicality of various data collection procedures before finalizing the data collection plan (see A3, Described Purposes and Procedures, and P2, Formal Agreements).

G. Try out procedures and instruments in a pilot test to determine their practicality and their time requirements.

❖ COMMON ERRORS

A. Choosing a data collection and analysis plan from a research methods textbook or other general guide without considering whether the plan can be carried out in the given setting

B. Failing to weigh practicality against accuracy (If circumstances will inhibit the collection of valid and reliable data, work with the client to remove or alter these circumstances. If this proves unsuccessful, seriously consider using other procedures or not doing the evaluation.)

C. Disrupting program activities in an attempt to collect information

---

Illustrative Case 1—Description

A state education department issued a request for proposals to evaluate a state-supported school aid program. This program was operating in 100 school districts in the state and provided about $100 per pupil to schools with high concentrations of economically disadvantaged students. It was due to be applied in an additional 100 districts, and the officials of the state agency wanted to control the expansion in such a way that the effects of the program could be ascertained. Accordingly, the request for proposals specified that the next 100 program grants to school districts would be made in accordance with the requirements of the selected evaluation plan.

An evaluation plan was selected from among several proposals submitted by evaluators in response to a request for proposals. The selected evaluation proposal specified that the state department should recruit 10 urban, 15 suburban, and 25 rural districts, dispersed geographically throughout the state, to participate in the evaluation. Each district was to be chosen only if its superintendent agreed to cooperate fully with the evaluators and to meet the requirements of their evaluation plan. Specifically, the superintendents were to do the following: identify two of their elementary schools matched for their concentrations of disadvantaged students and for similarity of program offerings; allow the evaluators to choose one of these schools at random to receive the financial aid; use this aid to enrich the programs of the disadvantaged students in the chosen school; and ensure that both schools would comply with the evaluators' data collection requests. The evaluator's plan specified that the students in all 100 schools would be pretested and posttested during each of three years, and that the results would be analyzed to determine whether the students in the 50 schools receiving the state aid achieved higher test scores than did the students in the other 50 schools.

The state department successfully recruited 50 districts that met the sampling requirements and whose superintendents agreed to the conditions specified in the evaluation plan. A grant was made to each school randomly chosen from the 50 matched pairs, and the evaluation was launched with the pretesting of all students in all 100 schools.

By the time the evaluators administered the posttest at the end of the first project year, they realized that their evaluation had been hopelessly compromised. The superintendents had lived up to the letter but not the spirit of their agreement with the state department. In the face of possible criticism from the parents and staff of schools in their district who were not benefiting from the new state grant, the superintendents had reallocated other discretionary monies so that no school was in a financially disadvantageous position. The result was that the difference between total per-pupil expenditures for the schools in each matched pair was negligible. Also, it was discovered that, by the time of the posttest, student populations in the schools were considerably changed. There were many new students in each school, while many others had left. Also, in several instances students starting out in one school of a matched pair had transferred to the other. Because so many assumptions of the original evaluation plan had been compromised, the state department officials and the evaluators agreed that a case study approach should be substituted for the originally planned comparative analysis.

Illustrative Case 1—Analysis

This evaluation illustrates some of the problems that can arise when an experimental design is imposed and applied in a complex, dynamic, and politically charged setting. It also illustrates violations of Standards P1, Service Orientation, and P3, Rights of Human Subjects. The evaluators should have known that providing preferential treatment to one school in a district was likely to generate political pressures to "equalize" the treatment across all schools. Moreover, they should have anticipated student attrition and mobility.

The evaluators originally might have considered an alternative evaluation approach such as a well-designed case study. This case study could employ interviews, observations, and document analysis as methods to collect information on the context, processes, and outcomes of the program. This approach would provide the state officials with information about the implementation of the program at each site, as well as about valued outcomes.

Illustrative Case 2—Description

A management team in a company designed a comparative evaluation of the effectiveness and costs of self-paced and instructor-led strategies for delivering computer programming training to employees with no prior programming experience. The 70 employees were to be randomly divided into two groups of 35, and each group was to receive one of the competing training programs. Due to space and computer hardware limitations, each group was to be subdivided into five subgroups of 7 participants each, and each subgroup was to attend a particular class using the assigned training approach. All classes were to be scheduled and completed during a four-week period. Of the seven available instructors, two were to be chosen randomly to supervise and assist the self-paced subgroups. The remaining five instructors were to be randomly assigned to teach one of the instructor-led subgroups.

At the end of the training, each participant would complete a series of computer programming problems. Their responses were to be scored for time required to complete each problem and quality of computer programs produced. Additional data would be collected through a questionnaire and a debriefing session with each subgroup. The date each self-paced participant completed training would be recorded, as would the hours of instruction/learning time involved for each participant in both groups. Hours and salary costs for the instructors working with both groups would also be recorded.

Before proceeding with the study, the two strategies were pilot tested with two small groups to identify and correct deficiencies. A number of improvements were made in each instructional program (e.g., clarification of printed instructions and provision of five to ten minutes at the beginning of each session when students could ask questions to make sure they understood the training objectives and procedures). The pilot test participants also completed the evaluation data collection procedures and gave their reactions and suggestions, which led to pertinent improvements.

As one more step toward assuring that the evaluation would be viable, the management team engaged an evaluation specialist to review the evaluation plan against a checklist of potential problems in comparative evaluation studies. This led to the following refinements in the plan:

1. To assure that all chosen trainees would be available to complete the training and evaluation and that they would not have been trained in computer programming before participating in the evaluation study, clear guidelines and agreement-to-participate forms were prepared and distributed to both supervisors and prospective participants. The responses were used to identify an appropriate study population from which to select participants.

2. Similarly, checks were made to assure that the instructors of the two training approaches and the persons who would collect the evaluation

information would be available for the duration of the evaluation. Consequently, the number of subgroups to receive each training approach was reduced to eight subgroups, each with seven members.

3. Training was provided to the evaluators so they would follow standardized procedures.

4. The complete schedule for the study was reviewed with appropriate authorities and participants, and their written approvals and agreements to participate were obtained.

5. Arrangements for facilities, equipment, and standby technical backup were made to assure that the programs could be run on schedule, without disruptions, and with immediate attention to any equipment failure that might arise.

6. Observers were trained and assigned to observe and make a written record of the training sessions, so that a judgment could be reached about the extent of implementation of each training approach.

7. A focus group, including instructors, managers, participants, and observers, was organized for the purpose of reviewing and discussing the draft evaluation report and providing joint interpretation and recommendations.

Due to the systematic and careful planning of this evaluation, it proceeded smoothly and resulted in an informative, defensible, and politically acceptable assessment of the relative effectiveness and costs of the two approaches. While both approaches proved to be effective, the self-paced approach cost less in instructor salary and student time, received higher acceptability ratings from the participants, and was recommended for adoption by the focus group.

Illustrative Case 2—Analysis

Many things can and do go wrong in even the most carefully planned evaluations. Preparing sound, realistic plans helps to avoid or minimize problems. Pilot testing the plans helps to make them more realistic and workable. Carefully preparing all the participants and getting their informed agreements to participate enhances the prospects for success. Involving representatives of the different interest groups in reviewing and interpreting findings helps to finalize a sound report and to gain support for it. And it is always wise to prepare contingency plans for dealing with unexpected problems. This example attests to the wisdom of deliberately and systematically making the evaluation plan as workable as possible. It also illustrates the amount of communication required to make an evaluation work. Planning sufficient time to communicate plans for data collection, revising data collection, and teaching it to others is important.

Supporting Documentation

Brinkerhoff, R. O., Brethower, D. M., Hluchyj, T., & Nowakowski, J. R. (1983). *Program evaluation: A practitioner's guide for trainers and educators.* Boston: Kluwer-Nijhoff.

Cook, T. D., & Reichardt, C. S. (Eds.). (1979). *Qualitative and quantitative methods in evaluation research.* Beverly Hills, CA: Sage.

Fetterman, D. M. (1989). *Ethnography: Step by step.* Newbury Park, CA: Sage.

Fitz-Gibbon, C. T., & Morris, L. L. (1987). How to design a program evaluation. In J. L. Herman (Ed.), *Program evaluation kit* (2nd ed.). Newbury Park, CA: Sage.

Frankel, B. (1982). On participant observation as a component of evaluation: Strategies, constraints, and issues. *Evaluation and Program Planning, 5*(3), 239-246.

Nagel, S. S. (1988). Evaluative decisions under conflicting constraints. *Evaluation Practice, 9*(2), 36-39.

Sanders, J. R. (1992). *Evaluating school programs.* Newbury Park, CA: Corwin.

F1   Practical Procedures

F2   Political Viability

> **STANDARD**   The evaluation should be planned and conducted with anticipation of the different positions of various interest groups, so that their cooperation may be obtained, and so that possible attempts by any of these groups to curtail evaluation operations or to bias or misapply the results can be averted or counteracted.

Overview

An interest group is any group of individuals that seeks to influence policy in favor of some shared goal or concern. An evaluation has political implications to the extent that it leads to decisions concerning reallocation of resources and influence. Evaluations are politically viable to the extent that their purposes can be achieved with fair and equitable acknowledgment of the pressures and actions applied by various interest groups with a stake in the evaluation.

In the case of a potentially volatile evaluation, if evaluators are not vigilant, they may find too late that their work has been manipulated, has been applied by one group to gain an unfair advantage over another, or has been seriously impeded by a group that is threatened by an evaluation. Consequently, the credibility of the evaluation will be reduced or destroyed. On the positive side, evaluators who are sensitive to political pressures sometimes will be able to make constructive use of diverse political forces in achieving the purposes of the evaluation.

❖ GUIDELINES

A. Before agreeing to do a potentially volatile evaluation, meet with as many interest groups as possible, provide them with an opportunity to express their positions and raise concerns regarding the evaluation, and

71

assure them that it will be conducted fairly (see U1, Stakeholder Identification; U7, Evaluation Impact; and A3, Described Purposes and Procedures).

B. Negotiate a contract that makes explicit and public the conditions that will govern the evaluation and that assures that the evaluators will have access to the required data and control over the editing and dissemination of their reports (see P2, Formal Agreements). In addition, be sure that the contract provides for periodic review and amendment as appropriate.

C. Provide clients and other key audiences with periodic reports on the progress of the evaluation—through such means as advisory panels and newsletters—to ensure that reported outcomes of the evaluation are not total surprises to the audiences and that their reactions to the reports are not unanticipated by the evaluators (see U2, Evaluator Credibility, and U7, Evaluation Impact).

D. Within available resources, identify, assess, and report different perspectives, when they exist, among stakeholder groups.

E. Discontinue the evaluation if political issues create such an unfavorable situation that it appears the interests of all concerned will be best served by withdrawal. However, be sure the public's right to know is upheld (see P6, Disclosure of Findings).

❖ COMMON ERRORS

A. Giving the appearance—by attending to one stakeholder group more than another—that the evaluation is biased in favor of one group

B. Failing to assess accurately and to take into account both the formal and informal organizational power structure

C. Insulating the evaluation from the possible influence of special interest groups to the extent that key stakeholders are not consulted and/or provided timely feedback that addresses their particular questions (see U1, Stakeholder Identification)

D. Assuming "objective" methodologies will ensure a fair evaluation

E. Failing to provide cautions with interim reports that further study or emergent questions may alter early conclusions

Illustrative Case 1—Description

A team of professors accepted an assignment in a school district to evaluate an innovative approach to reading instruction. The evaluation was mandated as part of state funding for the program. There were rumors that the district superintendent was opposed to the program because, although there would be fewer state funds available if it were not in operation, school district funds that were needed for the program could then be used with greater flexibility. Some teachers said the superintendent would do anything to scrap the program, even influence the evaluation so that it reflected adversely on the program. In order to try to mediate the influence of the superintendent on the evaluation, the evaluators met with the superintendent. The goal of the meeting was to gain an insight into the particular nature of the superintendent's opposition to the team teaching program. The evaluators then planned to include information in the evaluation report that could counter the superintendent's concerns.

As part of their evaluation, they built in a scheme to assess individual teachers' instructional skills. To their consternation, however, when the design was released it brought an immediate repudiation from the teachers' union, which was opposed to the scheme for appraising its members. A strike was threatened if the evaluation was to be carried out as planned. The incident was reported on the front page of one of the local newspapers and received much attention on local radio stations. Fearing the consequences, the evaluators backed down on their demands for the teacher assessments, even though they thought such an action would substantially reduce the evaluation's defensibility.

Based principally upon pupil achievement data, the evaluators concluded that the approach to reading instruction was a clear success. But, when the superintendent got a preview copy of the report, he issued a public statement to the newspapers isolating a number of alleged methodological deficiencies in the evaluation, repudiating its conclusion, and castigating the evaluators for incompetence. In particular, he stressed the omission of the assessment of individual teacher's instructional skills.

Illustrative Case 1—Analysis

While the evaluators tried to include the superintendent's concerns in the design, more could have been done to reduce the political volatility of the situation. Sensing the superintendent's bias in the matter, the evaluators might have developed a written evaluation plan and obliged him to approve the plan in writing or to suggest revisions so that it would be acceptable. By securing the superintendent's approval of their methodology, the evaluators might have precluded subsequent dismissal of findings.

With respect to the teacher appraisal part of their design, the evaluators should have involved teacher union officials early in their planning, so that, sensitized to the union's views, they could have evolved a strategy that was acceptable to all parties. The evaluators should have recognized the tensions that frequently exist between the needs of stakeholders and the requirements of a comprehensive evaluation and dealt with them before the study was conducted. However, the quality of the evaluation should not be compromised by political pressures.

Illustrative Case 2—Description

A newly formed in-house evaluation team was assigned the task of evaluating 14 remedial education and job training programs for economically disadvantaged youth. The evaluation was mandated by the state agency responsible for administering the federal funds used to implement these youth programs. While the administrative agency had regularly conducted compliance monitoring of these programs, this was the first attempt to evaluate them in any depth. The evaluation team was given three months to design and implement the evaluation.

The program operators were informed of the impending evaluation through a letter that requested their cooperation and stated that the evaluation was to provide the administrative agency with information on the quality of the programs as well as program outcomes. However, rumors began to reach the evaluation team that, given a budgetary crisis within the state, administrative agency personnel and state legislative representatives wanted to use the evaluation results to reduce the funds for a number of the youth programs.

The rumors quickly became public. The youth program operators immediately formed an ad hoc advocacy committee, hoping to enhance their authority by negotiating with the administrative agency on a collective rather than an individual basis. However, the director of the administrative agency refused to deal with this committee, stating that he was only obligated to work with the individual subcontracted to operate each program. Meanwhile, the program operators, through their ad hoc committee, charged that they had inadequate resources with which to participate in an in-depth evaluation and that the evaluation team was unqualified to evaluate their programs because team members were neither educators nor experienced in the actual implementation of youth remedial education and/or job training programs.

Confronted at the outset with this political standoff between the funding agency and program operators, the evaluation team sought to identify strategies for mediating the conflict and obtaining as much consensus as possible among stakeholders regarding the design and conduct of the evaluations.

First, the evaluation team formally requested agency administrators to clarify what they perceived to be the primary purpose of the evaluation and how they intended to use the evaluation results. In addition, they informed the agency administrators that, given the time lines and human resources available, the evaluation would not and could not provide any definitive basis for refunding any but those programs that were not performing at all. Confronted with this information, agency administrators responded by stating they expected the evaluation would generate information about the efficacy of the structure and processes of each program. The evaluation results would be used to assist program operators in making the changes necessary to improve the quality of service delivery and to enhance outcomes. Following a discussion, the evaluators and agency administrators agreed to this purpose.

The evaluation team then convened several meetings with program operators to ask them to identify the critical features of youth programs that they believed should serve as hallmarks of "quality" programs. This information was synthesized and became the basis upon which evaluation designs for individual programs were developed. Program operators were asked to review and comment upon the design for their respective programs.

The evaluations were conducted and the written reports of findings and recommendations were again sent to program operators for review and comment prior to finalization. In the few cases where differences of perspective with regard to findings could not be resolved, program operators were requested to prepare written comments that were ultimately included in the final report disseminated to agency administrators and state legislative representatives. To ensure fairness, the evaluation team included in these reports a discussion of issues related to state agency policies, rules, and practices that were found in the evaluation to hinder the programs' ability to be more effective.

Illustrative Case 2—Analysis

Much of the conflict that occurred prior to the beginning of the evaluation could have been avoided by the administrative agency informing program operators of the pending evaluations and their purposes. The first steps taken by the in-house evaluation team were appropriate. By involving agency administrators and program operators in the planning, definition, and design of the evaluation, much of the apparent conflict was eliminated. The antagonism was further reduced by including information about the role and efficacy of both the programs and the agency, and by sharing the findings of the evaluation with the program operators and including their comments in the final report prior to its release. Through these activities, the evaluation team was able to effectively mediate the conflict and demonstrate the utility and mutual benefit of the evaluation to both the program operators and the agency administrators.

Supporting Documentation

Alkin, M. C. (1990). *Debates on evaluation.* Newbury Park, CA: Sage.

Chelimsky, E. (1987). What have we learned about the politics of program evaluation? *Evaluation Practice, 8*(1), 5-21.

Cronbach, L. J., Ambron, S. R., Dornbusch, S. M., Hess, R. D., Hornik, R. C., Phillips, D. C., Walker, D. F., & Weiner, S. S. (1980). *Toward reform of program evaluation.* San Francisco: Jossey-Bass.

Delamont, S. (1992). *Fieldwork in educational settings: Methods, pitfalls and perspectives.* Bristol, PA: Falmer.

House, E. R. (Ed.). (1973). *School evaluation: The politics and process.* Berkeley, CA: McCutchan.

Scriven, M. (1993). *Hard-won lessons in program evaluation* (New Directions for Program Evaluation, No. 58). San Francisco: Jossey-Bass.

F3   Cost Effectiveness

STANDARD   The evaluation should be efficient and
produce information of sufficient value, so that the
resources expended can be justified.

Overview

An evaluation is cost effective if its benefits equal or exceed its costs. *Costs*
refer to the value of all of the resources used in the evaluation, including
the time of participants and volunteer workers, financial amounts actually
charged, and in-kind services. That is, *costs* refer to the total value, social
and monetary, of all the human and physical resources used to carry out the
evaluation. *Benefits* denote the value of all the results derived from the
evaluation. These include, but are not limited to, publicly identifying effective and ineffective educational and training programs, projects, materials,
and services; discovering how the monetary and nonmonetary costs of a
program might be reduced without decreasing its services; and fostering
understanding of activities and how they are perceived in a given setting
and from a variety of perspectives.

Often, evaluators have under consideration several alternative designs
they could choose from to conduct an evaluation. If none is judged to be
cost effective and no additional designs are identified, then the evaluation
should not be undertaken when there is a choice. Sometimes evaluations are
mandated whatever the cost. If more than one are judged to be cost effective,
then the design with the best combination of costs and benefits should be
chosen. When the design that is expected to provide the most useful information is also the most expensive, the extra information it will provide
should be worth the extra expense. In a situation where the benefits are
judged equal for alternative designs, the choice can be made on the basis of
cost alone.

Cost effectiveness analyses are often elusive and difficult to conduct. This
is because outcomes of evaluations are often numerous, intangible, and
valued differently by different stakeholders. These outcomes are often not

easily measured or observed. When confronted with such difficulties, the evaluator must use past experiences and approximations to make cost effectiveness judgments. It is always wise in such instances to ask for second opinions.

Even when it is not possible to fully evaluate cost effectiveness, it is important to be prudent and efficient in expending resources for evaluation.

❖ GUIDELINES

A. Investigate thoroughly initial costs of materials and services to be used (e.g., answer sheets, copy paper, interviewer time, training, budgeting and cost accounting, computer time, and films or tapes). If necessary, anticipate increases in costs due to inflation during the period of the evaluation.

B. Develop a budget in which all costs, including dollar amounts, time, and in-kind support are listed and, where necessary, explained (see P8, Fiscal Responsibility).

C. Minimize disruptions that evaluations can cause (see P4, Human Interactions).

D. Make an inventory of benefits—those agreed upon with the client as well as beneficial side effects for other stakeholders (e.g., increased interest of parents in a program or improvement of students' attitudes toward the program).

E. Weigh anticipated human and financial costs against projected benefits to the client and other stakeholders before deciding to do an evaluation.

F. Conduct evaluations as economically as possible (see P8, Fiscal Responsibility).

G. Maintain a proper balance between resources spent on the evaluation and resources spent on the program.

❖ COMMON ERRORS

A. Completely ignoring cost effectiveness just because an evaluation is mandated and will be done in spite of the cost

B. Selecting an evaluation method that is familiar without searching for alternatives that are more cost effective

C. Commencing an evaluation without a commitment of sufficient resources to complete it

D. Assuming that an initial commitment of adequate resources obviates the need to ensure that the evaluation is cost effective

E. Allowing concerns for cost effectiveness to deter evaluators and clients from trying new methods or doing evaluations that are important but difficult to do and that may lead to additional, useful data and information

F. Failing to recognize that cost effectiveness analyses are often difficult to complete because the outcomes considered in an evaluation are often numerous, intangible, and differentially valued by different groups, and because they are often not easily measured or observed

Illustrative Case 1—Description

A superintendent of a large school district contracted for an evaluation of a new elementary school mathematics program. While a part of the evaluation was the assessment of the computational skills of the district's third- and fourth-grade students, the performance of individual students was not at issue. In fact, only district-level results were to be reported.

A committee composed of one teacher selected from each school in the district chose, using a consensus model, a set of 300 computational problems from a large item bank. The items selected were judged to be appropriate for assessing the degree to which 30 computational objectives of the mathematics program were being met.

The evaluators assembled the 300 problems into a test that required three sessions of two and a half hours each to administer. This test was given to all third- and fourth-grade students in the district.

Illustrative Case 1—Analysis

While accomplishing the goal of assessing the degree to which the 30 computational objectives had been achieved, the evaluation required the investment of more student and teacher time than was necessary. This was especially true because the scores of individual students were not reported.

Rather than constructing a single test of 300 problems, the evaluators might have randomly divided the problems into 10 subsets of 30 problems each so that each objective was covered by each subset of problems. The 10 subsets could have been randomly assigned and administered to students in a random sample of classrooms, so that each participating student responded to a single subset of 30 items. Substantial savings of pupil and teacher time could have been achieved with little loss in the accuracy of the assessment.

Illustrative Case 2—Description

A medical school's educational policy requires that student achievement in third-year clerkships must be evaluated, in part, by the use of "objective measures of acquired knowledge." Instead of developing examinations locally, the five clerkship directors chose to purchase external examinations from a testing agency. The examinations are nationally standardized, produced in alternate forms, yield highly reliable scores, and are secure—their specific contents are not known prior to administration. Past research shows that correlations among the alternate forms are in the high .80s to low .90s, and that the forms historically correlate in the low .80s with locally prepared tests of acquired knowledge.

The cost for these examinations is $4,100 for each clerkship. With five clerkships per year, the medical school thus pays $20,500 each year to use these external examinations.

Illustrative Case 2—Analysis

The medical school, through the five clerkship directors, fulfills its policy of measuring knowledge acquisition among students by using examinations developed by an outside agency. However, at issue here is the reported finding that the external examination scores are highly correlated with scores from locally prepared tests. The clerkship directors should consider whether spending money on the external examinations is more cost effective than developing the examinations locally. Despite the convenience and faculty time savings, the directors might find that the local preparation would be less expensive. At the same time, they may find that, by preparing the examinations locally, other positive side effects, such as refinement of the clerkship content, may come about.

Supporting Documentation

Alkin, M., & Solomon, L. C. (1983). Conducting benefit cost analysis of program evaluation. In M. Alkin & L. C. Solomon (Eds.), *The costs of evaluation.* Beverly Hills, CA: Sage.

Levin, H. M. (1983). *Cost-effectiveness: A primer.* Beverly Hills, CA: Sage.

Monteau, P. (1987). Establishing corporate evaluation policy: Cost versus benefit. In L. S. May, C. A. Moore, & S. J. Zammit (Eds.), *Evaluating business and industry training.* Boston: Kluwer Academic.

Worthen, B. R., & Sanders, J. R. (1987). *Educational evaluation: Alternative approaches and practical guidelines.* White Plains, NY: Longman.

Propriety Standards

Summary of the Standards

P Propriety Standards The propriety standards are intended to ensure that an evaluation will be conducted legally, ethically, and with due regard for the welfare of those involved in the evaluation, as well as those affected by its results. These standards are as follows:

P1 Service Orientation Evaluations should be designed to assist organizations to address and effectively serve the needs of the full range of targeted participants.

P2 Formal Agreements Obligations of the formal parties to an evaluation (what is to be done, how, by whom, when) should be agreed to in writing, so that these parties are obligated to adhere to all conditions of the agreement or formally to renegotiate it.

P3 Rights of Human Subjects Evaluations should be designed and conducted to respect and protect the rights and welfare of human subjects.

P4 Human Interactions Evaluators should respect human dignity and worth in their interactions with other persons associated with an evaluation, so that participants are not threatened or harmed.

P5 **Complete and Fair Assessment**   The evaluation should be complete and fair in its examination and recording of strengths and weaknesses of the program being evaluated, so that strengths can be built upon and problem areas addressed.

P6 **Disclosure of Findings**   The formal parties to an evaluation should ensure that the full set of evaluation findings along with pertinent limitations are made accessible to the persons affected by the evaluation, and any others with expressed legal rights to receive the results.

P7 **Conflict of Interest**   Conflict of interest should be dealt with openly and honestly, so that it does not compromise the evaluation processes and results.

P8 **Fiscal Responsibility**   The evaluator's allocation and expenditure of resources should reflect sound accountability procedures and otherwise be prudent and ethically responsible, so that expenditures are accounted for and appropriate.

P1 Service Orientation

STANDARD Evaluations should be designed to assist organizations to address and effectively serve the needs of the full range of targeted participants.

Overview

EVALUATIONS should help assure that educational goals are appropriate, learner development is addressed, promised services are delivered, and ineffective or harmful programs are removed, thus providing accountability to community and society. Those who design, administer, use, and participate in evaluations must look beyond educators' or organizations' self-interests to enhance development of learners and society. In short, evaluations should serve program participants, community, and society.

❖ GUIDELINES

    A. Design evaluations to promote excellence in educational and training programs.

    B. Inform the stakeholders of the purposes of the evaluation (see A3, Described Purposes and Procedures).

    C. Focus evaluation efforts and resources on those program features most likely to affect participants and promote the organization's goals (see U3, Information Scope and Selection, and F3, Cost Effectiveness).

    D. Use evaluation to identify program effects on learners, intended or not.

    E. Examine program effects against the assessed needs of the targeted participants or other beneficiaries.

    F. Provide interim evaluation findings citing strengths and deficiencies and suggestions for improvement.

G. Periodically inform the stakeholders and the public about how program evaluation is promoting the best interests of the organization's constituents.

H. Minimize the interruption of instructional processes while still trying to promote the purposes of the evaluation.

❖ COMMON ERRORS

A. Failing to monitor the effectiveness of programs

B. Focusing on program goals and objectives identified only by program management and staff

C. Failing to include the perspectives of various stakeholders in evaluations

D. Recommending premature termination or curtailment of programs before attempting to improve their effectiveness

E. Failing to recommend termination of ineffective or detrimental programs

F. Failing to monitor the effectiveness of evaluations in improving programs serving students, adult learners, community, and society (see A12, Metaevaluation)

G. Failing to keep evaluation practices current with state-of-the-art information on teaching, learning, and evaluation

H. Advocating beliefs about the rights of participants or community when such beliefs represent a bias on the part of the evaluator

I. Overusing instructional time for data gathering to the detriment of student learning

Illustrative Case—Description

An urban school district implemented an in-service training program to prepare teachers to teach an alternative mathematics curriculum designed for the ninth grade. Teachers in four of the district's ten high schools were selected for the in-service. The program was funded by the district with board-approved funds for staff development activities. These funds were administered by the Division of Instruction, which reviewed proposals for staff development activities and required that they include an evaluation component to assess student outcomes.

The training program consisted of four after-school sessions for three hours each, provided over the course of the fall semester. Teachers were to implement the new curriculum in their algebra classes for the next semester. Largely unfamiliar with program evaluation, the district's mathematics director allocated a minimal amount of funds for the evaluation. He contracted with a local evaluation consultant in a newly established business to conduct the evaluation.

The evaluation consultant suggested that she and the director meet to discuss his goals for the evaluation and that she would provide a plan for the evaluation, based on those goals and the resources available to conduct the evaluation. On the day of the scheduled meeting, the district's assistant superintendent for instruction called a mandatory meeting of all central office instructional staff. As a result, the mathematics director was only able to meet with the evaluation consultant for 30 minutes, rather than the 90 minutes they had originally planned. During the meeting, he did state that the district intended to expand the new curriculum to all high schools if the evaluation results were favorable. Eager to be responsive to this new client, the consultant indicated she felt she could develop an evaluation plan based on their discussion and review of the proposal for the training program. Approximately two weeks later, the consultant mailed the director an evaluation plan. He reviewed it briefly and indicated his approval via telephone and asked the evaluator to proceed as specified in the plan.

The plan focused on provision of the training and the teachers' implementation of the training in the classroom. It included (a) trainers' and teachers' assessments of the training program itself (i.e., opinion surveys about the content, method, and setting for the training sessions) and (b) observation of teachers' use of the new teaching strategies in their algebra classes. No additional information was collected from teachers about their use of the new curriculum, nor were any student outcome data collected. The evaluator based the limited scope of the evaluation on two factors: the limited funds available and her belief that evaluating in terms of student outcomes was premature. However, she did not discuss this rationale with the mathematics director, nor did he inquire about it.

The final evaluation report provided at the end of the school year reflected favorably on the program. Basically, both teachers and trainers reported satisfaction with the training, and teachers appeared to be implementing the alternative algebra curriculum properly in their classes. The Division of Instruction decided to expand use of the alternative algebra curriculum to all district schools.

The following school year's (October) administration of standardized tests showed 10th-grade students' performance on the mathematics subsection to be significantly lower than in previous years. The mathematics director requested further analyses of scores for individual items and disaggregated by high school. Available the following March, these additional analyses revealed the lowest scores to be on the algebra items for students from the four high schools where the new curriculum had been implemented. The Division of Instruction was dismayed at this outcome, given the favorable evaluation of the training program for the alternative algebra curriculum. By this time, another class of ninth-grade students in all high schools was being instructed with the alternative curriculum.

Illustrative Case—Analysis

The evaluator's original intention for a 90-minute meeting was correct. Perhaps if she had had the opportunity to gather more information prior to submitting her design, some of the problems that occurred might have been avoided. Given the chain of events, the Division of Instruction based a decision about the mathematics curriculum on evaluation results too limited in scope to properly inform the decision. The decision affected all district ninth-grade students and potentially limited their ability to perform well on standardized achievement tests, the results of which could be used in future decisions (e.g., college entry based on SAT scores).

A number of factors contributed to the failure of this evaluation to sufficiently address the training program's implementation and its impact on students. Insufficient attention was given to evaluating the new curriculum, both in time and in monetary resources. Although the Division of Instruction required funded programs to be evaluated, it did not examine proposals for the adequacy of their evaluation components. Further exacerbating this circumstance, the mathematics director hired an inexperienced evaluator and did not devote sufficient time to working with her to design the evaluation. The evaluator was correct in suggesting a meeting with the mathematics director to discuss the goals and resources in order to design the evaluation. She was also correct in providing the director a copy of the evaluation plan for confirmation and approval. However, both the meeting to discuss the goals and resources and the director's feedback were inadequate. He approved the submitted evaluation plan essentially without discussion or modification. The plan did not meet the requirement of evaluating the program in terms of student outcomes.

Given the limited funds available for the evaluation, the consultant felt justified in the evaluation design she proposed. However, given further consideration of the program's impact on students and the Division of Instruction's stated intent to expand the program if evaluation results were favorable, the evaluator might have declined to conduct the evaluation. At the very least, the evaluator should have made clear the limitations of the evaluation. An appropriate evaluation plan would have addressed student outcomes and other data sources that could have alerted the district to problems with the new curriculum (e.g., more in-depth investigation of the teachers' ability to implement the new curriculum, parent opinion data that might have reflected student difficulty with the new approach, interviews with other mathematics teachers addressing the new curriculum's articulation with curricula in the seventh and eighth grades, and interviews with the students themselves).

Supporting Documentation

Alkin, M. C. (1990). *Debates on evaluation*. Newbury Park, CA: Sage.

Greene, J. C. (1991, April). *Responding to evaluation's moral challenge*. Paper presented at the annual meeting of the American Educational Research Association, Chicago.

Schwandt, T. A. (1989). Recapturing moral discourse in evaluation. *Educational Researcher, 18*(8), 11-16.

Stake, R. E. (1986). *Quieting reform*. Urbana: University of Illinois Press.

P2 Formal Agreements

STANDARD   Obligations of the formal parties to an evaluation (what is to be done, how, by whom, when) should be agreed to in writing, so that these parties are obligated to adhere to all conditions of the agreement or formally to renegotiate it.

Overview

A written agreement is a mutual understanding of the specified expectations and responsibilities of both the client and the evaluator. Having entered into such an agreement, both parties have an obligation to carry it out in a forthright manner or to renegotiate it. Neither party is obligated to honor decisions made unilaterally by the other.

Guidelines of federal, state, and local agencies for *external* evaluations often require that the evaluator and client enter into a formal contract. Matters to include in such contracts include responsibilities of agency personnel for conducting and participating in evaluations; approval of evaluation plans; protection of human subjects; data collection, storage, and retrieval; editing and disseminating reports; use of external evaluators; and financing the evaluation effort. But even when a formal contract is not mandated—commonly the case with *internal* evaluations—the parties to the evaluation should develop at least a brief memorandum of agreement spelling out what is to be done, by whom, how, and when. The agreement could even be based on minutes of a meeting.

It is desirable that both client and evaluator begin their relationship in an atmosphere of mutual respect and confidence. This is the best atmosphere in which to negotiate a contract (or to establish general policies) to guide the behavior of both. The process of developing a written agreement provides the evaluator and the client the opportunity to review and summarize the total evaluation plan and to clarify their respective rights, responsibilities, and expectations in the enterprise. A formal agreement can reduce and help resolve many of the day-to-day misunderstandings between the evaluator

87

and client. Included as an appendix to the final evaluation report, the evaluation contract or memorandum of agreement can promote understanding of the agreements that guided the evaluation.

❖ GUIDELINES

A. Include in the agreement (allowing for appropriate adjustments in emergent designs):

purposes of the evaluation;

identification of stakeholders and questions to be investigated;

specification of the deliverables to be produced;

data collection procedures, including information sources, participant selection, instruments and other data-gathering techniques, and, if appropriate, a site-visitation plan;

procedure for analyzing quantitative and qualitative data and information;

a management plan;

reporting plan, including a consideration of interim and final report formats and delivery (number and types of reports, length, audiences, and methods of presentation), anonymity of respondents, prerelease review of reports, rebuttal by those being evaluated, and editorial and final release authority over completed reports;

methods of quality control in data collection, analysis, and reporting;

services, personnel, information, and materials provided by clients, including access to data;

time line for work of both clients and evaluators;

contract amendment and termination procedures;

budget for the work, including amounts to be paid upon completion of certain tasks or on specified dates;

provision for periodic review and modification of the agreement as development of the work suggests desired changes.

B. Negotiate and document amendments to the agreement as the work proceeds if changing circumstances make alterations in work scope, cost, or timetable necessary or desirable.

C. Establish, within reasonable limits, what would constitute a breach of the agreement by either party and what consequent actions may be taken.

D. Ensure that the agreement conforms to federal and state statutes and local regulations applying to such contractual arrangements. Review by an attorney may be appropriate.

E. Consider having an outside party review the agreement for clarity and soundness.

F. Collaborate with educational administrators or management personnel in drafting policies for approval at the appropriate level covering the conduct of the evaluation.

❖ COMMON ERRORS

A. Allowing the evaluation proposal to constitute the full written agreement (see A3, Described Purposes and Procedures)

B. Omission of important contractual elements in the written agreement

C. Failing to consult with those who will be directly affected by the evaluation but who are not parties to the written agreement before the agreement is signed (see U1, Stakeholder Identification; U2, Evaluator Credibility; and F2, Political Viability)

D. Expecting participation in the evaluation by persons who have not previously agreed to do so

E. Acting unilaterally in any matter where it has been agreed that evaluator/client collaboration would be required for decisions

F. Changing the design, scope, or cost of the study without amending the agreement

G. Adhering so rigidly to the contract that changes dictated by common sense are not made or are unduly delayed

H. Developing contracts that are so detailed that they stifle the creativity of the evaluation team or require an undue amount of time and resources in their development, thereby taking time away from conducting the evaluation

Illustrative Case 1—Description

A state teacher education association, concerned about the ways in which school districts were holding teachers accountable for professional performance, decided to undertake a thorough appraisal of those procedures. Accordingly, an evaluation organization was commissioned to complete the task.

The state education association and the evaluators assumed that a formal agreement would be necessary before the study commenced. However, what should be included in the agreement was never fully addressed. Early discussions between the evaluators and the association officials centered on procedures to be pursued in conducting the study, rather than on all the specific agreements about who would do what, for what reason, and at what times. The discussions did include agreements related to data collection and analysis but failed to include specific arrangements for report dissemination.

Following a comprehensive investigation of accountability procedures used by school districts, the evaluators presented their report, as agreed, to the education association officials. The findings indicated that the school districts had employed teacher-appraisal instruments yielding unreliable information, and that association officials themselves had contributed to the general failure of the accountability strategies by encouraging teachers not to cooperate with school districts' initiatives to hold teachers professionally accountable.

As agreed contractually, the report was disseminated to specified audiences by the education association officials according to a prearranged time schedule. The evaluators soon discovered that those sections that were critical of the teachers' association had been removed from the report. Moreover, the evaluators were at a serious disadvantage in seeking redress because the matter of final editorial authority had not been included in the formal agreement. At this point, the evaluators considered either submitting to the action of the association or publicly condemning the behavior of the association officials.

Illustrative Case 1—Analysis

The evaluation team did have formal agreements for several phases of the evaluation, most notably data collection and data analysis. During preliminary discussions with the state education association authorities, the evaluators should have taken careful note of points for inclusion in the formal agreement. In particular, the contract should have included (a) a reporting plan to ensure that reports would be open, correct, and honest in their disclosure of pertinent findings (see P6, Disclosure of Findings) and (b) a procedure for considering possible difficulties that may have arisen given the controversial nature of the subject. Mutual agreement should have been reached, so that all crucial issues would have been fully and fairly settled in the contract. During the evaluation the contract might have been scrutinized by both parties and consideration might have been given to the possibility of review by legal experts.

Under such an agreement, if the education association officials had tried to persuade the evaluators to modify the report before it was disseminated, the evaluators could have refused to do so. No doubt, the education association officials would have then concluded that the integrity of the report would be damaged by their requested modifications. The evaluators' final editorial authority, by this contract, would have assured the right to contest the issues.

Illustrative Case 2—Description

The training director for a multistate company hired a consultant to evaluate the curriculum of the company's management training program. The director suspected that the curriculum was out of step with the developmental needs of the company's managers. The consultant had done several projects for the training director.

In response to the director's request, the consultant submitted a plan for how the evaluation would be conducted, including a fee schedule. The director and consultant signed a "memo of agreement" with the plan attached.

According to the plan, the consultant interviewed several instructors and their manager for their opinions about the curriculum. He also observed classes for a week, spending several hours in 10 different classes, and interviewed several students during lunch breaks and after class.

The student interviews led the consultant to recommend a mail survey to recent graduates of the management courses. The survey was not part of the original design. In a brief telephone conversation, the training director agreed to the survey without discussing details.

While the survey was in progress, the training director was transferred to a new position within the company. Her replacement arrived two months later.

The consultant arranged to meet with the new director to provide her with a progress report. He also used this meeting to submit a bill including charges for data processing of completed survey questionnaires. The director accepted the bill but later challenged the data processing charges. Neither the "memo of agreement" on file nor any staff member could substantiate the oral agreement between the former director and the consultant to conduct the survey. When contacted, the former director could recall that she had endorsed the idea of a survey but denied agreeing to any additional charge. The consultant eventually dropped the matter because he could not afford a legal fight nor did he want to jeopardize his professional reputation.

Illustrative Case 2—Analysis

This case illustrates the need to update contracts as changes are made to project plans. In this case, the original plan adequately covered the purpose, procedures, and time and fee schedules, but no thought was ever given to updating the agreement to reflect negotiated changes. The former training director and consultant trusted one another because they had had successful dealings in the past.

Another shortcoming was the failure of the former training director to brief others in the company on the details of the agreement. Indeed, no one had seen the agreement until the billing controversy arose. Therefore no one could resolve the issue before it became a crisis. In hindsight, an appropriate course of action would have been to amend the written agreement. Alternatively, other managers or training staff should have been involved in reviewing the proposed plan before it was approved and in any subsequent meetings at which possible changes to the evaluation plan were discussed and documented.

P2   Formal Agreements

Supporting Documentation

Bogdan, R. C., & Biklen, S. K. (1992). *Qualitative research for education* (2nd ed.). Boston: Allyn & Bacon.

Guba, E. G., & Lincoln, Y. S. (1989). *Fourth generation evaluation*. Newbury Park, CA: Sage.

House, E. R., Rivers, W., & Stufflebeam, D. L. (1974, June). An assessment of
   Michigan's accountability system. *Phi Delta Kappan*, pp. 663-669.
Worthen, B. R., & White, K. R. (1987). *Evaluating educational and social programs: Guidelines for proposal review, on-site evaluation, evaluation contracts, and technical assistance.* Boston: Kluwer Academic.

P2 Formal Agreements

P3 Rights of Human Subjects

> **STANDARD** Evaluations should be designed and conducted to respect and protect the rights and welfare of human subjects.

Overview

Rights of human subjects in an evaluation include those that apply specifically to their role in the evaluation as well as rights that apply generally to many other situations. Some such rights are based in law, while others are based in accepted ethical practice, common sense, and courtesy. Legal provisions bearing on rights of persons include those dealing with consent for participation, privilege of withdrawal without prejudice and without withdrawal of treatment or services, privacy of certain opinions and information, confidentiality of information, and health and safety protections. Ethical, common sense, and courtesy considerations include the right to determine one's physical and emotional preparedness for program activities, to place limits on time spans of involvement, and generally to avoid harmful or uncomfortable experiences.

Evaluators, for both moral and pragmatic reasons, should be knowledgeable about and adhere to both legal and other human rights requirements in their evaluations. Those who are not informed about the legal and personal rights of those affected by the evaluation may unwittingly ignore or abuse them, thereby harming participants in the process. The physical and emotional safety of participants must take priority. If evaluators violate legal and ethical rights, knowingly or unknowingly, they may be subject to legal prosecution and/or professional sanctions. Violations of these rights will create opposition and may cause discredit to the evaluation. In addition, conclusions and recommendations may be discounted if it is learned they were derived from information obtained illegally or unethically.

❖ GUIDELINES

A. Make every effort to understand the cultural and social values of all participants (see U4, Values Identification, and P1, Service Orientation).

B. Be knowledgeable about due process and civil rights laws.

C. Before initiating an evaluation, determine the pertinent ethical and legal principles that are applicable.

D. Do not deprive students of instructional or training methods that are beneficial and normally available, that is, assigning students to a control group in which treatment (or instruction) previously available from public resources is purposely withheld to assess the effect of such deprivation.

E. Develop formal written agreements that explain the procedures to be followed by the client and the evaluator to ensure that the rights of participants will be protected.

F. Assure communications are appropriate for language minority participants and/or parents.

G. Duly inform individuals of their intended participation.

H. Inform subjects or participants of their rights in the evaluation.

I. Secure appropriate written permission from relevant authorities (e.g., subjects, parents, guardians, relevant agency authorities) for access to individual records.

J. When permission of parents/guardians is needed in an evaluation, they are to be informed of the implications of the evaluation and a signed permission form is to be secured in order to involve their children in the evaluation. It is not enough to assume permission simply because parents/guardians do not specifically object to their children being tested.

K. Establish a procedure to guarantee confidentiality for participants who supply information for use in the evaluation.

L. Do not disclose identities of participants in reporting evaluation findings.

M. Guard against the possibility that other parties may use the collected data for purposes different than those agreed to by the persons who provided the data.

N. Respect the right of those who carry out the program to refuse to supply information about their effectiveness if they did not participate in the planning and implementation of the program.

O. Submit evaluation proposals for review by a human subjects committee.

P. Ask respondents to identify themselves only when necessary.

Q. Inform the organization's staff and constituents of the purpose of the evaluation, for example, monitoring, continuation or discontinuation, improvements (see A3, Described Purposes and Procedures).

❖   COMMON ERRORS

A. Confusing anonymity and confidentiality

B. Promising confidentiality or anonymity when it cannot be guaranteed

C. Guaranteeing that information will be used only to serve the stated purposes, when the courts may legally order that the information be released to serve other purposes

D. Failing to communicate clearly how the information contributed by the participants will be used

E. Jeopardizing the self-esteem and reputations of participants by publishing a report that questions their professional ability or their personal ethics without giving them an opportunity to present their perspective

F. Choosing methods that have a significant potential for violating the rights of human subjects

G. Collecting data from children without proper authorization

H. Failing to identify respondents when their identity is necessary for data analysis or reporting

I. Failing to attend to the needs of language minority participants or parents

Illustrative Case 1—Description

A board of education decided to examine which of two organizational approaches to education ("self-contained" or "open area") worked best with which kinds of elementary school children. The district hired an outside evaluator to plan and conduct the needed study. As part of his plan, the evaluator recommended that a stratified random sampling plan be followed to assign students to self-contained and open area classrooms. He suggested using student achievement, personality, and socioeconomic status as the stratification variables.

To obtain the necessary data for this sampling design, he administered a test of achievement, a personality scale, and a socioeconomic questionnaire to all elementary students in the school district in June. Using this information, students were then assigned to follow one of the organizational plans.

Although there was a clear directive in the evaluation agreement to obtain prior approval from the district superintendent or her designated representative before any measures were administered to students, the evaluator bypassed this directive in order to complete data collection in time to meet other contractual agreements. Specifically, the evaluator carried out parts of the testing program under the guise of field testing "draft" instruments.

Shortly after the data were collected, a principal at one school requested a particular student's scores on one of the experimental personality measures used, so that he could better understand why the student was frequently in trouble. The evaluator was happy to comply with this request, as doing so might enhance relations between the evaluator and the district staff.

The evaluator decided to discuss that student's data in the final report to illustrate specific findings. In doing so, he provided enough information to reveal the student's identity to anyone casually acquainted with the student. The parents of the student sued the school district for rights violations.

Illustrative Case 1—Analysis

While the evaluator's desire to meet contractual obligations is admirable, standards must sometimes be weighed against each other. In this case, all data collection instruments should have been reviewed and approved prior to their use. Time to carry out this process should have been planned by the evaluator in developing the schedule of activities. If delays did occur, then he could have discussed with the superintendent the impact of eliminating the district's review as a way of completing the June data collection on time.

The evaluator should have denied the principal's request for information about a particular student, thereby respecting the confidentiality of this information. The same respect for confidentiality should also have guided the evaluator's judgments regarding how to illustrate specific findings in the final evaluation report.

Illustrative Case 2—Description

A dental school received a generous gift from an alumnus for replacement of out-of-date dental equipment. Part of the gift was set aside to do an evaluation study of available dental chair systems to discern which system most successfully helped the dentist working from behind the patient rather than at the patient's side. Research had shown that this operating style caused less back strain than traditional styles. One clinic was established that had multiple chairs from each of the commercial chair systems available for purchase. Several people from an evaluation unit in another university were asked to conduct the study.

During the study, the evaluators observed students and faculty working in pairs while using "simulated patient heads" and interacting with the "patient." Numerous observational scales were used to record how well the chair system accommodated students and faculty working from behind the "patient." Records were kept of how often students and faculty were forced to practice in less than the optimal position because of the design of the chair.

The final step in the evaluation involved observing student-faculty pairs working on actual patients. Each student-faculty pair and patient were observed for one 3-hour clinic session. To make optimal use of student and faculty time, the faculty decided to use this observation period in a second manner: to grade the students' patient management and operating skills through the presentation of the patient as a case study. The clinic session began with each student introducing the patient, describing the patient's medical and dental history, and explaining the particular procedure being accomplished that day. The completed case studies were graded by a clinician hired by the faculty.

Following their session, numerous patients complained directly to the school's clinic administrator that they were not told that their medical and dental histories would be discussed and that the evaluators present had been privy to this information in violation of confidentiality. Embarrassed by this violation of patients' rights, the clinic administrator became angry with both the faculty and the evaluators and requested that the evaluation be stopped.

Illustrative Case 2—Analysis

The United States Privacy Act states that information from a patient's medical and dental chart may only be revealed to outside parties on a "need-to-know" basis. The school should not have combined the dental chair evaluation and the student evaluation. Administrators and faculty should have been aware of the restrictions of the Privacy Act and should not have allowed patient histories to be heard by the evaluators.

Nonetheless, the evaluators, while possibly not cognizant of all parts of the Privacy Act, should have sought information about and considered the confidentiality rights in the field in which they were working. They should have made themselves aware of the restrictions imposed on information coming from the special relationship between doctor and patient and declined to continue the evaluation where patient histories were being described.

Further, the evaluators should have objected to the use of their observation time for the additional purpose of grading. Their original observation design appropriately focused on the usefulness of the various chair types during simulated patient activity. It is quite likely that student operating procedures were different than their habitual styles, given that the students were aware that their "case" study was to be graded. Therefore the observational scale results would not reflect the typical behavior necessary for a valid and accurate evaluation of the chair systems. Had the evaluation team been more sensitive to the issues that could potentially affect their project as a result of the multiple use of observation time, they would have been able to avoid the resultant deterioration of the working relationship with their clients.

Supporting Documentation

Code of fair testing practices for education. (1988). Washington, DC: American Psychological Association, Joint Committee on Testing Practices.

Ethical standards of psychologists. (1989). Washington, DC: American Psychological Association.

Principles for fair student assessment practices for education in Canada. (1993). Edmonton, Alberta, Canada: University of Alberta, Centre for Research on Applied Measurement and Evaluation, Joint Advisory Committee.

Weinberger, J., & Michael, J. A. (1977). Federal restrictions on educational research: A status report on the Privacy Act. *Educational Researcher, 6*(2), 5-8; also see *5*(11), 3-8.

P4   Human Interactions

> **STANDARD**   Evaluators should respect human
> dignity and worth in their interactions with other
> persons associated with an evaluation, so that
> participants are not threatened or harmed.

Overview

Human interaction in the context of this standard pertains to evaluators' interpersonal transactions that affect the feelings and self-respect of those who participate in an evaluation or are affected by an evaluation. Most evaluations have the potential for reflecting either positively or negatively on individuals or groups and their work. The point of this standard is that evaluators must guard against potentially threatening or harmful effects of their interactions with participants. Enhancement of interpersonal and communication skills is vital to adherence to this standard.

Evaluators who neither understand nor respect the feelings of participants in an evaluation may needlessly offend these persons or provoke hostility toward the evaluation. Such offense violates the moral imperative that a person's essential dignity is to be respected.

❖   GUIDELINES

A. Make every effort to understand the culture, social values, and language differences of the participants (see U4, Values Identification; P1, Service Orientation; and P3, Rights of Human Subjects).

B. Take time to learn about particular concerns about the evaluation held by participants (see U1, Stakeholder Identification; U3, Information Scope and Selection; and F2, Political Viability).

C. Maintain good communication through established channels with participants in an evaluation.

D. Become familiar with the organization where the evaluation is to be done, and plan the evaluation activities for minimum disruption of the organization's staff procedures, routines, and work schedules (see A2, Context Analysis).

❖ COMMON ERRORS

A. Behaving attentively and respectfully toward those in positions of authority while largely ignoring their subordinates

B. Assigning greater or lesser importance to some persons because of their age, sex, ethnicity, cultural background, or language differences

C. Violating legal requirements or protocol in contacting and addressing participants

D. Reporting findings as personal evaluations of, or attacks on, people involved in the program evaluated

E. Discussing with others one's opinions of the personal attributes—such as intelligence, physical attractiveness, taste, and social skills—of persons whose work is being evaluated

F. Collecting information that might embarrass participants, when this information is not needed to evaluate the program

G. Avoiding the embarrassment of individuals by allowing incompetence, unethical behavior, fraud, waste, or abuse by program participants to be ignored or, perhaps, covered up, thereby compromising the validity and utility of the evaluation

Illustrative Case 1—Description

A university's curriculum department undertook an evaluation to determine the impact of a history course on the achievement of poverty-level secondary school students as part of an evaluation of a new federal program. By arrangements with the curriculum department and its team of evaluators, the local school district agreed to subcontract for the evaluation.

The evaluators developed an operational definition of a poverty-level student, identified all the students in the eleventh grade in the participating district who met this definition, and then randomly assigned half of these students to be taught using the history course.

All the poverty-level students who had been identified were brought together at the beginning and at the end of the evaluation for testing. On each occasion, they were told that they were being tested to help determine the school's effectiveness.

In addition to the testing, the evaluation design included extensive classroom observation and pupil interviews. To ensure that the teachers would not make unusual preparations for the observations, the evaluators visited classrooms unannounced and conducted their observations without any advance agreements with either the teachers or their school principals. Similarly, the evaluators went unannounced to the homes of students to interview them about their school experiences.

When the final report was published, criticisms of the evaluators' insensitivities toward participants began to arrive at the school district's central office. The critics charged, for example, that the evaluators had

— disconcerted teachers by extensive classroom observation,

— made thinly veiled criticisms to some teachers about their implementation of the history course, and

— caused acute embarrassment to poverty-level pupils by separating them from other pupils, publicly labeling them as disadvantaged, and intruding on their homes unannounced.

In the light of these persistent criticisms, the school administration and the school board tended to place less confidence than they might have in the evaluators and thus in the evaluation report. Later, they discounted the report altogether when they learned that the teachers and students who allegedly had been demeaned had not cooperated with the evaluators. As a consequence of these problems, the relationship between the university and the school district was weakened.

Illustrative Case 1—Analysis

The evaluators were careful not to label the students as disadvantaged during their interaction with the students but did not extend this protection to the students during data analysis. They might have selected students randomly from the total student population and assured that no students were labeled or identified publicly with respect to income level or other sensitive characteristics. The test results then could have been analyzed and reported so as to assess the program's comparative effects on poverty-level and non-poverty-level students without embarrassing any student. The interviews with students should have been conducted privately in the students' schools. If there was a compelling reason to use their homes, these interviews should have been arranged carefully with the full knowledge and consent of the students, parents/guardians, and school officials.

Teachers, parents, students, and school principals should have been involved in the planning of the evaluation, especially those aspects related to the classroom observations and interviews. Conferences involving teachers, principals, and the evaluators could have been held periodically to report progress and to deal with problems, fears, threats, and insecurities. If some teachers had expressed embarrassment at overambitious observing and probing by the evaluators, an alternative strategy could have been agreed upon and implemented.

Illustrative Case 2—Description

Several managers in the human resource department of a large corporation wanted to improve the training and development programs that they offered centrally to secretaries who worked in all company divisions. An internal evaluator was asked to examine the training needs of secretaries, and then to use this information to assess the effectiveness of current programs and make recommendations for change.

The primary method for assessing needs was focus group interviews with secretaries in each of the various divisions. Interview questions were developed with input from the human resource managers and the questions and procedures were pilot tested with groups of secretaries in the human resource department. Then interviews were scheduled with groups of secretaries representative of the company.

When one of the senior managers in the employee relations department learned about the study, he asked that it be stopped. He said that he did not see a need for secretaries to be interviewed and that the process would stir up problems for him that he did not want to deal with at that time. However, once the purpose of the study was explained to him and he had an opportunity to review the evaluation materials, he became supportive and offered to cooperate. But by that time the secretaries were complaining that they had not all been given a chance to participate and their input had not been given any consideration by the company. Further, much goodwill had been lost between the human resource and employee relations departments.

Illustrative Case 2—Analysis

The evaluators were careful to gain input on focus group questions as well as to pilot test the questions and procedures. However, the senior employee relations manager and secretaries should have been involved early in the design and planning of the evaluation. Both were key stakeholders and should have been included. Not including them sent the message that they were not respected either for who they are as individuals or for their positions within the organization. This message, intended or not, probably had more to do with resistance to the study than did an initial lack of understanding of the purposes or potential results of the study. Further, by stopping the evaluation work in progress, negative feelings among the secretaries about the evaluator and managers in the company were created.

A stakeholder advisory group should have been created at the beginning of the project. The employee relations manager, other key managers, and two or three secretaries appointed or elected by the secretaries could have been invited to participate in this group. This would have provided a forum for discussing issues related to the purpose and methods of the evaluation. By listening to them and responding to their concerns, the evaluator would have conveyed her responsibility to the entire organization. Further, she would have had their help in designing an effective evaluation. In addition, their cooperation could have been enlisted, which would have been useful later during data collection.

Supporting Documentation

Punch, M. (1986). *The politics and ethics of fieldwork* (Qualitative Research Methods Series, 3). Beverly Hills, CA: Sage.

Rodman, H., & Rolodny, R. L. (1964). Organizational strains in the researcher-practitioner relationship. *Human Organization, 23*(2), 171-182.

Ulschak, F. L., & Weiss, R. G. (1976). The interpersonal aspects of evaluation: A transactional analysis model for viewing evaluator-client relationships. *Educational Technology, 16*(11), 18-25.

Worthen, B. R., & Sanders, J. R. (1987). *Educational evaluation: Alternative approaches and practical guidelines*. White Plains, NY: Longman.

P5   Complete and Fair Assessment

Overview

Balancing an evaluation does not mean generating equal numbers of strengths and weaknesses. It means being thorough and fair in assessing and reporting both negative and positive aspects of the program being evaluated.

Even when the primary purpose of an evaluation is to determine the weaknesses of an object, it is essential to identify strengths as well. One reason for this is that strengths can sometimes be used to correct weaknesses. Another is that actions taken to correct weaknesses may inadvertently diminish some unidentified strengths.

The methods used in the evaluation should be described by the evaluator along with their strengths and weaknesses so that their impact on findings and conclusions can be assessed.

❖ GUIDELINES

A. Fully report findings that indicate both strengths and weaknesses, whether intended or unintended, and justify each (see U5, Report Clarity, and A11, Impartial Reporting).

B. Solicit critical comments about the thoroughness and fairness of reports from knowledgeable parties representing diverse perspectives before submitting reports.

C. When relevant data are inaccessible because of time or cost constraints, report these omissions, and estimate the effect of such omissions on the overall judgment of the program.

❖ COMMON ERRORS

A. Manipulating the reporting of strengths and weaknesses to please partisan individuals or interest groups or allowing deletion from the report of weaknesses that might prove embarrassing or to further or protect the evaluator's personal interest or biases

B. Furthering or protecting the evaluator's personal interest or biases

C. Reporting a judgment about or interpreting findings as either a strength or weakness without considering alternative perspectives that might change that conclusion

D. Reporting speculative or tentative findings for the purpose of achieving a balance of strengths and weaknesses

E. Failing to report completely the methods used in the evaluation and the impact their strengths and weaknesses may have had on findings and conclusions

F. Reporting only negative findings as if evaluators were only to report weaknesses

Illustrative Case 1—Description

A school district committee undertook an evaluation of a two-week workshop designed to train teachers to teach in teams. The trainer's materials and the teachers' materials developed for the workshop were to be evaluated. The evaluation group was asked to find the weaknesses in the materials and to suggest improvements.

Following the workshop, the evaluators interviewed the trainers and the teachers to discover deficiencies in the materials and collect suggestions for changes. Their evaluation report listed the weaknesses they identified in those interviews and the recommended changes to correct them.

Later, when the developers of the materials tried to use the report to guide revisions, they discovered that, if they made the recommended changes, they would destroy characteristics that they considered to be primary strengths of the materials. However, the report offered no data on whether the trainers and teachers shared that view or how these characteristics related to the identified weaknesses. Lacking that balance, the report could not be used as a blueprint for revising the materials.

Illustrative Case 1—Analysis

The evaluation team did a thorough job identifying the training material's weaknesses. However, the evaluators should have asked the trainers and the teachers to identify both strengths and weaknesses in the materials, and to rate sections of the materials according to their effectiveness or usability. Furthermore, the evaluators should have gathered data on how the materials were, in fact, used during the workshop and on whether teachers learned what the materials were designed to teach them. Relative strengths and weaknesses could then have been identified and recommendations for change made, supported by data and information on the actual effects of the materials in producing skillful teachers with favorable attitudes toward team teaching. The materials then could have been revised accordingly.

Illustrative Case 2—Description

An evaluation consultant from another state was hired by a university administrator to evaluate a professional degree program in a state university. The administrator described the evaluator's purpose generally, saying that the use of out-of-state external evaluators was part of the "routine internal institutional evaluation system used at the university," and that the out-of-state evaluators were expected to complete a site visit as part of their evaluations.

A catalog and a hastily assembled set of program information and materials were sent to the evaluator a few days prior to his evaluation visit. Due to institutional cost constraints, the evaluator was scheduled to be at the university on one evening and the next day through the late afternoon. Appointments were made for the evaluator by the university administrator with individuals that the institution felt were important to the evaluation. These individuals included representatives of the faculty, current students, alumni, program administrators, and university administrators. Appointments took place during the evening and the following day, with a final summarization scheduled with the university chancellor during the last part of the afternoon. Students were to be interviewed in two groups, as were alumni. Faculty were interviewed singly or in pairs.

Upon arrival, the evaluator was presented with the "standard" state university form that he was to use to summarize his judgments about the program. The form comprised 60, 5-point Likert-type items. No criteria or explanation of the categories were provided.

During his interviews with the faculty representatives, the evaluator found that his evaluation was also going to be used as part of a larger review of several programs to determine which should continue to be funded. The faculty also reported that the quality of their program would be compared with the quality of similar programs at the other state-supported universities.

The evaluator found it difficult to produce a balanced report using the form provided to him. He found many items on the checklist dealt with areas that were not directly applicable to the professional program he had been asked to evaluate. Of particular concern to him was the use of the total score formed by simply summing across all 60 items.

In his meeting with the university chancellor, the evaluator strongly emphasized the need to consider more than the results obtained using the standard form. He again emphasized this view when he submitted his final report. As well as the completed university form, the final report included a written report in which he provided a summary of what he had learned about the program and suggestions of how the information from the standard form and his report might be put together to better represent the program and its operation when it was compared with other similar programs in the state.

Illustrative Case 2—Analysis

The evaluator attempted to rectify the situation by including comments in his final report addressing the weaknesses of the standard form. However, at the outset, the evaluator should have clarified all of the purposes of the evaluation so that he could be sure that relevant data and information were collected and analyzed to allow more complete and therefore fair reporting. Given that his work was part of a routine procedure, he also should have sought information about any evaluation procedures that were in place. In addition, it might have been more helpful to have the evaluator work with the university administrator to plan who would be interviewed and the sequence of the interviews, in order to obtain information from a broader base that was pertinent to addressing the multiple purposes of the evaluation. For example, the large groups of students and alumni and the setup of the room made it difficult to assess their perceptions about the adequacy of the program.

The use of the standard "generic" checklist that was not specifically designed for the professional program being evaluated made it difficult to provide a balanced reporting of the strengths and weaknesses of the program. The oral report provided to the chancellor prior to leaving the campus and the written report attached to the standard form assisted in providing more balance to the report. In spite of the standard checklist, the evaluator provided recommendations concerning the enhancement of the quality and applicability of evaluation information stemming from this standardized process. However, it was not certain whether the addendum would be considered in the statewide review.

Supporting Documentation

Kleinfeld, J., & McDiarmid, G. W. (1986). Living to tell the tale: Researching politically controversial topics and communicating the findings. *Educational Evaluation and Policy Analysis, 8*(4), 393-401.

Morris, L. L., Fitz-Gibbon, C. T., & Freeman, M. E. (1987). How to communicate evaluation findings. In J. L. Herman (Ed.), *Program evaluation kit* (2nd ed.). Newbury Park, CA: Sage.

Stake, R. E. (1982). How sharp should the evaluator's teeth be? *Evaluation News, 3*(3), 79-80.

P6   Disclosure of Findings

> **STANDARD**   The formal parties to an evaluation
> should ensure that the full set of evaluation findings
> along with pertinent limitations are made accessible
> to the persons affected by the evaluation, and any
> others with expressed legal rights to receive the
> results.

Overview

Persons who will be affected by the evaluation and persons and agencies
with a legal right entitling them to the findings of the evaluation should be
fully informed about how and why it was done and about its full set of
results, except where the disclosure of such information would endanger
public safety or abridge individual freedoms.

Stakeholders for the evaluation are entitled to reports that present clearly
and frankly the evaluator's judgments and recommendations, and the information and methods that were used to formulate them. *Disclosure of findings* means telling what one thinks and believes, as candidly as possible,
based on one's best informed judgment. It requires that all acts, public
pronouncements, and written reports of the evaluation adhere strictly to a
code of directness, openness, and completeness. Such disclosure in reporting is essential if the evaluation is to be defensible. Its absence will severely
threaten the evaluation's credibility.

If persons or groups who will be affected by the evaluation cannot get
information about it, then they cannot detect flaws in its procedures or data,
nor can they make constructive use of its findings. As a consequence, these
persons may unwittingly become the victims of unwarranted conclusions
and actions, or may perform their functions less well than if they had been
informed of the evaluation findings. Evaluations should be expected to
withstand the critical examination of those whose lives they may affect and
to provide them with useful information.

The evaluator's ability to identify and properly serve all persons affected by the evaluation greatly influences the fairness and utility of the evaluation. In turn, the evaluator's ability to release or publish information is often partially controlled by the client. Therefore both the evaluator and the client bear responsibility for meeting this standard. This is an issue that should be negotiated as part of the formal agreement (see P2, Formal Agreements).

❖ GUIDELINES

A. Reach a formal agreement with the client during the planning stages of the evaluation covering the client's and evaluator's roles in assuring compliance with right-to-know requirements, including identification of stakeholders for interim and final reports; authority to edit reports; documentation of intents, procedures, and outcomes; and when, how, and to whom information about the evaluation will be released (see P2, Formal Agreements).

B. Report the evaluation completely in writing and, if possible, orally with full disclosure of pertinent findings and without omissions or other alterations.

C. Show clearly the basis for the perceived relationship between the purposes of the evaluation, methods used, data collected, and findings (see A10, Justified Conclusions).

D. Present relevant points of view of both supporters and critics of the program being evaluated (see U3, Information Scope and Selection).

E. Report judgments and recommendations that represent broad, balanced, and informed perspectives.

F. Report key factors that might significantly detract from or add to the evaluation's defensibility, whether discovered before or during the evaluation, and discuss frankly their implications for the findings and recommendations (see A2, Context Analysis).

G. Prepare, where appropriate, interim reports corresponding to development or implementation stages that contribute to bringing about needed changes in the program.

H. Encourage clients to provide all affected persons with information that is appropriate, timely, in appropriate linguistic form, and that helps them to be enlightened contributors, consumers, critics, and observers (see U6, Report Timeliness and Dissemination).

I. Become knowledgeable about the statutes bearing on the right to know, and how these statutes relate to, or are tempered by, other statutes related to privacy, civil and human rights, and health and safety.

J. Be prepared to recognize and affirmatively address situations in which information obtained in an evaluation may require an evaluator to exert an independent obligation to disclose information against the wishes of the client, such as the circumstances of discovering evidence of illegal or unethical conduct.

❖   COMMON ERRORS

A. Determining stakeholders for the evaluation reports on the basis of convenience or economy, rather than on the basis of ethical and legal considerations

B. Failing to be involved in the control and release of information about, or resulting from, the evaluation

C. Agreeing to allow the client to select and release parts of the evaluation report without consulting the evaluator

D. Giving the client unilateral authority to edit, censor, or in any other way change the evaluation report before its release

E. Providing selected information to some members of a group affected by the evaluation and not to other members of the group

F. Issuing reports that have been altered to reflect the self-interest of the evaluator, the client, or the program staff

G. Allowing premature disclosure of information in a condition that may lead to misinterpretation and misunderstanding

H. Making so much of the limitations of the evaluation that the evaluation loses credibility

I. Violating any individual's right to privacy (see P3, Rights of Human Subjects)

J. Failing to be considerate of the client's rights, responsibilities, and needs (see P4, Human Interactions)

K. Failing to consider pertinent social and political factors when designing evaluations and preparing and releasing reports (see A2, Context Analysis)

Illustrative Case 1—Description

For almost two years, the residents of a school district had been complaining about the injustices of the district's desegregation strategies. The most prominent minority group insisted that the integration plans were a farce, while the majority group was equally vehement that there was reverse discrimination favoring the minority children. The board of education decided to have the situation evaluated so that problems might be placed openly in their proper perspective. Moreover, it was hoped that, as a result of an evaluation, decisions could be made that would alleviate the tense situation.

The evaluation was completed by an outside agency. Three evaluators were assigned to the study. In their formal agreement with the school board, the matter of information dissemination to the public was described as follows: "Interested parties will be informed of outcomes of the evaluation in due course and at the discretion of the Board."

During the early stages of the evaluation, the evaluation team became aware of the strong negative feelings between the minority and majority groups with respect to the issue of desegregation. They felt it necessary to concentrate their efforts on the schools and their students. Correspondingly, they devoted little time to obtaining information from parents/guardians and the general public.

Upon completion of the analysis of the data and information obtained during their study, the evaluators submitted their report to the board. After some changes had been made in deference to the board's requests (e.g., elimination of the mention of questionable decisions about busing), the evaluators presented their findings at a public meeting. A large crowd attended, demanding to know why they had not been consulted about the planning of the evaluation, why they had not been involved in data and information collection activities, why intermediate reports had not been released, and why the final report failed to address findings about the propriety of board decisions on busing. The evaluators and board were accused of violating laws covering public disclosure of information and their credibility and integrity were questioned.

Illustrative Case 1—Analysis

The evaluators, whether or not they sensed the intensity of public interest over the desegregation issue, should have made sure that the formal agreement with the school board complied with federal and state laws relating to disclosure of public information. With the board's concurrence, the evaluators might have formed an advisory group—consisting of representatives of the school and community—and consulted the group about what questions should be addressed in the evaluation. Such a component of the evaluation would have served as a check on the narrowness of the data collection procedures and on an inclination to avoid controversies or change reports. While perhaps increasing the complexity of the evaluation, such a component would likely have resulted in more open and honest reporting. During the course of the evaluation, intermediate reports might have been issued in which completed aspects of the evaluation were described. Interim reports could also have been used to address specific issues of the evaluation. For example, the history of busing in other jurisdictions might have been distributed as an intermediate report, thereby providing the audiences with information to reflect upon prior to the final report for their school district. Representatives of both the minority and the majority groups could have been invited to respond to these reports as well as to other important findings during the course of the evaluation.

The final report should have been presented in an open, public meeting without being altered, even though many of the recommendations might have been unpalatable to the majority and/or minority groups, and to the board. If the public had been openly, honestly, and fairly informed at all stages of the evaluation, the final report would not have been likely to contain many surprises. It then would have been accepted by more people, and its credibility would not have been so susceptible to attack.

Illustrative Case 2—Description

The Faculty of Medicine at a large public university spent considerable undergraduate medical teaching time on teaching students at patient bedsides in clinic groups. Much of the teaching in these bedside sessions focused on medical and surgical subspecialties. In fact, the curriculum specified how many sessions were to be devoted to teaching each subspecialty (e.g., cardiology, rheumatology, orthopedics). Clinical group teaching represented the total undergraduate commitment for many faculty clinicians.

After consulting all relevant constituencies, an evaluation system was established by an interdepartmental curriculum committee to address two issues: (a) the extent to which experiences of clinic groups were consistent with the educational objectives of specific clinical specialties and (b) the need to provide assessments yielding valid information about the faculty clinicians. Information about the first issue was primarily of interest to the curriculum management committee and chairs of specialty course committees. Information about the second issue was primarily of concern to individual departments where it was to be used in promotion decisions and other forms of academic reward.

The students in each clinic group were asked to respond to a questionnaire following the completion of the session for each medical specialty. The questionnaire contained two sections. In the first, the students described the activities in which they were engaged. They rated their faculty clinician in the second part. This information was collected over a three-year period. Participation rates exceeded 90%. Analysis of the results across the three years revealed a high degree of consensus, and the information provided was determined to be both valid and reliable.

The evaluators reported the information obtained from the two parts of the questionnaire separately to the two intended audiences. Overall summaries of educational experiences were prepared for the interdepartmental curriculum committee and detailed summaries of subspecialty teaching results were provided to course committee chairs. Faculty clinicians received original questionnaire results related to their teaching along with a single-page report comparing their results with those of their professional peers. No results were released until the end of the academic year after the students had received their marks.

Detailed explanations of evaluation results were provided in writing and at meetings with the various audiences. Summaries at the course and hospital levels were presented at departmental faculty meetings. The evaluation system was reviewed each year by the education committees of participating departments and the interdepartmental curriculum committee. Modifications to the system were introduced and documented as necessary to reflect changes in the educational environment.

Illustrative Case 2—Analysis

The evaluation described in this case was designed to respond to two clearly defined needs and to operate effectively in the context of a particular clinical teaching format. Important stakeholders were identified and consulted in the development and implementation of the evaluation. Information requirements for each audience were carefully defined.

Following standard guidelines to report evaluations completely, results in their original form were returned to faculty clinicians along with information that allowed comparison of their results with the distributions of results of their professional peers. No information was released until the end of the academic year.

Supporting Documentation

Morris, L. L., Fitz-Gibbon, C. T., & Freeman, M. E. (1987). How to communicate evaluation findings. In J. L. Herman (Ed.), *Program evaluation kit* (2nd ed.). Newbury Park, CA: Sage.

Stake, R. E. (1976). *Evaluating educational programmes: The need and the response*. Paris: Organization for Economic Cooperation and Development.

P7   Conflict of Interest

> **STANDARD**   Conflict of interest should be dealt with openly and honestly, so that it does not compromise the evaluation processes and results.

Overview

Conflict of interest exists in an evaluation when the personal or financial interests of an evaluator might either influence an evaluation or be affected by the evaluation. A conflict of interest can also exist when a client or stakeholder has an inappropriate personal or financial interest in an evaluation or a program being evaluated. The following are examples.

— Evaluators might benefit or lose financially, long term or short term, depending on what evaluation results they report, especially if the evaluators are connected financially to the program being evaluated or to one of its competitors.

— The evaluators' jobs and/or ability to get future evaluation contracts might be influenced by their reporting of either positive or negative findings.

— The evaluators' personal friendships or professional relationships with clients may influence the design, conduct, and results of an evaluation.

— The evaluators' agency might stand to gain or lose, especially if they trained the personnel or developed the materials involved in the program being evaluated.

— A stakeholder or client with a personal financial interest in a program may influence the evaluation process.

— A stakeholder or client with a personal professional interest in promoting the program being evaluated may influence the outcome of an evaluation by providing erroneous survey or interview responses.

The breadth of the above examples indicates that many evaluations contain the potential for conflict of interest. Thus the problem is frequently not a matter of how to avoid conflict of interest but of how to deal with it.

It is a prevalent concern in internal evaluations where close friendships and personal working relations are commonplace and may influence the outcomes of the evaluations. It is also a frequent problem in external evaluations, because clients have much freedom to choose external evaluators and external evaluators must win evaluation contracts in order to stay in business. Conflicts of interest can bias evaluations by corrupting their processes, findings, and interpretations.

❖ GUIDELINES

A. Identify and clearly describe possible sources of conflict of interest in initial discussions with clients.

B. Agree in writing on procedures to protect against problems associated with conflict of interest (see P2, Formal Agreements).

C. Seek advice from persons who have different perspectives on the evaluation in order to stay open to evaluation alternatives and philosophies and thus plan and conduct a more balanced evaluation.

D. When appropriate, release evaluation procedures, data, and reports publicly, so they can be judged by other independent evaluators.

E. Whenever possible, obtain the evaluation contract from the funding agency directly, rather than through the funded program or project.

F. Assess what advantages (monetary, social, moral, political) various parties may gain or lose as a result of the evaluation, and be prepared to resist pressures they might exert (see F2, Political Viability).

G. Make internal evaluators directly responsible to agency heads, thus limiting the influence other agency staff might have on the evaluators.

H. Arrange for metaevaluations in cases where conflict of interest is unavoidable.

❖ COMMON ERRORS

A. Believing that calling the attention of the client to a real or potential conflict of interest will be sufficient to correct the problem, especially when public disclosure or corrective action may reflect adversely on the client

B. Assuming that following well-established evaluation procedures will eliminate all conflicts of interest

C. Assuming that independent, nationally known experts are unbiased and free from conflict-of-interest problems

D. Excluding persons who are uniquely qualified to be involved in the evaluation solely because of the fear of conflict-of-interest allegations

Illustrative Case 1—Description

A school district curriculum director was working with the district's reading specialist and several teachers to develop a curriculum guide and materials for a three-stage individualized reading program to be introduced in grades 1 through 4 in two years. To ensure that the materials and processes were valid and appropriate, he suggested that each stage be evaluated by a group of their colleagues.

The director commissioned a team of teachers to evaluate the first stage, with the idea that if their work was satisfactory they would be engaged for the evaluations of the second and third stages of the development of the reading program—with considerably larger voice in the future of the program. The team of evaluators realized that the curriculum director had been the major architect of the new curriculum guide and accompanying materials, that he believed strongly in their value, and that he would play a key role in determining whether they continued for the evaluations of the second and third stages of the program.

The evaluation team then sought the involvement of other staff in developing criteria for evaluating the guide and materials produced at the first stage. From this participation, the evaluation team formalized the criteria that focused on the program's strengths rather than its weaknesses.

The evaluation report was highly favorable. However, when it was released, a substantial number of teachers complained to the superintendent of schools that major controversial elements of the curriculum guide as well as deficiencies in the materials had been glossed over during the evaluation, that the objectives of the teachers themselves had not been properly considered, and that one of the evaluators had been influential in writing the curriculum guide.

The superintendent concluded that the evaluators had been too eager to win the favor of the curriculum director, had compromised their fairness, and had destroyed their credibility. He directed that they not continue as the evaluators.

Illustrative Case 1—Analysis

At the beginning, the evaluators should have assessed and dealt openly with their own potential conflicts of interest, that of their client, and those of other involved parties. If they were not successful in instituting procedures that would keep the evaluation reasonably free from being influenced by vested interests, they should have declined to proceed with the evaluation. Certainly they should not have designed and staffed the evaluation so that a positive report was virtually assured.

The process of involving key staff persons was an appropriate action for the evaluation team to take. The team's treatment of the staff persons' involvement contributed to the overall favorable review that was criticized by staff. They could have developed a design by which to describe and assess the guide and materials that included collecting and reporting judgments of the material from a wide spectrum of participants in the reading program. They might have asked one or two reading specialists and, perhaps, teachers from another district to apply the criteria to the guide and materials, thereby obtaining an "outside" point of view to further increase the credibility of their report.

Illustrative Case 2—Description

A group of evaluators from an educational research and development department in a medical school won a competitive contract to evaluate courses included as part of a continuing medical education (CME) program offered by a professional association in CME. Under the terms of the contract, the evaluators were to assess the impact of the association's program and to make recommendations for future, more in-depth evaluations of the program.

Oversight for the project was provided by an advisory group consisting of five physician members of the association and three external consultants. The study design called for an evaluation of two courses, one for each of the two years of the contract. The design specified that practicing physicians would be used as trained telephone interviewers. For each course, physician attendees were randomly divided into two groups. Physicians assigned to Group 1 were interviewed both before and after the course, while the physicians assigned to Group 2 were interviewed after the course only. As a control group, physicians who did not attend their courses were also interviewed before and after the course they should have attended. Following completion of the postcourse interviews for Groups 1 and 2, copies of office patient charts were requested from 50% of the physicians to provide a check on the veracity of the interview data. Case studies were written for each physician participant in the study.

In general, the program went well. The attendance rates for both Group 1 and Group 2 were slightly greater than 80%. Physicians in both groups reported during their interviews that they had changed their practices. Further, the changes reported were consistent with those called for in the course objectives. In contrast, physicians in the control group corresponding to each course reported they had made no changes in their practices. However, little confirmation of the interview data was visible in the sample of patient charts examined. While this raised troubling questions about the validity of the interview responses, the evaluators pointed out that typical office patient charts are somewhat limited in the information they contain. As such, the evaluators felt the checks lacked validity as an evaluation tool and, as a result, they tended to weight the interview data more and the office chart data less.

Despite the generally favorable results, problems arose when the evaluators were asked to recommend a more long-range plan for evaluation of the association's program. One of the findings of the evaluation study pointed to the need for a more thorough assessment of potential attendees' learning needs. The evaluators found, for example, that official course objectives and actual course content often did not match what practicing physicians indicated in their interviews they needed to learn. Further investigation revealed that the courses were designed by high-profile academic physicians who were longtime leaders in the association and who carried with them assumptions about practitioners' needs that were not always congruent with the day-to-day practices of community physicians. Thus a cornerstone of the evaluators' recommendations was a plan for systematic needs assessment based on periodic surveys of community physicians. However, the evaluation oversight committee resisted this recommendation. They argued strongly that to implement such a plan would threaten the autonomy of the association faculty responsible for preparing the course. Further, the oversight committee strongly suggested that these faculty would possibly leave the association. This was particularly troublesome given that, if they did leave, the association's role as a lobbying force with the National Institutes of Health and with Congress would be considerably weakened. The clear, if unstated, message to the evaluators from the committee and association officers was this: "Design an evaluation that employs only token field-based needs assessment and we will let you continue working with us. Otherwise we will shelve your results and find someone else." The evaluators declined and their relationship with the college ended.

Illustrative Case 2—Analysis

Clearly, the evaluators found themselves in a position of having their private interests—renewal of a lucrative contract—affected by their potential evaluation plan. Their decision not to pursue another contract, while principled, was a response to an impasse that might have been avoided by consideration of the following three points.

First, while the initial two-year contract was awarded as a one-time project, with no plan for renewal or follow-up, the evaluators should have realized the long-term implications and should have initiated discussions with association leaders about implications of findings for the conduct of association programs.

Second, as findings that suggested programmatic changes began to emerge, the evaluators should have communicated these informally with both the evaluation oversight committee and the association leaders, and looked for evidence of potential political problems.

Third, the evaluators needed to work more closely with the faculty conducting the programs under study, all of whom were highly respected opinion leaders within the association. Specifically, they should have sought ways in which their study could better inform course design, and explore alternative forms of needs assessment acceptable to these faculty. When the issue of needs assessment arose in the renewal discussions, the evaluators would then have had a negotiating position strengthened by faculty support, and thus could have challenged the assumptions made by association leaders without facing the uncomfortable consequence of choosing between compromising their professional principles and dropping their involvement altogether.

Supporting Documentation

Clark, W. W., Jr., & Beers, C. D. (1976). *Ethical considerations in the anthropological evaluation of educational programs*. Paper presented at the annual meeting of the American Educational Research Association.

Scriven, M. (1976). Evaluation bias and its control. In G. V Glass (Ed.), *Evaluation studies review annual* (Vol. 1). Beverly Hills, CA: Sage.

Windle, C., & Neigher, W. (1978). Ethical problems in program evaluation: Advice for tripped evaluators. *Evaluation and Program Planning, 1*(2), 97-107.

Worthen, B. R., & Sanders, J. R. (1987). *Educational evaluation: Alternative approaches and practical guidelines*. White Plains, NY: Longman.

P7 Conflict of Interest

P8   Fiscal Responsibility

> **STANDARD**   The evaluator's allocation and
> expenditure of resources should reflect sound
> accountability procedures and otherwise be prudent
> and ethically responsible, so that expenditures are
> accounted for and appropriate.

Overview

Evaluators are fiscally accountable when funds are used for the purposes
and procedures stated in the evaluation agreement, expenditures are in
compliance with pertinent state and federal statutes and associated rules and
regulations, and financial transactions are verified by generally accepted
accounting and auditing procedures.

There is always the possibility that evaluators will misuse the funds for
which they are responsible. In addition, alleged misuse of funds can be used
in attempts to discredit an evaluation. Therefore it is important that evaluators exercise extreme care in their use of and accounting for funds.

❖   GUIDELINES

A. Specify major costs for the evaluation in agreements with the clients,
including personnel, consultants, travel, supplies, postage, telephone, data
processing, conferences and meetings, public information, printing, metaevaluation, and overhead (see P2, Formal Agreements).

B. Maintain accurate records of sources of funding and expenditures in a
clear and understandable format.

C. Maintain adequate personnel records with respect to job allocations
and time spent on the job.

D. Use contract bidding or comparison shopping for the purchase of
resources and services.

E. Include an expenditure summary as part of the public report to enhance public confidence in the evaluation. If private evaluators prefer not to do this, they should, at a minimum, have such information available upon request.

F. Be frugal in expending resources for the evaluation.

❖ COMMON ERRORS

A. Commencing a study without a carefully planned and approved budget that details specific amounts to be spent by category

B. Changing the evaluation activity plan without making necessary budgetary adjustments

C. Being unaware of laws applicable to the expenditure of and accounting for funds

D. Showing favoritism in the expenditure of project funds (see P7, Conflict of Interest)

E. Failing to ensure that the budget is sufficiently flexible to permit appropriate reallocations for the purpose of successfully completing the evaluation

F. Failing to discuss openly and frankly with clients any unexpected occurrences that threaten the financial viability of the evaluation

G. Failing to assign responsibility for fiscal management

H. Agreeing to a contract amount based upon senior-level evaluation staff working on the project and then transferring the work to less qualified associates

I. Failing to obtain approval for substantial changes in expenditure from those originally planned and approved

J. Inflating the evaluation budget to cover unanticipated costs and not returning the money or not using it appropriately

Illustrative Case—Description

A medical school faculty member submitted a proposal to a federal agency for funds to support the development of an innovative curriculum for medical residents. One of the requirements for the proposal was that an evaluation section be included. The faculty member asked the school's evaluation specialist, who was not in his department, to write the evaluation plan.

The evaluation specialist prepared a comprehensive evaluation plan, which included a substantial commitment of medical faculty effort for which funds were not requested. She discussed the details of the plan with the principal investigator. He then included the plan that he and the evaluation specialist discussed. The proposal was funded, but at a reduced amount. The principal investigator made the necessary adjustments to the budget by reducing the time allocated to various personnel including the time for the evaluation specialist. He did not explicitly negotiate any changes in the planned program, or its evaluation, with the funding agency.

Because of the reduced funding, many of the planned evaluation activities could not be implemented. In addition, the medical faculty members did not place a high priority on the evaluation. The evaluation specialist periodically discussed the need to begin data collection with the principal investigator, but could not independently initiate any activities. Toward the end of the contract period, the principal investigator wanted the evaluation specialist to conduct an evaluation that could be presented to the funding agency during an upcoming site visit. However, it was too late to obtain baseline data or any formative evaluation data that were part of the original evaluation plan.

Given the time remaining, the evaluation specialist mailed a hastily developed questionnaire to each participant in the program. Only half were returned. Moreover, there was no time to complete a follow-up study of nonrespondents prior to the site visit, or to conduct analyses comparing the characteristics of respondents with those of nonrespondents or with the total sample.

When the evaluation specialist presented her findings during the site visit, the funding agency team was surprised and disappointed that the evaluation plan presented in the proposal was not followed. The evaluation specialist's credibility was damaged, relations with the medical school department were strained, and the funding agency no longer considered applications from either the faculty member or the evaluation specialist.

Illustrative Case—Analysis

The evaluation specialist and principal investigator did discuss the evaluation plan prior to submission, but neither critically examined the budget. Once it was known that the proposal was not fully funded, the evaluation specialist should have developed an evaluation plan that was feasible within the budget constraints. Then she should have encouraged the principal investigator to get the approval of the funding agency for the modified evaluation. As with many failed evaluations, this one suffered because of poor communication between the evaluator and several parties. Communication is often most difficult when it involves touchy subjects, such as money; but it is precisely these touchy subjects that require the most conscientious and clear dialogue.

Supporting Documentation

Sludek, F. E., & Stein, E. L. (1981). *Grants budgeting and finance: Getting the most out of your grant dollar*. New York: Plenum.

P8   Fiscal Responsibility

Worthen, B. R., & Sanders, J. R. (1987). *Educational evaluation: Alternative approaches and practical guidelines*. White Plains, NY: Longman.

Worthen, B. R., & White, K. R. (1987). *Evaluating educational and social programs: Guidelines for proposal review, on-site evaluation, evaluation contracts, and technical assistance*. Boston: Kluwer Academic.

P8   Fiscal Responsibility

Accuracy Standards

Summary of the Standards

A Accuracy Standards The accuracy standards are intended to ensure that an evaluation will reveal and convey technically adequate information about the features that determine worth or merit of the program being evaluated. The standards are as follows:

> **A1 Program Documentation** The program being evaluated should be described and documented clearly and accurately, so that the program is clearly identified.

> **A2 Context Analysis** The context in which the program exists should be examined in enough detail, so that its likely influences on the program can be identified.

> **A3 Described Purposes and Procedures** The purposes and procedures of the evaluation should be monitored and described in enough detail, so that they can be identified and assessed.

> **A4 Defensible Information Sources** The sources of information used in a program evaluation should be described in enough detail, so that the adequacy of the information can be assessed.

A5 Valid Information The information gathering procedures should be chosen or developed and then implemented so that they will assure that the interpretation arrived at is valid for the intended use.

A6 Reliable Information The information gathering procedures should be chosen or developed and then implemented so that they will assure that the information obtained is sufficiently reliable for the intended use.

A7 Systematic Information The information collected, processed, and reported in an evaluation should be systematically reviewed and any errors found should be corrected.

A8 Analysis of Quantitative Information Quantitative information in an evaluation should be appropriately and systematically analyzed so that evaluation questions are effectively answered.

A9 Analysis of Qualitative Information Qualitative information in an evaluation should be appropriately and systematically analyzed so that evaluation questions are effectively answered.

A10 Justified Conclusions The conclusions reached in an evaluation should be explicitly justified, so that stakeholders can assess them.

A11 Impartial Reporting Reporting procedures should guard against distortion caused by personal feelings and biases of any party to the evaluation, so that evaluation reports fairly reflect the evaluation findings.

A12 Metaevaluation The evaluation itself should be formatively and summatively evaluated against these and other pertinent standards, so that its conduct is appropriately guided and, on completion, stakeholders can closely examine its strengths and weaknesses.

A1 Program Documentation

STANDARD   The program being evaluated should
be described and documented clearly and accurately,
so that the program is clearly identified.

Overview

It is necessary for the evaluator to gain a solid understanding of the program
being evaluated, including both the way it was intended to be and the way
it actually was implemented, and to convey this description to others.
Failure to gain such understanding will lead to an evaluation that, when
completed, is likely to be of questionable use.

A valid characterization of a program as it actually was implemented will
describe its unique features and component parts in order to facilitate
comparisons of the program with similar programs. A good description of
the program will also facilitate attempts to associate components of the
program with its effects.

❖ GUIDELINES

A. Ask the client and the other stakeholders to describe—orally, and, if
possible, in writing—the intended and the actual program with reference to
such characteristics as personnel, cost, procedures, location, facilities, setting, activities, objectives, nature of participation, and potential side effects.

B. Collect and analyze for differences and similarities available descriptions of the program, including proposals, public relations reports, slide-
tape presentations, and staff progress and final reports.

C. Engage independent observers to describe the program if time and
budget permit.

D. Set aside time at the beginning of the evaluation to observe the program and the staff and participants who are involved.

E. As part of the ongoing evaluation process, maintain up-to-date descriptions of the program from different information sources (e.g., participant observers, minutes of staff meetings, interviews of participants, and progress reports), giving particular attention to changes in the description.

F. Consider developing separate descriptions for each aspect of the program being studied.

G. Ask the client and stakeholders to check the accuracy of recorded descriptions of both the intended and the actual program.

H. Record obtained descriptions of the object in a technical report, paying special attention to discrepancies between intended characteristics of the program and characteristics of the program as implemented.

❖ COMMON ERRORS

A. Relying solely on the client's or the funding proposal's description of the program

B. Failing to check the accuracy of the obtained description of the program through direct examination or observation, or by confirmation by program personnel

C. Glossing over a description of the program by saying, for example, that "the treatment was all that occurred between Time 1 and 2," without describing the actual events

D. Forcing too precise a description when the program is under development

E. Concentrating so much on describing the program that insufficient time is available for assessing its strengths and weaknesses

F. Assuming that the program was uniformly implemented as intended

Illustrative Case 1—Description

A school district contracted to have a tutorial program at the secondary level evaluated over a two-year period. The evaluators conducted a comparative study in the district's secondary school.

All students in the school were screened, by means of teacher judgments and grades in school, to identify those students who needed help. The chosen students were then randomly divided into a tutorial group and a control group (students who would receive no special tutoring but whose school performance would be compared with that of the tutorial group).

The evaluators asked the school principal to administer the tutorial program so that the students selected for this program would be tutored for the whole two-year period. At the end of the two years, the evaluators gathered grades and teacher judgments of progress for students in both the tutorial group and the control group.

The evaluators found "no statistically significant differences" between the tutorial and control groups. Grade point averages for the students in both groups had improved considerably, but about equally. Also, the teachers judged that most students in both groups still needed special remedial instructional assistance.

At no stage during the evaluation did the program staff or the evaluators clearly describe the special assistance that students in the tutorial group were receiving. Likewise, the evaluators did not describe the instructional experiences of the members of the control group.

The evaluators concluded that the tutorial program had not enhanced the educational development of the students, and recommended that it be dropped.

Following release of the evaluation report, the Parent and Teacher Association (PTA) in the secondary school sent a letter of protest to the district superintendent. They charged that the evaluators' conclusions and recommendations were unjustified. They stated that the progress in grade point averages for the tutorial group was evidence that the tutorial program had been effective. They asserted that the teachers' reports that most students still needed special assistance was an indication that there was a continuing need for the program. They further argued that the evaluators should not have expected the tutorial and control groups to differ in their educational gains; they claimed that their association, in cooperation with the school principal, had gotten former teachers from the community to voluntarily tutor those students who needed and wanted tutoring but were assigned to the control group. The PTA questioned the overall validity of the evaluation, arguing that the evaluators had not learned what actually took place in the program.

Illustrative Case 1—Analysis

While the use of grades was appropriate and was considered as one component of the students' experience, the evaluators should have monitored both the tutorial and the control programs throughout the two-year project. This was essential for testing their assumptions about differences between tutorial and control conditions. In addition, such monitoring might have led them and their clients to adjust the purposes and procedures of the evaluation.

Even if the decision was not to change the original evaluation plan, the evaluators should have reported, along with their conclusions and recommendations, accurate descriptions of the tutorial services that were received by students in both the tutorial group and the control group. These descriptions should have identified the activities that made up the tutorial program and the amount of time and resources that had been devoted to them. The descriptions would have aided the evaluators and their audience to assess whether the tutorial program was well implemented, whether it provided tutorial services to students in the tutorial group beyond those provided to the control group, and whether the absence of differences in educational gains could be explained by the absence of differences in the amounts and kinds of remedial tutorial services delivered to the two groups. By describing the tutorial service provided to the control group, the evaluators would have been better able to evaluate its effectiveness, practicality, and costs relative to those of the tutorial program.

The evaluators could have done a number of things to obtain adequate descriptions of the tutorial program and the tutoring provided to members of the control group. At different times during the two years, they could have asked the superintendent, the school principal, and selected teachers, students, and parents to provide oral descriptions of the tutorial program and tutorial services being provided to both groups. The evaluators could have tape-recorded and transcribed these descriptions for future reference. They might have maintained case histories of the tutorial experiences of selected students in both groups. Classroom observations and interviews with teachers, students, and parents could have added to the evaluators' understanding of how the tutorial program operated and whether it differed from the instructional services received by students in the control group. The evaluators could have incorporated the descriptions obtained by all these procedures into their report and used them in reaching conclusions.

Illustrative Case 2—Description

An evaluator was awarded a contract by a company to provide assistance in conducting an evaluation of one of the company's technical training programs. This program consisted of three phases, two of which were delivered using a traditional classroom-instructor format, and a third that was delivered using individually paced, computer-based training (CBT). The CBT was to be the focus of the evaluation.

The company's training specialist and the evaluator established an evaluation task force consisting of seven people from various divisions of the organization. At the first meeting of the evaluation task force, the evaluator facilitated a discussion focused on the background of the training program and the CBT process. It was discovered through this discussion that five members of the task force did not fully understand the goals of the training program and the CBT process. As a result, the entire task force participated in a demonstration of CBT. Following this hands-on experience, the team was able to develop three key evaluation questions that then guided the evaluation.

At the next meeting of the task force, the evaluator asked a series of questions regarding political and organizational constraints bearing on the evaluation. The responses suggested that some staff and administrators within the organization believed that the CBT approach should be expanded to include the other technical training programs within the company. With this more thorough understanding of the training programs and potential implications of the evaluation findings, the task force expanded the breadth of their study to meet the needs of audiences not considered earlier in their discussions. The evaluation report included a full description of the operation and effectiveness of the CBT process. Strengths and weaknesses were identified, and recommendations were made for application of the CBT process in all the company's training programs.

Illustrative Case 2—Analysis

The program being evaluated was well defined at an early stage. During the first meeting of the task force, the training specialist and evaluator recognized the low level of understanding that most members of the evaluation task force had of the CBT process. By arranging for a demonstration in which the task force members gained hands-on experience with CBT, the experience and a level of understanding needed to identify key evaluation questions were acquired. Further, discussion of the political and organizational constraints helped task force members understand the need for an expanded evaluation and the need to identify a new set of "real" issues regarding actions to be taken as a result of the evaluation. The needs of the task force members and the company were better served because of these preliminary evaluation activities.

Supporting Documentation

Henderson, M. E., Morris, L. L., & Fitz-Gibbon, C. T. (1987). How to measure attitudes. In J. L. Herman (Ed.), *Program evaluation kit* (2nd ed.). Newbury Park, CA: Sage.

Herman, J. L., Morris, L. L., & Fitz-Gibbon, C. T. (1987). Evaluator's handbook. In J. L. Herman (Ed.), *Program evaluation kit* (2nd ed.). Newbury Park, CA: Sage.

King, J. A., Morris, L. L., & Fitz-Gibbon, C. T. (1987). How to assess program implementation. In J. L. Herman (Ed.), *Program evaluation kit* (2nd ed.). Newbury Park, CA: Sage.

A2   Context Analysis

STANDARD   The context in which the program
exists should be examined in enough detail, so that its
likely influences on the program can be identified.

Overview

The context of the program includes the geographic location of the program, its timing, the political and social climate surrounding it, competing activities in progress, the staff, and pertinent economic conditions. These and other contextual factors must be studied, described, and taken into account during the design, conduct, and reporting of an evaluation. A program is embedded in and intertwined with its context in ways difficult to disentangle. An understanding of context is necessary if the evaluation is to be realistic and responsive to the conditions within which the program is found. Contextual information is also needed to help audiences interpret the evaluation. Difficulties in separating context from programs should be acknowledged. For example, an audience would want to know whether a program's success or failure had been influenced by such things as impoverished economic conditions, a divisive relationship between teachers and school administrators, parental support, apathy, or resistance, or a community-wide campaign to promote the program being evaluated.

Explication of the contextual conditions should help stakeholders judge whether the context for the study is similar to other settings in which the findings might be applied. Moreover, this explication should help keep evaluators from claiming wider applicability for their findings than the context justifies.

This standard sometimes has implications for choosing where and when to conduct an evaluation. If evaluators have any options, they should select a context most like those where the program might be adopted.

❖ GUIDELINES

A. Describe the technical, social, political, organizational, and economic context of the program using multiple sources of information (logs, records, demographic studies, newspaper clippings, legislative bills).

B. Maintain a log of unusual circumstances—such as a strike, a student protest, the passing of a tax increase, a snowstorm, or a breakdown of equipment—that might influence the findings.

C. Record instances in which individuals, intentionally or otherwise, interfered with the program or gave special assistance.

D. Analyze how the context of the program being evaluated is similar to and different than selected contexts where the program might be adopted, and report those contextual factors that appear to have significant influence on the program and that are likely to be of interest to anyone who might adopt the program.

❖ COMMON ERRORS

A. Viewing the program's context too narrowly and ignoring potentially important influences, such as political pressures or the restrictive influences of inadequate physical space or costly equipment

B. Accepting as adequate the descriptions of context found in public relations documents

C. Concentrating so much on analyzing the context of the program that not enough time is left for assessing its effectiveness

Illustrative Case 1—Description

A state education agency formed a panel to evaluate a group of innovative public school programs, all sponsored by the agency. Each panel member was assigned the task of evaluating only one project; this task, including the submission of a report to the state agency, was to be completed within two months.

One of the programs to be evaluated was located in a secondary school of approximately 1,500 students and 90 faculty. This program, which had been developed by a mathematics teacher, was intended to familiarize students and faculty with computer programming and the many functions that computers can perform. The hardware supporting the program was to consist of a single computer in a network with several terminals. Although the computer was installed six months prior to the evaluation, the first terminal had been connected only a month before the evaluator arrived on the scene. The panel's report stated that the program was not achieving its purpose. This judgment was based on the fact that, during the six months since the installation of the computer, only eight students and one faculty member had been involved in the project. No attempt was made to interpret this finding in light of such contextual factors as the following: The school was heavily engaged in the school district's campaign to pass a school tax, and a new, inexperienced principal had just been appointed.

Illustrative Case 1—Analysis

The panel gathered accurate data but did not accurately interpret the data given the program's context. To accomplish this, the panel should have compiled a file of contextual information, including reports of conditions and events in the school, school district, and community during the life of the program. Then the panel could have noted in the report the fact that terminals had not been available for all but one of the six months, that the school had been preoccupied during the time with the tax issue, and that the administration of the school had changed. With the context taken into consideration, the report to the state education department might have recommended a further trial of the program, during a time when all the terminals are in place, the school administration is stable, and the school faculty are not preoccupied by the tax issue. By considering the contextual factors, the panel might have provided constructive feedback and not simply rendered a negative judgment.

Illustrative Case 2—Description

The sales division of a large corporation contracted with an external evaluator who had no prior contact with the corporation to assess the effectiveness of a one-day training program for sales representatives in which they were trained to identify new customers. Evaluation feedback from early training sessions was to be used to influence the design and delivery of later training sessions. The evaluator observed five training sessions, asked the 75 people in attendance at each session to complete a questionnaire, and enlisted the participation of 12 people at each session in a postsession focus group.

The first of the five training sessions was to provide a site for pilot testing both the design of the training and the methods of evaluation to be used. This training session involved sales staff working out of the company's home office. Based on the evaluation feedback from this meeting, minor changes were made in the design of the training session, but the evaluation data indicated that the training was achieving its goals.

The second training session involved sales staff from one of the district offices. During the focus group session following this training session, the evaluator learned that a major reorganization of field personnel was under way and that some of the employees in attendance at the training session were being reassigned within the company. These individuals were more concerned about their new jobs and, in some cases, reduced income and status, than they were with the content of the training program. Consequently, this training session was evaluated much more negatively than the first one had been.

In the beginning, the evaluator should have asked the client about conditions in the company that might affect response to the training sessions. The evaluator should also have found out who was being invited to participate in the training sessions and what their expectations were likely to be. The design using observations, questionnaires, and focus group interviews was a good approach for collecting feedback to help implement and revise the training sessions, but it would have been enhanced by information concerning conditions in the company. This information would have guided the evaluator both in designing the evaluation—more information about the impact of contingent factors could have been collected—and in advising the client on the scheduling of training for sales staff. Indeed, early awareness of the company reorganization might have led the evaluator to recommend delaying the training sessions until the negative effects of the reorganization had dissipated.

Supporting Documentation

Harrison, M. I. (1987). *Diagnosing organizations* (Applied Social Research Methods, 8). Newbury Park, CA: Sage.

King, J. A., Morris, L. L., & Fitz-Gibbon, C. T. (1987). How to assess program implementation. In J. L. Herman (Ed.), *Program evaluation kit* (2nd ed.). Newbury Park, CA: Sage.

A3 Described Purposes and Procedures

> **STANDARD** The purposes and procedures of the evaluation should be monitored and described in enough detail, so that they can be identified and assessed.

Overview

The purposes of an evaluation are stated in terms of the evaluation objectives and intended uses of its results. For example, the objective for a particular evaluation may be to judge the relative merits of competing textbooks for a short, three-week training course; the corresponding use of the findings is to help the instructors choose a textbook. The evaluation procedures include the ways in which the data and information are gathered, organized, analyzed, and reported to meet or satisfy the evaluation purpose.

Because differences of opinion sometimes exist about an evaluation's purposes and procedures, the points of agreement and disagreement need to be identified and assessed. Minimally, evaluators and clients at the outset of an evaluation should record their understanding of its purposes and procedures. It is also desirable (when feasible, especially in large-scale evaluations) to have independent evaluators monitor, describe, and judge the purposes and procedures of the evaluation. When descriptions of purposes and procedures are obtained from persons with different responsibilities, underlying disagreements can be identified and reconciled or, at least, taken into account when interpreting findings.

The purposes and procedures of an evaluation should be described and recorded at different stages during the evaluation. These descriptions should occur at the beginning of the evaluation—at least in general terms—so that all participants will know what they are expected to do. Purposes and procedures should also be reviewed periodically during the evaluation to provide a realistic view of the appropriateness of the original plans, the extent to which they were implemented, and the extent to which they were altered. At the conclusion of the evaluation, the audiences will need an up-to-date description of what the evaluators actually did and with what intent, so that the findings and recommendations can be judged and interpreted accordingly.

Such descriptions of purposes and procedures also have a number of other uses. They provide vital information to anyone who wishes to evaluate the evaluation. They can inform the conduct of similar evaluations in other settings. They define the purposes and procedures to be observed in replications of an evaluation. And the descriptions of evaluation purposes and procedures can constitute good case materials for use in instructing evaluators.

❖ GUIDELINES

A. Discuss thoroughly and record the client's initial conceptions of the purposes of the evaluation, and the intended uses of the findings from the evaluation.

B. Discuss thoroughly and record the client's initial conceptions of how the evaluation's purposes will be achieved.

C. Keep a copy of the evaluation plan and the evaluation contract (if one was negotiated).

D. Keep field notes on actual implementation procedures.

E. Reach a clear understanding with the client about major changes in evaluation purposes and procedures as the changes are made.

F. Record any major changes in purposes and procedures and the date on which they occurred.

G. Preserve (unless legal or contractual stipulations forbid doing so) field notes about the procedures followed in collecting and analyzing information, and make these notes available (unless legal or contractual stipulations forbid it) to persons engaged in reviews and in secondary analyses of the evaluation.

H. Describe purposes and procedures at the conclusion of the evaluation in both a summary report (executive report) and a full technical report, noting deviations from original plans (see U5, Report Clarity).

I. Engage independent evaluators to monitor the purposes and procedures of the evaluation, and evaluate them whenever feasible, especially in the case of large-scale evaluations.

❖ COMMON ERRORS

A. Assuming that a funding proposal contains a full description of the purposes and procedures of a completed evaluation

B. Assuming that the purposes and procedures agreed to by the client and the evaluator at the outset of an evaluation will not change during the evaluation

C. Failing to allow for the adjustments in purpose and procedure that may be needed during the evaluation

D. Concluding that purposes and procedures are sound simply because they are carefully described

Illustrative Case—Description

An independent study approach to teaching was under consideration for a district's high school mathematics program. Before adopting the program on a system-wide basis, the assistant superintendent of instruction decided that the approach should be evaluated in competition with the instructional approach then in use.

The assistant superintendent and the district's evaluation staff arrived at a written formal agreement including the following:

— The purpose of the evaluation was to help the high school mathematics department decide whether to adopt the independent study approach.

— A district-wide comparison of the two approaches was to be made. This comparison was to involve a randomly selected 20% of the district's high school mathematics teachers together with the students enrolled in all the classes taught by these teachers.

— The teachers chosen were to be assigned randomly to one of the two approaches to teaching.

— Mathematics achievement, student attitude, and teacher enthusiasm were to be assessed at the end of the school year.

The assistant superintendent, without telling the evaluator, subsequently decided that the purpose of the evaluation should be narrowed and that it should only provide feedback for strengthening the experimental program. He also changed the procedure for assigning teachers and students to the two approaches, so that the final assignment to a teaching approach was not random.

The evaluator, assuming that purposes and procedures, once agreed upon, would remain constant, collected and analyzed the data on the assumption that the original plan for selecting teachers and assigning them (and their students) to a teaching approach had been followed. She found that student attitudes toward the two approaches were about the same, but that student achievement and teacher enthusiasm were significantly higher for the independent study approach. Consequently, it was recommended that the independent study approach be adopted on a district-wide basis.

The assistant superintendent was disappointed with the report because it did not provide adequate direction for improving the independent study approach. Further, several teachers complained that the findings were not accurate for two reasons: First, many of the teachers assigned to the independent study approach were biased in favor of this approach before the study began, and, second, students in the independent study classes were higher achievers on average than the students in the classes taught by the traditional approach.

Illustrative Case—Analysis

The evaluation plan, as originally designed, was thorough and appeared to meet the needs of the client. The difficulty arose because the evaluator should not have assumed that purposes and procedures, once agreed upon, would remain constant throughout a project. Steps should have been taken to monitor and record changes in purpose and procedures as they occurred during the year. She should have met periodically through the year with the assistant superintendent to review and check on the planned implementation of those procedures (namely, the assignment of teachers and students to instructional approach) that were not directly under her control. Finally, prior to analyzing the data and formulating conclusions and recommendations, the evaluator should have met with the assistant superintendent and others involved in the study to verify that the method of instruction and the procedures for administering tests and questionnaires had been followed faithfully throughout the year. The evaluator should have described any differences among stakeholders in perceptions of the purposes and procedures of the evaluation.

Supporting Documentation

Brewer, J., & Hunter, A. (1989). *Multimethod research: A synthesis of styles.* Newbury Park, CA: Sage.

Patton, M. Q. (1990). *Qualitative evaluation and research methods* (2nd ed.). Newbury Park, CA: Sage.

Smith, M. L. (1986). The whole is greater: Combining qualitative and quantitative approaches in evaluation studies. *New Directions for Program Evaluation: Naturalistic Evaluation, 30,* 37-54.

A3 Described Purposes and Procedures

A4 Defensible Information Sources

> **STANDARD** The sources of information used in a program evaluation should be described in enough detail, so that the adequacy of the information can be assessed.

Overview

Many different sources of information are tapped by evaluators. Possible sources include individuals and groups, records, documents and films, audio- and visual tapes, and the like.

It is desirable that information be obtained from a variety of sources, so that the information from different sources can be compared for congruity or added perspectives. For example, the test scores of a class of students may take on added meaning if accompanied by a qualitative account of activities in the classroom prior to testing.

Information sources can be tapped in many different ways. People and groups can be tested, surveyed, observed, and interviewed; documents, films, and tapes can be content-analyzed; and situations can be observed.

Evaluators can usually expect to obtain only a portion of the information that is potentially available. For example, evaluators normally cannot test, interview, survey, and observe everyone who is in the population of interest. They must select samples of the population. These may be drawn according to a formal procedure, as by random sampling, or they may be drawn informally as in the use of "man on the street" interviews. Samples can change during an evaluation, as when students leave or enter a school or employees turn over. These changes should be documented by the evaluator.

Evaluators should document, justify, and report their sources of information, the criteria and methods used to select them, the means used to obtain information from them, and any unique and biasing features of the obtained information. These descriptions should be sufficient to permit others to determine the adequacy of the information for the evaluative questions to be answered. Poor documentation and description of information sources can reduce an evaluation's credibility. These inadequacies might also mislead careless or uninformed stakeholders to assume that the evaluation's conclusions and recommendations are based on sound information, even though this is not true.

❖ GUIDELINES

A. For each source, define the population (e.g., the third graders in a school for a specified year) and describe the procedure by which the sample was drawn (e.g., a stratified random sample was taken of the population, with the stratifying variables being the gender of the student and socioeconomic status of the student's home; or "snowball" sampling was used starting with the Board of Directors for the corporation).

B. Describe the sources of information (e.g., 50 patients, six medical wards, three hospitals, four occasions, one-hour videotapes, and the characteristics of each) that were used in the particular study.

C. Document the process (e.g., interview, content analysis, or test) by which information was collected from each source, and retain copies of the information gathering instruments for inclusion in a technical appendix to the evaluation report.

D. Document changes in the sample during the study (e.g., employee turnover or students moving from a school), and assess the impact of the changes upon the evaluation results.

E. Report and justify the criteria used to decide when to stop collecting information (e.g., redundancy, marginal returns, and saturation) in cases where information was collected through an iterative, evolving process instead of according to a fully prespecified plan.

F. Use previously collected information that is pertinent to the evaluation once its soundness has been determined.

G. Assess the adequacy of the information sources as part of the technical documentation of the evaluation, acknowledging limitations that may exist.

❖ COMMON ERRORS

A. Labeling information sources (e.g., fourth-grade portfolio assessments) but not describing them

B. Assuming without supporting evidence that different information sources (e.g., progress reports from staff of the evaluation project and program reports from staff of the evaluation office of the organization) are comparable and equally sound

C. Labeling information sources as adequate or inadequate and discarding the latter, thus failing to recognize that all information sources are only partially adequate

D. Assuming that information based on personal interviews, testimony, observations, or document analysis contains distortions and hence is not worthy of consideration. Conversely, assuming that "hard" quantitative data lack distortion and hence should be weighted heavily in evaluation.

E. Concentrating so much on documenting the sources of information and assessing the appropriateness of each source that the message contained in the information is either obscured by the documentation or overlooked in the documentation/assessment effort

F. Using a percentage of the population as a sampling procedure without calculating the required sample size needed to meet evaluation requirements

Illustrative Case—Description

A school district principal was called upon by the chairperson of a state's Board of Higher Education to evaluate a controversial teacher education program. This program had been designed to educate graduates suited for teaching in open area classrooms. The purpose of the evaluation was to inform future decisions about the allocation of funds to the program.

The evaluator launched an extensive data collection effort, including questionnaire surveys of superintendents, principals, and students as well as interviews of the program director, her staff, recent graduates, and students still in the program. While the response rates to the questionnaire surveys were low, the data from all sources generally showed the program to be successful, and the evaluator's report influenced the state board's decision to continue the program.

Critics of the program attacked the evaluation report in the state legislature. They charged that the evaluation was inconclusive because the samples of respondents to the questionnaire surveys did not represent the populations of which they were a part. The critics questioned the credibility of the questionnaire results, both because response rates were low and because no attempt had been made to determine the comparability of respondents and nonrespondents. Also, it was charged that the recent graduates who were interviewed had been chosen because of their positive feelings toward the program.

Board members, smarting under the critics' attack, refused to reverse their decision publicly but failed to allocate funds at the level previously set. Further evaluations were not commissioned, and at a subsequent board meeting the program was terminated.

Illustrative Case—Analysis

The evaluator should have described the procedures used to select each sample and then compared the characteristics of each sample that was actually obtained with the same characteristics of the population from which it was chosen. He should also have checked whether those who did not respond to the survey were in some way different than those who did. This could have been done by choosing a random sample of both groups—those who responded and those who did not—and seeing whether they were different with respect to variables that might have biased their responses. Having done this, the evaluator could have reported whether or not he had found differences that might have caused the respondents to answer in a more positive way than the nonrespondents would have. He could then have offered an informed judgment as to whether the actual samples were broadly representative of the populations surveyed.

Supporting Documentation

Bednarz, D. (1985). Quality and quantity in evaluation research: A divergent view. *Evaluation and Program Planning, 8*(4), 289-306.

Brannen, J. (Ed.). (1992). *Mixing methods: Qualitative and quantitative research.* Brookfield, VT: Avebury.

Guba, E. G. (Ed.). (1990). *The paradigm dialog.* Newbury Park, CA: Sage.

Patton, M. Q. (1990). *Qualitative evaluation and research methods* (2nd ed.). Newbury Park, CA: Sage.

Shadish, W. R., Jr., Cook, T. D., & Leviton, L. C. (1991). *Foundations of program evaluation: Theories of practice.* Newbury Park, CA: Sage.

A5   Valid Information

STANDARD   The information gathering procedures should be chosen or developed and then implemented so that they will assure that the interpretation arrived at is valid for the intended use.

Overview

Validity concerns the soundness or trustworthiness of the inferences that are made from the results of the information gathering process. The processes that might be used in an evaluation include, but are not limited to, administration of standardized tests and paper-and-pencil tests and questionnaires selected from available instruments or developed specifically for the evaluation, performance-based assessments, observations, interviews, and analysis of documents. Validation is the process of compiling evidence that supports the interpretations and uses of the data and information collected using one or more of these instruments and procedures.

In general, the validation process should include the following elements:

— a detailed description of the constructs and behaviors about which information will be acquired;

— an analysis of what type of information a particular data collection procedure purports to acquire;

— a detailed description of how the procedure was implemented, how responses and observations were judged or scored, and how interpretations were made (see U4, Values Interpretation);

— a presentation of evidence—both qualitative and quantitative—that justifies the use of the particular procedure; and

— an overall assessment of the validity of the interpretation and use of the information provided by the procedure, with reference to the evaluation questions and processes.

From the preceding elements, it is incorrect to say that a specific instrument or information collection procedure is valid. Instead, it is the inference that is validated. Further, it is not appropriate to conclude that the inferences drawn from the information obtained from a particular procedure are valid just because a publisher or researcher has reported high validity. Rather, in a given evaluation, the validity of an inference depends upon the evaluation questions being addressed, the procedure used, the conditions of data collection, the judging and scoring procedures followed, the analyses procedures used, and the characteristics of the persons who provided the data or information.

It is highly desirable that evaluators measure multiple outcomes and use multiple information gathering procedures. Inferences from all of the procedures used must be validated, singly and in combination, to ensure that collectively the information required to answer the evaluation questions has been provided.

One major reason for using multiple procedures and information sources is to assure that all important variables are assessed. It is highly unlikely that a program, project, or material can be adequately characterized and assessed by reference to a single variable. Many kinds of variables typically need to be considered, such as program characteristics, student activities, and program costs, as well as outcome variables such as knowledge possessed, skills acquired, and attitudes toward the subject.

A different but equally important reason for using multiple procedures is that any one information source is fallible. For example, conclusions regarding student achievement in working with fractions have greater validity if results are obtained using a combination of (a) a multiple choice test, which allows coverage of many exercises in a given time; (b) a completion test in which the students have to show the work they used to find the answers; and (c) interviews of students to clarify the actual thought processes used by the students. Similarly, findings regarding program implementation have greater validity if they are based on data and evidence collected from analysis of program documents, observation of classes, and interviews with instructors. Using a combination of procedures increases validity as the strength of one approach compensates for the weaknesses of another approach.

❖ GUIDELINES

A. Check information collection procedures against the objectives and content of the program being evaluated to determine the degree of fit or congruence between them. This check should be informed at least in part by personnel responsible for the program and its operation and by representatives of important stakeholder groups.

B. Report the reasons for selecting each procedure, and highlight the evidence that supports the use of each in a methodology section of the evaluation report, an appendix to the report, or a technical report (see U5, Report Clarity).

C. Consider the *Standards for Educational and Psychological Testing* and other available sets of standards, and apply them when making decisions about educational and psychological tests to be used in the evaluation.

D. Consider validity evidence from other similar evaluations in which proposed procedures were used.

E. When collecting opinions, consider whether the respondents are motivated to tell the truth. Word questions to maximize understanding and minimize bias in responses.

F. Ensure that the individuals who will administer or use a particular procedure are qualified and adequately prepared (in terms of knowledge, training, and practice) to do so (see U2, Evaluator Credibility).

G. For newly developed procedures, present the rationale for the extent of validity claimed. Point out that such procedures are exploratory, and that results obtained from them must be interpreted cautiously and with a clear understanding of the limited validity evidence. Further, proper account must be taken of the context (see A2, Context Analysis), the characteristics of the subjects or groups with whom the procedure was used, and the qualifications and training, if needed, of the individuals who administered or used the procedure. Use multiple measures to help clarify the validity of the inferences drawn from the information yielded by the new procedure.

H. Use multiple procedures to obtain a more comprehensive assessment, but do so in as nondisruptive and parsimonious a manner as possible. Often it is desirable to employ nonreactive procedures, and to assess samples instead of populations of respondents. Use existing records, if relevant (see F3, Cost Effectiveness).

I. Assess the comprehensiveness of the information provided by the procedures as a set in relation to the information needed to answer the set of evaluation questions.

J. Consider respondent characteristics, such as reading ability, language proficiency, or physical handicaps, that may affect the validity of evaluation results.

K. Establish meaningful categories of information by identifying regular and recurrent themes in information collected using procedures calling for open-ended responses (e.g., essays, interviews).

❖ COMMON ERRORS

A. Accepting an information collection procedure for its general characteristics (e.g., title, format, and reputation) or for convenience (e.g., used previously) without first establishing the validity of the inferences drawn from the information obtained in relation to the evaluation questions

B. Basing important decisions on only one procedure or operational definition of a critical variable

C. Expecting that procedures yielding valid inferences can be constructed or developed quickly and easily

D. Failing to use existing procedures yielding valid inferences when they are available

E. Failing to ensure that personnel responsible for collecting information are adequately qualified and prepared to perform their assigned tasks

F. Failing to ensure that observations and descriptions of a process or event are adequately conducted and completed

G. Failing to allow qualified stakeholders the opportunity to review an instrument or procedure prior to its use

H. Failing to consider characteristics of respondents that may affect their ability to understand or respond to a procedure as implemented (e.g., reading ability, language proficiency, physical handicaps)

Illustrative Case 1—Description

Units on ecology were introduced for the first time in all grades in a middle school. The school's curriculum committee requested that the school district's evaluation department evaluate the effectiveness of these units. Specifically, the committee wanted to know whether the students who had completed the units had increased knowledge of environmental issues (e.g., preservation of endangered species and conservation of scarce resources) and had actually changed their behaviors (e.g., decreased their practice of littering the school grounds).

The evaluators administered a test and a questionnaire to the students before they took the ecology units and after they had completed these units. The test, a subtest of a national standardized science achievement test, covered hygiene, biology, and earth science. The questionnaire, a self-report instrument, included items on which the students rated themselves and their classmates on factors related to school citizenship. The questionnaire also included items on respect for other students, respect for teachers, and respect for school property. Following the collection and analysis of test scores, the evaluators reported no change from preinstruction to postinstruction scores on two parallel forms of the subtest. They reported further that the students' ratings on the citizenship questionnaire did not change with instruction. The curriculum committee expressed disappointment in the evaluation, pointing out that it did not really answer their questions.

Illustrative Case 1—Analysis

The information provided by the evaluators to the school's curriculum committee possesses little validity in that inferences drawn from the test scores and questionnaire ratings fail to address the evaluation questions asked. The evaluators should have chosen or developed data-gathering procedures that responded directly to the curriculum committee's questions. They should have checked the content of the test and questionnaire against the content and objectives of the ecology unit and asked the curriculum committee and the middle school teachers to offer judgments about whether the two instruments together would adequately address the evaluation questions. Further, the evaluators should have observed the ecology units as they were taught, and observed or received reports about the students in and out of school during the time the students were enrolled in the ecology units to discover possible unintended effects of the units on the students' behavior. They should have collected data on the quantity of wastepaper, bottles, and cans found in specific locations around the school plant and the extent to which students used both sides of notebook paper during the period of the evaluation to monitor changes, if any, in these student behaviors.

Illustrative Case 2—Description

A group of evaluators agreed to accept the assignment of evaluating collaboration activities of several interagency projects aimed at coordinating education and training services for economically disadvantaged populations. The purpose of the evaluation was to identify those collaborative activities that facilitated the desired coordination. The information to be used was to be gathered from the descriptions of each of the projects obtained by a combination of interviews of project staff and participants, observation of five sessions of each project, and an analysis of the initial proposal for each project.

In developing the procedures to be used to analyze the obtained information, the evaluators first reviewed a number of conceptual models and hypotheses identified in the literature. These models explained the dynamics of interorganizational cooperation, and particular attention was given to those models that offered explanations of why and where interorganizational collaboration was or was not successful. This literature was synthesized to identify a core of "critical features of interorganizational collaboration" thought to significantly affect the nature and level of collaborative effort.

Next, the evaluators selected and analyzed a purposeful sample of 15 case studies to identify additional critical features and to refine the core identified in the literature review.

As a next step, the evaluators convened a number of focus groups comprising representatives of, and persons with a stake in, each of the individual collaborative projects. In these groups, participants were first asked to identify and to rank in importance the factors that they felt had most hindered attempts to collaborate effectively. They were then asked to identify those factors that they felt had most facilitated collaboration within their localities and service domains.

Information obtained within each focus group was analyzed in terms of emergent themes focusing on factors hindering or facilitating successful collaboration. Themes were then analyzed across focus groups for comparability. While emergent themes reflected each local situation, they nevertheless displayed a remarkable consistency across all focus groups and related to such issues as authority distribution, consensus over goals and functions, and level of commitment to collaboration by key administrators. The evaluators juxtaposed the themes and the group discussion that focused on themes against the critical features identified from the literature and the 15 case examples. The coding categories were once more revised and clarified based on this comparison.

As a final step, the evaluators asked a small group of evaluators not familiar with the project to spend some time using the critical feature categories to code similar portions of raw group interview data from individual focus groups. The results of this coding exercise were then compared for consistency and discussed in a team setting. A final round of revisions and refinement of the coding system was conducted based on the results of this exercise.

The coding system was then used in the evaluation of the individual collaborative projects. While the evaluator assigned to each project was instructed to use the coding scheme, each was also asked to note aspects of the project that could be coded for later corroboration by a second observer. Four local codes were identified and subsequently corroborated.

Illustrative Case 2—Analysis

Given the time lines and resources available, the evaluators attempted to ensure that the validity and reliability (see A6, Reliable Information) of the final coding schema were assessed as rigorously as possible. This assessment was accomplished through the several iterative steps of using theoretical hypotheses as a starting point and validating coding categories based on the literature through focus group information. Moreover, validity was assessed in terms of both theoretical significance and meaningfulness to local stakeholders in the individual collaborative projects, and provision for emergent categories during data collection was made.

Use of the literature and prior case studies as a starting point for identification of critical features and processes helped to ensure that evaluation findings spoke, in general, to theoretical issues involved in interorganizational collaboration. By developing a theoretical baseline (i.e., the coding system) against which to analyze information obtained from singular projects, while at the same time allowing unique factors to emerge, the evaluators were able to identify both common and unique local patterns of interaction that were significantly affecting attempts at collaboration in individual projects.

Supporting Documentation

American Counseling Association/Association for Assessment in Counseling. (1991). *Responsibilities of users of standardized tests.* Washington, DC: Author.

American Psychological Association. (1985). *Standards for educational and psychological testing.* Washington, DC: Author.

Bradburn, N. M., & Sudman, S. (1979). *Improving interview method and questionnaire design.* San Francisco: Jossey-Bass.

Code of fair testing practices for education. (1988). Washington, DC: American Psychological Association, Joint Committee on Testing Practices.

Hambleton, R. K., & Zaal, J. N. (Eds.). (1991). *Advances in educational and psychological testing.* Boston: Kluwer Academic.

Howe, K., & Eisenhart, M. (1990). Standards for qualitative (and quantitative) research: A prolegomenon. *Educational Researcher, 19*(4), 2-9.

Kirk, J., & Miller, M. L. (1986). *Reliability and validity in qualitative research* (Qualitative Research Methods Series, 1). Newbury Park, CA: Sage.

LeCompte, M., & Goetz, J. (1982). Problems of reliability and validity in ethnographic research. *Review of Educational Research, 52,* 31-60.

Lincoln, Y. S., & Guba, E. G. (1986). But is it rigorous? Trustworthiness and authenticity in naturalistic evaluation. *New Directions for Program Evaluation: Naturalistic Evaluation, 30,* 73-84.

Linn, R. L. (Ed.). (1989). *Educational measurement.* New York: Macmillan.

Linn, R. L., Baker, E. L., & Dunbar, S. B. (1991). Complex, performance-based assessment: Expectations and validation criteria. *Educational Researcher, 20*(8), 5-21.

Morris, L. L., Fitz-Gibbon, C. T., & Lindheim, E. (1987). How to measure performance and use tests. In J. L. Herman (Ed.), *Program evaluation kit* (2nd ed.). Newbury Park, CA: Sage.

Patton, M. Q. (1990). *Qualitative evaluation and research methods* (2nd ed.). Newbury Park, CA: Sage.

Principles for fair student assessment practices for education in Canada. (1993). Edmonton, Alberta, Canada: University of Alberta, Centre for Research in Applied Measurement and Evaluation, Joint Advisory Committee.

Shadish, W. R., Jr., Cook, T. D., & Leviton, L. C. (1991). *Foundations of program evaluation: Theories of practice.* Newbury Park, CA: Sage.

Sudman, S., & Bradburn, N. M. (1982). *Asking questions.* San Francisco: Jossey-Bass.

A6   Reliable Information

STANDARD   The information gathering procedures should be chosen or developed and then implemented so that they will assure that the information obtained is sufficiently reliable for the intended use.

Overview

A generic term, *reliability*, refers to the degree of consistency of the information obtained from an information gathering process. Most important when assessing the reliability of the information obtained is to distinguish unwanted variability that is attributable to noise or random error in the information collection procedure from variability due to systematic, explainable sources. Systematic sources include differences attributable to different instructional effects, characteristics of program participants, and conditions in the environment or context of the program being evaluated. Reliability will be called into question whenever the evaluation procedures yield information and results that cannot be explained by these systematic sources.

Different information gathering procedures are sensitive to different sources of this random error. It is thus important that the form of reliability to be considered takes into account the sources of error present in each procedure. For example, in some instances, the primary concern may be with stability of a measurement from one occasion to another. In other situations, the concern may be with the equivalence of scores from alternate forms of a test, the internal consistency of items in an achievement test or an attitude scale, the consistency of ratings provided by different judges when scoring open-ended responses, the consistency of descriptions provided by different observers, or the consistency of themes extracted from a set of transcribed narratives by different analysts. Efforts should be devoted to reducing and/or describing the amount and impact of these unwanted sources of variability upon the evaluation results and findings.

It is also important when assessing the degree of reliability to take into account the unit of analysis or target group on which the evaluation is

153

focused. If the unit of analysis is a group, it is not appropriate to assess reliability analyses that focus on individuals as the unit of analysis. Similarly, reliability estimates derived from procedures used with adults cannot automatically be extended to adolescents.

❖ GUIDELINES

A. Whenever possible, evaluators should choose information gathering procedures that have, in the past, yielded data and information with acceptable reliability for their intended uses; however, the generalizability of previously favorable reliability results may not be simply assumed. Reliability information should be collected that is directly relevant to the groups and ways in which the information gathering procedures will be used in the evaluation.

B. For newly developed information gathering procedures, present the rationale for the type and extent of reliability claimed. Proper account must be taken of the content or behavior assessed by the procedure, of the ways in which the procedures were administered to the subjects or groups, and of the heterogeneity of the persons in terms of the characteristics being measured or observed, for these factors all influence reliability.

C. Evaluators should be familiar with the *Standards for Educational and Psychological Testing* and the *Responsibilities of Users of Standardized Tests* and apply them when making decisions about instrument selection and development.

D. Discuss developing propositions, interpretations, and conclusions with an impartial peer to help clarify one's own posture and values and their role in the inquiry.

E. Periodically record what the evaluator expects to find throughout the evaluation as a check on a predominant influence of the evaluator's own perspective. Maintain sensitivity to the perspectives of the stakeholders and alternative explanations for the phenomenon observed.

F. In the case of open-ended instruments and procedures, check the consistency of scoring, categorization, and coding by two or more qualified persons independently analyzing the same set of information or by an outside auditor verifying that the data have been consistently analyzed (see A11, Impartial Reporting).

G. Provide adequate training to scorers and analysts to ensure that they are sensitized to the kinds of mistakes they are likely to make, and know the procedures to avoid these mistakes.

❖ COMMON ERRORS

A. Interpreting evidence of one type of reliability (e.g., internal consistency, stability over time, interobserver agreement) as evidence of another type; that is, different reliabilities reflect different sources of measurement error, which influence the interpreting of information in different ways

B. Relying upon the reliability evidence that is reported for a published instrument or procedure taken at face value without considering the likely effects of differences between the setting and sample of the reported reliability study and those of the evaluation

C. Failing to take into account the fact that the reliability of the scores provided by an instrument or procedure may fluctuate depending on how, when, and to whom the instrument or procedure is administered

D. Assuming that because the reliability of individual scores for an instrument is low, the reliability of mean scores for a group will also be low

E. Interpreting reliability coefficients for measures of continuous variables as evidence of the reliability of dichotomous decisions (e.g., pass-fail, mastery-nonmastery) based on these measures

F. Failing to recognize that the reliability of a set of difference scores is typically less than the reliability of either of the two sets of scores used to compute the differences

G. Using scores with low reliabilities as influential outcome information

H. Assuming that because reliability is high, validity is also high

I. Assuming that the observations of one evaluator are not affected by the evaluator's perspective, training, or previous experience

J. Failing to consider all relevant information in interpreting and drawing conclusions

Illustrative Case 1—Description

Evaluators constructed an observation checklist and two forms of each of several objectives-referenced tests for use in evaluating an innovative instructional technique. The objectives-referenced tests each contained ten objectives with five items per objective.

The evaluators pretested the objectives-referenced tests by administering each form of each test to a different sample of students at grades 2 and 4 in six schools. They used a standard formula to compute an internal consistency coefficient for the total score based on 50 items (10 objectives with 5 questions each) for each form of the test. The internal consistency of each form was found to exceed .80.

To assess the reliability of the information provided by the observation checklist, the evaluators sent a different observer into each of six schools. Each observer studied a single domain in the school on two occasions. An interval of three weeks separated the first and second observations. Correlations between the observation reports for the two occasions were computed for each item on the observation checklist over the six schools. All correlations were found to exceed .60. Based on these results, the evaluators concluded that their tests and observation checklist yielded scores and information of sufficient reliability for use in the evaluation.

This conclusion was later attacked. A group of teachers who participated in the evaluation charged that the different forms of the tests were not equivalent and that they yielded unfair comparisons of classrooms and of schools. The teachers said they could not see the point of assessing the reliability of scores from each test as a whole, because the tests were constructed to yield subscores for specific objectives. They doubted that the items assigned to each objective provided consistent measurements of student mastery of the objective. The teachers also claimed that the results of the observations were more a function of the observers sent to each school than of what was happening in the classroom. The evaluators were unable to defend themselves against these charges.

Illustrative Case 1—Analysis

Both forms of each test might have been pretested by administering them to a single sample of students on two occasions. This would have made it possible to estimate the consistency of the results from one form to the other, for scores on each objective separately, and for scores on the 10 objectives combined. Because the tests had been developed to determine whether certain instructional objectives had been achieved, the percentage of students who were identified by both forms of the test as having achieved or having failed to achieve each objective would have been an appropriate index of the consistency of pass-fail judgments provided by the tests.

The observation checklist might have been pretested by having two or more different observers make the observations independently but simultaneously in each classroom involved in the pilot study. The percentage of interobserver agreements could have been calculated as an index of rating consistency for each item on the checklist. These results would indicate whether the rating of a classroom was independent of the rater.

Overall, the evaluators should have been more discriminating in choosing the types of reliability evidence to be considered in their evaluation. They should not have made the common error of treating internal consistency and test-retest reliability as the only ways of assessing consistency of pass-fail decisions and observational ratings.

Illustrative Case 2—Description

A radiologist was interested in evaluating the extent to which lectures in a course designed to introduce medical students to the fundamentals of clinical medicine contained instruction regarding the use of diagnostic imaging procedures. To do this, he developed a procedure in which an observer counted the number of each of four different types of diagnostic images used in a lecture (radiographs, ultrasound, magnetic resonance imaging, and computed tomography) and the content area discussed (e.g., cardiology or neurology). The counts were recorded on a standard form. The form listed, but did not define, each type of diagnostic imaging procedure. The radiologist hired two first-semester medical students as observers. He provided each student with sufficient copies of the forms to rate a series of lectures, and gave the students the times and locations for the lectures. The students were to make their observations independently.

When the course was completed, the radiologist had his secretary count the number of different types of images recorded for each content area. Based upon these counts, he concluded that large numbers of diagnostic images were being presented that were too advanced for students in an introductory course in clinical medicine. He also concluded that too few diagnostic images were being used in some content areas. He prepared a report and sent it to the medical school curriculum committee with a call for action.

The curriculum committee discussed the report with the course instructors, who were confused by the findings. They disagreed with the count data contained in the report. Prompted by this reaction, the committee more carefully scrutinized the report, and spoke with the radiologist and the medical students who made the observations. These discussions revealed that the medical students did not fully understand the differences among the four types of diagnostic imaging, and they did not consistently categorize instances of the diagnostic imaging presented during the lectures. Embarrassed, the radiologist agreed to retract his report and reconduct the study.

Illustrative Case 2—Analysis

The radiologist committed at least three errors in his execution of the study. First, prior to using the data collection instrument, the radiologist should have trained the observers and conducted an analysis of interrater agreement using a pilot study. By doing so, he very likely would have seen that the students had made their categorizations inconsistently and would have been prompted to seek reasons or explanations for the low level of agreement. This information should have signaled the radiologist to design better training procedures for the observers prior to the full study. Second, he should have done some of the observations himself to make sure he was satisfied with the procedures as implemented and to spot check the performance of the observers. Third, he should have discussed the findings and his conclusions with a colleague who had not been involved in the work. The colleague might have raised questions regarding possible errors in the data-gathering technique used and saved the radiologist the embarrassment of presenting and then retracting his findings and conclusions.

Supporting Documentation

American Counseling Association/Association for Assessment in Counseling. (1991). *Responsibilities of users of standardized tests*. Washington, DC: Author.

American Psychological Association. (1985). *Standards for educational and psychological tests*. Washington, DC: Author.

Hambleton, R. K., & Zaal, J. N. (Eds.). (1991). *Advances in educational and psychological testing*. Boston: Kluwer Academic.

Howe, K., & Eisenhart, M. (1990). Standards for qualitative (and quantitative) research: A prolegomenon. *Educational Researcher, 19*(4), 2-9.

Kirk, J., & Miller, M. L. (1986). *Reliability and validity in qualitative research* (Qualitative Research Methods Series, 1). Newbury Park, CA: Sage.

LeCompte, M., & Goetz, J. (1982). Problems of reliability and validity in ethnographic research. *Review of Educational Research, 52*, 31-60.

Lincoln, Y. S., & Guba, E. G. (1986). But is it rigorous? Trustworthiness and authenticity in naturalistic evaluation. *New Directions for Program Evaluation: Naturalistic Evaluation, 30*, 73-84.

Linn, R. L. (Ed.). (1989). *Educational measurement*. New York: Macmillan.

Lipsey, M. W. (1990). *Design sensitivity*. Newbury Park, CA: Sage.

Morris, L. L., Fitz-Gibbon, C. T., & Lindheim, E. (1987). How to measure performance and use tests. In J. L. Herman (Ed.), *Program evaluation kit* (2nd ed.). Newbury Park, CA: Sage.

Shadish, W. R., Jr., Cook, T. D., & Leviton, L. C. (1991). *Foundations of program evaluation: Theories of practice*. Newbury Park, CA: Sage.

Shavelson, R. J., & Webb, N. M. (1991). *Generalizability theory: A primer*. Newbury Park, CA: Sage.

A6 Reliable Information

A7 Systematic Information

STANDARD   The information collected, processed, and reported in an evaluation should be systematically reviewed and any errors found should be corrected.

Overview

Systematic information control implies that steps will be taken to assure that all information, whether already existing or newly collected, is as free from error as is possible and kept secure.

The possibilities for error are numerous in collecting, scoring, recording, coding, filing, collating, analyzing, and reporting information. Information may be collected from an unintended group of respondents. Intended procedures for administering tests and other procedures may not be followed because of unclear directions or inadequate training of personnel. Scoring guides and categorization systems may be misapplied. Clerical errors may occur; files may subsequently be lost. Errors may be made during the analysis of information. Summaries and results of analyses may be misinterpreted and reported incorrectly. These are but a few of the ways that avoidable errors can occur. Evaluators should eliminate as many of these errors as possible. Their presence can lead to erroneous conclusions and recommendations, which, in turn, can result in misguided decisions and actions.

Evaluators should not assume that even highly qualified and dedicated persons will perform (see P1, Service Orientation) in an error-free manner, nor should it be assumed that such persons will closely monitor their own work. Prudent evaluators will institute a systematic program of training, controls, and accuracy checks so as to eliminate as many errors as possible and/or to assess the probable effect of the errors that are not detected.

The information collected and the results of the analyses of this information should be kept secure to avoid subsequent tampering. In this way the completeness and accuracy of the information and results will be maintained.

❖ GUIDELINES

A. Take the steps necessary to ensure that evaluation staff are adequately trained to carry out their roles and are sensitized to the kinds of mistakes they are likely to make.

B. Systematically check for errors in the collecting, processing, and reporting of information and results using the quality control plan.

C. Use another person to verify data entry.

D. Monitor outside agencies or individuals responsible for information collecting, scoring and categorization, and/or quantitative or qualitative analyses.

E. Maintain control of original information and results so that their integrity can be protected.

F. Adopt and implement standard procedures for storing and retrieving information.

G. Check with stakeholders routinely to make certain information collected from them is represented accurately, and allow time to do so.

❖ COMMON ERRORS

A. Assuming that people who collect information follow administration instructions correctly

B. Assuming that respondents read, understand, and follow all the directions they are given

C. Failing to verify data entry for accuracy

D. Assuming that results from test-scoring machines and computers are accurate just because they have been produced by machine

E. Failing to manage the large volume of data generated through qualitative fieldwork methods

F. Failing to verify and proofread data tables generated from computer output

G. Assigning analysis and reporting functions to inexperienced staff, or consultants unfamiliar with the overall study, who would not recognize data-related errors

H. Failing to retract reports with inaccurate results or to assure substitution of accurate results

I. Ignoring systematic information control due to time pressures

J. Failing to control access to information

Illustrative Case 1—Description

A government agency announced its intention to provide $100,000 contracts to three school districts in each state for the purpose of field testing a nationally developed program in career education. The agency received many proposals and assigned four judges to rate each proposal on 13 specified criteria. The agency then summed and averaged the four ratings for each proposal. The proposals within each state were then ranked from highest to lowest. Contracts were awarded to the three school districts with the three highest ranked proposals in each state.

The authors of the proposal for a school district were disappointed to learn that their school district was not awarded a contract, especially because much time and effort had gone into the development of the proposal. One of the authors traveled to Washington seeking an explanation. She learned from a government official that her district's proposal had been given a very low overall rating. Not accepting this report, the author demanded an audit of the four individual ratings that had been assigned to her proposal. The government official complied and, much to his embarrassment, found that the overall rating for this proposal had been calculated by dividing the summed ratings by 6 instead of 4 (judges). The corrected mean rating for the district moved it to the top of the rank-ordered list for the state. Moreover, a subsequent check of the mean ratings for all the proposals revealed five more cases of proposals ranked on the basis of averages obtained by dividing the summed rating by 6, instead of 4, judges.

Illustrative Case 1—Analysis

While the procedure used to reach a funding decision was sound in light of the analysis done, the accuracy of the analysis was not. The officials of the government agency should have ensured that their funding decisions accurately reflected the collected judgments. The accuracy of the calculations, as well as the original ratings, should have been independently verified. The agency could have employed an independent evaluator to verify the accuracy of the entire process of collecting and analyzing judgments. And two staff members of the agency could have independently calculated the overall ratings for each proposal.

Illustrative Case 2—Description

A state legislature had recently enacted legislation establishing child support guidelines. Shortly thereafter, a law school in the state developed a special 12-hour training course to prepare family court professionals (lawyers, judges, and mediators) in the implementation of the law. Two years later, a professor at an out-of-state law school was funded to evaluate the implementation of the law. The evaluation sought to discover whether different third party interveners were implementing the child support guidelines similarly and whether the guidelines were affecting other terms of settlement in disparate ways.

The evaluator hired law students from the in-state law school to conduct semistructured interviews of matrimonial lawyers, judges, and family mediators. The students were trained in interview techniques, provided with information on the substantive legal issues of interest, and given three hypothetical cases around which the interviews would be conducted. The students were also given rules for assigning code numbers to the typed transcripts of interview tapes. Arrangements were made for the interview tapes to be transcribed and returned to the original interviewers (students). The interviewers were asked to check the transcripts for accuracy and to add comments as appropriate. After the transcripts had been checked, they were sent to the out-of-state evaluator for analysis, but the tapes themselves were deposited in sealed cartons in the library of the in-state law school.

When the evaluator reviewed the transcripts, he was impressed by the thoroughness of the interviews, the quality of the data, and the clarity of the responses. He proceeded immediately to analyze the data and write the final report. One of the most significant findings was that the judges were not systematically implementing the new guidelines as mandated in the legislation. The report created a furor among the state judiciary, and the state bar association demanded an audit of the evaluation.

At first, the evaluation auditor found the evaluation dependable and credible. Design decisions had been well documented and met professional standards. Furthermore, the log books of the evaluation contained ample evidence of triangulation and procedures to control bias. The evaluation auditor found that the transcripts, findings, and conclusions agreed, but then an error was detected. When the auditor listened to a sample of the interview tapes while reading the associated transcripts, he discovered that one of the transcribers had systematically reversed the coding categories for family mediators and judges. Thus one entire set of interviews had been erroneously attributed to judges, when they were in fact interviews with family mediators. When the error was corrected, it was found that judges were correctly interpreting and implementing the new law. The amount of child support assigned in mediator-assisted agreements, on the other hand, was found to be significantly below the standards set in the guidelines. The evaluator published the new findings together with a retraction of his first report and a note of apology to the judges maligned in the first report.

Illustrative Case 2—Analysis

As stated in the description section, the auditor found that design decisions were well documented and met professional standards. The problem arose in the transcription of the interviews. The evaluator made fundamental errors when he failed to train the student interviewers to check the accuracy of all aspects of the transcripts, including the code numbers, and when he neglected to check for errors in the transcripts prior to the analysis. The interviewers should have been prompted to check the transcripts against the tapes to ensure correct attribution. The evaluator could have had a systematic check made for such errors by having someone not involved in the interviewing and transcribing process listen to the tape of each interview while reading the associated transcript, checking all the codes assigned to the transcript against those in the interview tape.

Supporting Documentation

Ball, S. (1975). Audit of evaluation. In S. B. Anderson et al. (Eds.), *Encyclopedia of educational evaluation*. San Francisco: Jossey-Bass.

Hopkins, K. D., & Glass, G. V. (1978). *Basic statistics for the behavioral sciences*. Englewood Cliffs, NJ: Prentice Hall.

Murphy, R. T. (1975). Quality control. In S. B. Anderson et al. (Eds.), *Encyclopedia of educational evaluation*. San Francisco: Jossey-Bass.

Weller, S., & Romney, A. K. (1988). *Systematic data collection* (Qualitative Research Methods, 10). Newbury Park, CA: Sage.

A8 Analysis of Quantitative Information

STANDARD   Quantitative information in an evaluation should be appropriately and systematically analyzed so that evaluation questions are effectively answered.

Overview

Many evaluations produce and analyze quantitative information. This information may include, for example, the age and socioeconomic characteristics of respondents; measures of achievement, attitude, and behavior; and descriptions of characteristics of the program, project, or instructional materials being evaluated. The task of quantitative analysis is to organize, summarize, and interpret this information.

The analytic methods chosen should be appropriate for the evaluation question(s) being addressed and the characteristics of the information being analyzed. The analysis should begin with preliminary exploratory analyses to gain a greater understanding of the data and to ensure its correctness (e.g., to identify outliers and verify their correctness), and then be followed by more sophisticated and complex analyses designed to provide clear and interpretable results. Visual displays and analysis should also be used to gain an increased understanding of the data and to clarify the presentation and interpretation of statistical results in the evaluation report.

Evaluations often involve comparing different groups in different programs. The groups being compared are seldom formed by random assignment. Rather, they tend to be natural groupings that are likely to differ in various ways. Analytical methods may be used to adjust for these initial differences, but these methods are based upon a number of assumptions. As it is often difficult to check such assumptions, it is advisable, when time and resources permit, to use several different methods of analysis to determine whether a replicable pattern of results is obtained.

165

Overall comparisons of average performance of groups in different programs are generally insufficient. At times, the effects of a program may influence variability of performance, but not average performance. Analyses of effects for identifiable subgroups should also be considered, because a program may have differential effects for various subgroups. While there is no one best method for analyzing a given set of data, evaluators should ensure that they can defend the methodology, the underlying assumptions, the calculations they used, and the interpretations, inferences, and conclusions drawn from the results of their analyses.

❖ GUIDELINES

A. Choose analytic procedures that are appropriate to the evaluation questions and the nature of the data.

B. Conduct multiple analyses of the data, as is usually warranted.

C. Report potential weaknesses in the research design or data analysis and describe their possible influence on interpretations and conclusions (e.g., unexpected attrition, violation of assumptions).

D. Consider practical significance (e.g., effect sizes) and replicability as well as statistical significance when drawing inferences and formulating conclusions from quantitative analyses.

❖ COMMON ERRORS

A. Allowing data collection and analysis techniques to dictate the evaluation process

B. Assuming that significant statistical results are necessarily of practical significance

C. Interpreting nonsignificant statistical results because they happen to have practical significance, unless there is evidence of replicability

D. Assuming that gain scores, matching, or analysis of covariance will necessarily provide an adequate adjustment for preexisting differences among groups

E. Using an incorrect unit of analysis

F. Interpreting group means on the basis of norm distributions for individuals rather than for groups

G. Using complex statistical techniques when the audience would be better served by the use of simpler analytical methods and graphs

H. Emphasizing rigor at the expense of relevance, and vice versa

I. Concluding that all evaluations need to use statistical analyses

J. Concluding that all evaluations should be comparative studies

K. Failing to recognize and exploit the complementarity between qualitative and quantitative analyses and that interpretations and conclusions should be supported by both

Illustrative Case 1—Description

A company was contracted by a school to run a special five-week project for improving the reading performance of low achieving fourth-grade children. The school regularly administered a reading test to all students at the beginning of the year, and those students who scored below a prespecified level were enrolled in the special project. A parallel form of this test was administered to both the participants in the five-week project and the nonparticipants at the end of the five weeks.

The project evaluator computed a gain score for each student. Analyses of these scores revealed that the gain scores of participants in the special project were more frequently positive than the gain scores of nonparticipants. Moreover, the average gain score of the participant group was positive and larger than the average gain score of the nonparticipant group, the mean of the latter group being near zero, but negative. The evaluator concluded that the special project had the effect of improving the reading skills of poor readers relative to the skills of better readers.

Illustrative Case 1—Analysis

The conclusion of the evaluator was very likely faulty due to the fact that the effect of regression was not accounted for in the analysis he performed. When subjects for a treatment program are chosen because they have extremely low scores on a test that yields unreliable information, then it can be expected that these subjects will score higher on retest, even if the performance being tested has not been changed by an experimental program. To estimate the effect of the special project on the reading performance of low scoring students, the evaluator could have obtained more information about the effect of the program had he used a different evaluation design. The altered design would involve randomly dividing the initially low scoring students into two groups. One group would be assigned to the special project while the other group would continue in the regular program. The test scores collected from the two groups could be directly statistically compared, using the scores from the second test, gain scores, and analysis of covariance, with the results from the three approaches compared. Graphic techniques could be used to enhance the interpretability of the statistical results obtained (e.g., stem-and-leaf or box-plot displays).

Illustrative Case 2—Description

A large school district developed a program to encourage girls to enroll, participate, and achieve in physical science courses in high school. Some of the schools in the district organized their first-year physical science courses as coeducational, others provided class sections for girls only, and some schools allowed girls to choose single-sex or coeducational sections. Information was collected from the participating girls on three types of variables: student background characteristics (e.g., parental education, previous achievement in mathematics, previous achievement in science, vocational aspiration); program and instructional variables (e.g., instructional time per week, laboratory time per week, attendance, gender of instructor, number of university science courses taken by instructor); and outcome measures (e.g., scores on a common physical science test and enrollment in a science-related course in the following year).

In an attempt to develop a policy on the use of single-sex classes for instruction in physical science at the high school level, the district board sought assistance in the analysis of the data. The contractor carried out a hierarchical regression analysis (e.g., Bock, 1989; Bryk & Raudenbush, 1992; Goldstein, 1987) to determine the relative effect of single-sex and coeducational organization with and without choice on the outcome measures. When all of the student, program, and instructional variables were held constant, the difference in favor of the same-sex program was about one quarter of a standard deviation on the physical science tests, and about one fifth of a standard deviation on the enrollment criterion. Further examination of the results revealed that the variation of mean parental education across schools accounted for approximately 15% of the variance among class achievement means after student-level factors had been taken into account. It was suggested that, holding all other things constant, increasing mean parental education by one standard deviation would not only improve the class mean achievement by .18 standard deviations but would also decrease the gap between the achievement means for single-sex and coeducational schools by one third of a standard deviation.

Illustrative Case 2—Analysis

Although the evaluators correctly noted the multilevel nature of the problem, and analyzed the data in a consistent fashion, reporting the results either as causal links, or even as residual effects, may not serve the audience well. The three kinds of organization (single sex, coeducational, and choice) are confounded with various combinations of background and instructional characteristics. Statistical adjustments and residual effects are complex and may not even present an accurate picture of how a school would operate, or how a student would achieve, under unconfounded circumstances. These problems may make it difficult for the district board to engage in a meaningful debate on policy implications. In circumstances such as these, it is generally appropriate to go beyond the complex techniques and examine the results in their simplest form using visual displays broken down according to the background and instructional variables as they actually occurred (e.g., Cleveland, 1985). Policy decisions often arise from informed debate. An important goal of statistical analysis is to inform the debate by making the information available to the participants. Policy-makers may not be easily conversant with notions of partialing out, holding constant, accounting for variance, and estimating corrected effects. Expression of results in those terms can act to curtail debate or, worse, encourage participants to disregard the data altogether. It is also possible that the analysis did not address issues within the control of policy-makers.

Supporting Documentation

Bock, R. D. (1989). *Multilevel analysis of educational data.* New York: Academic Press.

Bryk, A. S., & Raudenbush, S. W. (1992). *Hierarchical linear models: Applications and data analysis methods.* Newbury Park, CA: Sage.

Campbell, D. T., & Erlebacher, A. (1975). How regression artifacts in quasi-experimental evaluations can mistakenly make compensatory education look harmful. In M. Guttentag & E. L. Struening (Eds.), *Handbook of evaluation research.* Beverly Hills, CA: Sage.

Cleveland, W. S. (1985). *The elements of graphing data.* Monterey, CA: Wadsworth.

Fitz-Gibbon, C. T., & Morris, L. L. (1987). How to analyze data. In J. L. Herman (Ed.), *Program evaluation kit* (2nd ed.). Newbury Park, CA: Sage.

Freed, M. N., Ryan, J. M., & Hess, R. K. (1991). *Handbook of statistical procedures and computer applications to education and the behavioral sciences.* New York: Macmillan.

Goldstein, H. (1987). *Multilevel models in educational and social research.* London: Oxford University Press.

Hopkins, K. D., & Glass, G. V. (1978). *Basic statistics for the behavioral sciences.* Englewood Cliffs, NJ: Prentice-Hall.

Jaeger, R. M. (1991). *Statistics: A spectator sport.* Newbury Park, CA: Sage.

Journal of Experimental Education. (1993). The role of statistical significance testing in contemporary social science: A special issue.

Thompson, B. (1992). Misuse of ANCOVA and related "statistical control" procedures. *Reading Psychology, 13*(1), iii-xviii.

Wiersma, W. (1991). *Research methods in education* (5th ed.). Boston: Allyn & Bacon.

A9   Analysis of Qualitative Information

STANDARD   Qualitative information in an evaluation should be appropriately and systematically analyzed so that evaluation questions are effectively answered.

Overview

Qualitative information consists of descriptions and interpretations that are in narrative rather than numerical form. This information comes from many sources: structured and unstructured interviews; participant and nonparticipant observations; hearings, documents and records; and unobtrusive data collection procedures of various kinds. It may be gathered intentionally, or it may come to one's awareness quite unexpectedly. It may focus on decisions, objectives, plans, processes, and/or outcomes; and it may be recorded as descriptions, logical arguments, interpretations, and/or impressions.

Qualitative analysis in an evaluation study is the process of compiling, analyzing, and interpreting qualitative information about a program that will answer particular questions about that program. The result is a narrative presentation, in which numbers are rarely assigned to any of the information. While qualitative data can sometimes be quantitatively as well as qualitatively analyzed, qualitative analysis may give depth and perspective to the data that quantitative analysis alone is not able to provide.

One of the important distinctions between qualitative and quantitative analysis is that for qualitative analysis the observation protocols, categories of information, and methods of summarization are often not predetermined. Qualitative analysis often involves an inductive, interactive, and iterative process whereby the evaluator returns to relevant audiences and data sources to confirm and/or expand the purposes of the evaluation and test conclusions. It often requires an intuitive sifting of expressed concerns and relevant observations; it cannot always be accomplished by application of prespecified rules for data reduction although systematic procedures do exist. The evaluator must assure the accuracy of findings by seeking confirmatory evidence from more than one source and by subjecting inferences to independent verification.

In general, qualitative information has been appropriately analyzed when a set of categories have been derived that are necessary to account for the information that has been uncovered and sufficient to document, illuminate, and respond to the evaluation questions; when the information has been classified into these categories, and the categories themselves have been tested for validity and reliability; and when the meaningfulness of conclusions and recommendations has been demonstrated with reference to these categories.

The essence of this standard is both to enrich understanding of the phenomena under study and to avoid faulty conclusions. When this standard is met, evaluations are safeguarded from inappropriate analysis methods that may lead to premature closure or inadequate cross-checking of findings.

❖ GUIDELINES

A. Choose an analytic procedure and method of summarization that is appropriate to the questions to be addressed in the study and to the nature of the qualitative information to be collected.

B. Report potential weaknesses in the data, for example, a single source of information that seemed important but could not be cross-checked, or contradictory findings that could not be reconciled.

C. Focus the analysis on clear questions of interest and define the boundaries of information to be examined, for example, time period, funded activities, target student or other client population, and geographic location.

D. Establish meaningful categories of information—for example, parental support, home/career conflict, intrinsic rewards, and dominance—by identifying regular and recurrent themes in the qualitative data (see A5, Valid Interpretations).

E. Test the consistency of findings when possible by having two or more independent evaluators analyze the same set of information or by having an external auditor verify that the data have been consistently analyzed (see A6, Reliable Information).

F. Communicate frequently with representatives of the stakeholders to ensure that they find the intermediate qualitative analyses appropriate, and the tentative conclusions and recommendations meaningful (see U2, Evaluator Credibility).

G. Seek corroboration of qualitative evidence using independent methods and sources.

H. Allow for emergent questions to shape evaluation and analytic processes.

❖ COMMON ERRORS

A. Regarding qualitative data analysis as relatively nonrigorous and as something that can be accomplished well enough on an intuitive basis without training, choosing information to reinforce preconceptions rather than to examine the validity of preconceptions or working hypotheses

B. Failing to consider alternative interpretations of reality and the multiple value perspectives that may exist in an evaluation situation

C. Failing to distinguish among different sources of qualitative information on such bases as credibility, degree of expertise, and degree of involvement

D. Failing to recognize that qualitative and quantitative data are complementary and that interpretations should be supported by both

E. Overstressing the details of a situation at the expense of more general working hypotheses or inferences

F. Concentrating so heavily on describing the unique feature of a situation that its generalized features are not examined

G. Overstressing relevance at the expense of rigor, or vice versa

H. Redirecting the evaluation to address interesting new questions that emerge from the analysis without first discussing this with the client

I. Collecting so much qualitative data that analysis would be prohibitively expensive and time consuming

J. Attempting to quantify all qualitative information

K. Forcing responses into a priori categories when they do not fit

Illustrative Case 1—Description

Two members of a school district's evaluation office were assigned by the school superintendent to help her analyze a set of qualitative information that had been gathered to evaluate a special crime prevention project in the district. The project had an emergent format, with the activities carried on within it changing over time as the staff gained insight and experience. The superintendent needed accurate information about the nature of the project activities for inclusion in a progress report to the funding agency. This report was due in three months. That agency also wanted to know whether contacts between youngsters enrolled in the project and various law enforcement agencies—the police, the courts, and juvenile officers—had been reduced during the first operational year.

A considerable amount of information was available for analysis. Each staff member had kept a daily diary of project activities. Four times during the year, written and oral testimony had been received at hearings attended by students, teachers, counselors, parents, juvenile officers, health officials, and representatives of the business community. Staff members had maintained a file of pertinent newspaper clippings, and they had kept detailed case study records for a sample of 10 youngsters. A community advisory council had met monthly to hear and discuss project progress reports, and minutes of the meetings had been maintained. School cumulative files for each enrolled youngster were also available, as were official records of police, court, and juvenile probation officer contacts.

The evaluators spent more than a month getting acquainted with these materials and perusing the contents. They developed a set of descriptive categories within which virtually every entry in the staff logs, hearings records, newspaper articles, case study records, and cumulative files could be classified. They also developed a frequency count for the number of times each enrolled youngster had contact with a law enforcement agency during the first year of the project and in the immediately preceding year. Two results were soon evident: (a) Only a small proportion of the classified materials provided any insight into the nature of project activities and how they had changed over the year, and (b) the number of law enforcement agency contacts was virtually identical in each of the two years. The evaluators, running out of time, were able to provide only sketchy accounts of activities, and informed the superintendent that the project was unsuccessful in reducing law enforcement agency contacts. When the superintendent reported these findings to the funding agency, support was withdrawn and the project was aborted.

Project staff were stunned by this development, especially because the count of contacts had weighed so heavily in the decision. They pointed out that, during the first of the years examined (the preproject year), these contacts primarily took the form of arrests and court appearances for trial, while during the second of the years examined (the first project year), these contacts were primarily supervisory and counseling sessions with juvenile officers. The juvenile officers declared that they had in fact been well pleased with the changes they were witnessing in the attitudes and demeanor of the youngsters enrolled in the project.

Illustrative Case 1—Analysis

The evaluators carrying out this analysis made two fundamental errors. First, they failed to recognize the need to bound their inquiry and so wasted a great deal of time in organizing data irrelevant to their purposes. Perhaps this difficulty would have been avoided if the evaluators had met more frequently with the client. Second, they permitted frequency counts to substitute for an adequate analysis of the nature of the contacts between enrolled youngsters and law enforcement agencies. The evaluators should have attended first to the questions that they needed to answer. They should have entered only those records most likely to furnish the information they sought—for example, staff logs to answer the question of what sorts of activities were mounted and how they changed over the year—and they should have used other sources of information such as participant interviews. They should have been less hasty in converting contact records to numbers that failed to reflect differences in kinds of contacts. Even the most cursory thought about the kinds of contacts being recorded should have led the evaluators to classify the contacts, an effort that, had they engaged in it, would have quickly led them to a very different conclusion about the project's effectiveness.

Illustrative Case 2—Description

For well over 100 years, American law schools have used the "case method" of teaching law. This method involves the study of cases that demonstrate legal principles and the development of legal doctrine. With the case method, the predominant law school pedagogy continues to be the Socratic method used to help students develop legal reasoning and analysis, legal argumentation, and litigation skills. Over the last 20 years or so, however, these traditional methods for teaching law have been called into question by various segments of the legal community. It is alleged that modern legal practice more often than not requires skills in negotiation and mediation rather than skills in more adversarial techniques, and that traditional methods fail to prepare lawyers for this type of practice.

In an effort to bring empirical data to bear on the controversy, a law school professor recently obtained funding to evaluate the methods used by federal judges in pretrial settlement conferences. The evaluator collected data during the observation and recording of pretrial conferences with judges and attorneys for the parties in federal district court cases and during recorded interviews with federal district court judges.

The evaluator, schooled in quantitative methods, hired a qualitative methodologist to guide the analysis of the qualitative data. The methodologist worked with the evaluator to develop detailed procedures for systematic preservation and analysis of qualitative data, including the preparation of raw data logs and a category system for analysis. The evaluator expressed skepticism regarding the necessity for such time consuming procedures and gradually stopped consulting the methodologist.

The tapes were subsequently transcribed and the resulting transcripts cleaned by the evaluator to correct errors and to improve the flow of the narrative. An iterative, intuitive process was used during the analysis, and a report was published that confirmed that prevailing law school methods and pedagogy were inadequately preparing lawyers to fulfill the expectations of modern legal practice.

Illustrative Case 2—Analysis

The evaluator in this case violated four of the six guidelines for the handling and analysis of qualitative information. First, the evaluator, unschooled as he was in the rigors of qualitative data collection and analysis, tampered with the raw data to enhance the narrative quality of the data logs themselves. Second, the evaluator implemented a nonrigorous and nonsystematic data analysis strategy based on the assumption that qualitative data were merely anecdotal and that the analysis of such data could be accomplished on an intuitive basis. Third, the methodologist's suggestions regarding the systematic development of categories for analysis represented time consuming efforts that had been anticipated in neither the budget nor the time lines for the project. These feasibility considerations mitigated against fully observing the procedures developed by the consultant. Finally, the analytic strategy failed to consider alternative interpretations for the data such as might have been presented by, for example, a search for negative evidence or by discourse analysis. Therefore the findings reported for this study are suspect on every dimension.

Supporting Documentation

Crabtree, B. F., & Miller, W. L. (1992). *Doing qualitative research*. Newbury Park, CA: Sage.

Fielding, N. G., & Lee, R. M. (1991). *Using computers in qualitative research*. Newbury Park, CA: Sage.

LeCompte, M., & Goetz, J. (1982). Problems of reliability and validity in ethnographic research. *Review of Educational Research, 52*, 31-60.

Leninger, M. (Ed.). (1985). *Qualitative research methods in nursing*. Orlando, FL: Grune & Stratton.

Miles, M. B., & Huberman, A. M. (1984). *Qualitative data analysis: A source book of new methods*. Beverly Hills, CA: Sage.

Patton, M. Q. (1987). How to use qualitative methods in evaluation. In J. L. Herman (Ed.), *Program evaluation kit* (2nd ed.). Newbury Park, CA: Sage.

Patton, M. Q. (1990). *Qualitative evaluation and research methods* (2nd ed.). Newbury Park, CA: Sage.

Strauss, A. L. (1987). *Qualitative analysis for social scientists*. New York: Cambridge University Press.

Tesch, R. (1990). *Qualitative research: Analysis types and software tools*. New York: Falmer.

Yin, R. K. (1991). *Case study research: Design and methods*. Newbury Park, CA: Sage.

A10   Justified Conclusions

> **STANDARD**   The conclusions reached in an evaluation should be explicitly justified, so that the stakeholders can assess them.

Overview

The conclusions of an evaluation, which represent judgments and recommendations, must be defensible and defended. If stakeholders do not receive sufficient information for determining whether the conclusions are warranted, they may disregard them. Second, conclusions with inadequate justifications may be incorrect, thereby leading the audience to inappropriate actions. Conclusions must be based on all the pertinent information collected, must incorporate results of sound analysis and logic, and must be accompanied by full information about how the evaluation was conducted (i.e., an account of the evaluation's procedures, information, and underlying assumptions). Where possible, the conclusions should be accompanied by discussion of plausible alternative explanations of the findings and why these explanations were rejected.

❖   GUIDELINES

A. Develop conclusions that both respond to the audience's questions and faithfully reflect the evaluation procedures and findings.

B. Report information that relates to the conclusions (see A5, Valid Information).

C. Generate, assess, and report plausible alternative explanations of the findings and, where possible, indicate why these explanations should be discounted.

D. Limit conclusions to those situations, time periods, persons, contexts, and purposes for which the evaluation findings are applicable.

E. Advise the audience to be cautious in interpreting equivocal findings in the evaluation report.

F. Solicit feedback from a variety of program participants about the credibility of interpretations, explanations, conclusions, and recommendations before finalizing the report. Point out common misinterpretations and inappropriate inferences that may be drawn from the information collected.

❖ COMMON ERRORS

A. Concentrating on answering audience questions without taking appropriate account of the limitations of the evaluation procedures and data

B. Ignoring possible side effects of the program in reaching conclusions about its effectiveness

C. Basing conclusions on insufficient or unsound information

D. Being too cautious in interpreting the findings of an evaluation

E. Failing to report the limitations of the evaluation study

Illustrative Case—Description

An evaluation firm was contracted to field test a federally financed K-12 program in ecological education. The field test was to take place in three urban, four suburban, and ten rural school districts.

Officials of the government agency that financed the program's development wanted to know whether it was sufficiently meritorious to warrant widespread dissemination. Specifically, they wanted to know whether students participating in this program would achieve program objectives, whether teachers using the program would incorporate the ideas on ecology presented in the program into their existing courses, and how a sample of curriculum specialists would rate the program against other approaches to ecological education.

A representative of the government agency suggested that the evaluators review an earlier report describing the results of a pilot test of the program. The evaluators scanned this report but questioned its utility, because the pilot test was completed while the program was still under development. They decided, however, to include the pilot test report as an appendix to their own report.

The evaluators subsequently implemented a four-part evaluation study over a two-year period. First, they employed a test-retest design in each year, using the program's end-of-course test on both testing occasions. Second, they held periodic discussions with groups of participating students, teachers, and administrators, in which they asked about the implementation of the ecology program. Third, they conducted annual interviews with teachers and curriculum specialists in each of the participating schools. Finally, they conducted a cost analysis of the program.

A10 Justified Conclusions

The evaluators presented their findings at the end of the two-year evaluation in a main report and an appendix. Their main report concentrated on the results of the repeated measures analysis of variance, controlled for type of district, completed for each of the two years. Their analyses produced the following results: Pretest to posttest gains were statistically significant at the .01 level for nine of the twelve grades during the first year; corresponding gains were similarly statistically significant for all twelve grades during the second year; and the pattern of significance was similar for the three types of districts. Based on these findings, the main report concluded that the program was successful and recommended that it be widely disseminated.

Several staff members in the sponsoring agency criticized this field test report. They charged that the conclusion and recommendation were unjustified. They questioned the apparent total reliance upon an insufficient quantitative analysis and pointed to results of the pilot test and to other information in the appendix that raised serious questions about the adequacy of the program. This information suggested that the teachers—in both the pilot and the field studies—taught the program's test but failed to engage in planned activities; the curriculum specialists were only lukewarm in their appraisal of the program; and the school principals in both studies doubted that the program materials could be kept up to date at a reasonable cost. Based on the apparent disagreement between the main report and the appendix, the funding agency rejected the field test report.

Illustrative Case—Analysis

The evaluators did gather data that allowed them to draw conclusions about certain components of the program. But, in addition to the components included, the evaluators who conducted the field test should have used all pertinent prior information about the program in formulating their conclusions and recommendations. Moreover, they should have formulated their conclusions and recommendations to reflect all the findings of the field test—not just those reflecting student performance. Further, there also was no mention of the cost analysis they conducted.

Supporting Documentation

Hendricks, M., & Papagiannis, M. (1990). Do's and don'ts for offering effective recommendations. *Evaluation Practice, 11*(2), 121-125.

Smith, M. F. (1989). *Evaluability assessment: A practical approach.* Boston: Kluwer Academic.

A11 Impartial Reporting

> **STANDARD** Reporting procedures should guard
> against distortion caused by personal feelings and biases
> of any party to the evaluation, so that evaluation reports
> fairly reflect the evaluation findings.

Overview

Reports can be distorted in a variety of ways. The report may not reflect all the perspectives that should be taken into account, or may favor one interpretation over others. Distortions may occur because of carelessness or client/sponsor/audience pressure, which the evaluator cannot resist. Bias may be introduced if there is continuous reporting of evaluation findings; early reports may constrain later reports. Or, if the findings from earlier reports are used to hone a program, the evaluators may bias later reports because they are then evaluating, at least in part, their "own" program.

❖ GUIDELINES

A. Reach agreement with the client during the initial stages of the evaluation about the steps to be taken to ensure the fairness of all reports.

B. Clarify the nature of and authority for editing.

C. Ensure the evaluation report includes perspectives independent of the perspectives of those whose work is being evaluated.

D. Seek out and report alternative, perhaps even conflicting, conclusions and recommendations (see A10, Justified Conclusions).

E. Strive to establish and maintain independence in reporting, using techniques such as adversary-advocacy reports, outside audits, or rotation of evaluation team members over various audience contacts.

F. Describe and explain the steps taken to protect the integrity of reports.

181

❖ COMMON ERRORS

A. Assuming that all parties to an evaluation are neutral

B. Failing to safeguard reports against deliberate or inadvertent distortions

C. Surrendering the authority to edit reports

D. Failing to be involved in public presentations of the findings as the situation warrants

E. Being so isolated from the program developer that potentially useful information from the developer is not reported to the evaluator, and there is no good way for feedback to be transmitted from the evaluator to the program developer

F. Wanting to please the client to the extent that it becomes difficult to report negative findings

Illustrative Case 1—Description

A superintendent of a small school district decided to have a special reading project evaluated. The project had been introduced three years earlier within the elementary grades of one of the district's three elementary schools. It was now time for a decision about whether to institutionalize the project as the district's reading program. A reading specialist from a neighboring school district agreed to conduct the evaluation.

As she began collecting data, the evaluator formed the initial conclusion that the project had not been successful, and in fact was producing serious and undesirable side effects. Of particular concern was her impression that the project was destroying the motivation of children to read. She thought it wise to check this impression with the project staff, who, when she made a presentation to them, became very defensive and hostile. They suggested that heavy reliance on test scores had seriously constrained the evaluator's ability to understand what the project was about. Moreover, project staff asserted that the evaluator's bias in favor of highly structured approaches to the teaching of reading rendered her incompetent to judge the project's approach, which was not highly structured. The evaluator capitulated to the pressures brought to bear by the project staff and submitted a report to the superintendent recommending that the project be adopted as the reading program for the district.

Illustrative Case 1—Analysis

The evaluator's decision to check her assumption about the program with program staff was a wise one. However, the evaluator, perhaps because of her inexperience, was too quick to accept the criticism from project staff, who, as it turned out, had an axe to grind. Her reaction to their comments should not have been to capitulate but to test the extent to which the staff's observations were valid, not merely self-serving. Other information could have been compiled to check their assertion that test scores did not adequately represent project outcomes—an assertion that was probably true. She might have recognized the possibility that her own philosophical predilections about methods of teaching reading had influenced her judgment, and sought confirmation by employing—or at least consulting—other experts who could have confirmed or refuted her judgment. She should have realized that project staff would probably have developed a strong commitment to what they were doing, and discounted their reactions accordingly. Finally, if the conflicts introduced by the staff's reactions could not be resolved, she could have developed a final report that openly presented the conflicts, including her own value position, and noted their unresolved state. While not definitive, such a report would have reflected the true state of affairs to the superintendent and would have avoided providing a warrant for a project whose effectiveness was still in doubt.

Illustrative Case 2—Description

A large state medical school decided to assemble a library of videotapes of emergency room cases, together with supporting materials to be used in training medical students in the treatment of trauma cases. At the time that the medical school faculty created a committee to build the library, they also hired a panel of outside experts to evaluate both the process by which the content of the library was determined and the training materials that were produced. The evaluation panel was to provide formative feedback throughout the process of building the library as well as submit a summative evaluation report once the library had been assembled.

Two years later, the library was completed and the evaluation panel assembled its final report. Each member of the panel took responsibility for writing a section of the report. The panel then met to review each other's work and collaboratively assemble the final product. During that meeting, it became apparent to the panel chair that one of the team members had taken his "formative feedback role" too seriously. Because of this panel member's expertise and experience as a producer of nonprofit television documentaries in the field of science, the committee responsible for assembling the tape library called on him frequently for advice. Both from the written section he had contributed to the report and from his comments during the meeting, it was apparent that this panel member had gotten too involved in the project to be an objective evaluator.

The chair of the evaluation panel pointed this out to the panel member and said she felt that it would be best if he abstained from having any hand in the content of the final report. After some discussion with other members of the evaluation panel, most of whom agreed with the chair, the panel member concurred.

Illustrative Case 2—Analysis

This is a subtle, but not uncommon, trap that evaluators can fall into, particularly in the process of formative evaluation. Members of a formative evaluation panel must deliberately and frequently remind themselves of this possibility. The actions taken by the evaluation panel and the panel member in the case—once the impartiality of a member appeared to have been compromised—were correct.

Supporting Documentation

Scriven, M. (1976). Evaluation bias and its control. In G. V Glass (Ed.), *Evaluation studies review annual* (Vol. 1). Beverly Hills, CA: Sage.

A12   Metaevaluation

STANDARD   The evaluation itself should be formatively and summatively evaluated against these and other pertinent standards, so that its conduct is appropriately guided and, on completion, stakeholders can closely examine its strengths and weaknesses.

Overview

Program evaluation is difficult to do well but may provide critical support to effective programs or result in modification or cancellation of ineffective systems. Program evaluation soundly performed can appropriately guide decisions, but flawed program evaluation can mislead decision makers. Consequently, the program evaluation itself should be evaluated.

Metaevaluation is evaluation of an evaluation. The program evaluation should be evaluated by those who design and carry it through. And, inasmuch as program evaluations often are subject to outside scrutiny, criticism, and legal action by program supporters, detractors, and metaevaluators, separate concurrent review of the program evaluation process by external metaevaluators can help program evaluators avoid critical mistakes. Clients can also conduct metaevaluations. Documentation of the effective/ineffective application of program evaluation procedures facilitates the proper interpretation of data. Regular employment of metaevaluations should enhance the credibility of particular program evaluations and the overall evaluation profession.

Metaevaluations play two major roles: The formative role is to guide the planning and implementation of a program evaluation. Necessarily, the formative metaevaluation role is performed during the conduct of the program evaluation and, ideally, it should be performed by an evaluator external to the program evaluation itself. If resources are not available for an external metaevaluator, a metaevaluation process should be followed and executed by a program evaluation team member.

The summative role of metaevaluation is to assess the worth and merit of a completed program evaluation. In this role, metaevaluation addresses such questions as the following: Were the findings of the program evaluation clear? Were the design and implementation of the design appropriate for the study? Were the conclusions justified by the data? Were the results adequately disseminated? Were they used? Summative metaevaluations may be undertaken by one or more persons acting independently of the team responsible for the program evaluation. Alternatively, metaevaluation may be conducted by one or more members of the team that did the program evaluation. Both internal and external perspectives are desirable, as are multiple external perspectives. Metaevaluations may also be formal or informal depending on what is at stake. Formal metaevaluations are conducted as systematically as the program evaluations covered by these Standards. Informal metaevaluations may only involve an application of a checklist, such as the one provided earlier in this book, by a program evaluator periodically during the program evaluation.

The audiences for a metaevaluation include all who will, or should, be guided by the program evaluation in making decisions. Additional audiences include all those with stakes in the program evaluation plus those responsible for conducting the program evaluation.

Metaevaluation can be expected to facilitate early identification and correction of potentially fatal flaws in a program evaluation plan, increase the likelihood that evaluator conclusions are valid, and enhance the acceptance by users and stakeholders, and they may increase the cost effectiveness of the program evaluation. Detailed documentation of the program evaluation process itself will aid proper user interpretation of the results and may mitigate against legal action or misguided use of flawed program evaluation reports. It can support fair treatment of competent evaluators when users want to discredit results because they are unfavorable, and can also support subsequent advances in state-of-the-art program evaluation processes. Metaevaluation can serve the valuable function of helping prevent or terminate while still in process a program evaluation whose results predictably would never be used.

❖ GUIDELINES

A. Budget sufficient money and other resources to conduct appropriate formative and summative metaevaluations.

B. Assign someone responsibility for documenting and assessing the program evaluation process and products.

C. Consider asking a respected professional body to nominate someone to chair a team of external metaevaluators in large evaluations. Failing that, either (a) appoint a team and have it elect the chair, or (b) carefully and judiciously select as chair someone who will be competent and credible, and work with this individual to appoint other team members.

D. Determine and record the rules by which members of the metaevaluation team will reach a consensus and/or issue minority reports.

A12 Metaevaluation

E. Stipulate that any member of the metaevaluation team who does not fulfill contracted obligations can be dismissed at the discretion of the chair.

F. Reserve final authority for editing the metaevaluation report for the metaevaluators.

G. Determine and record which audiences will receive the metaevaluation reports and how the reports will be transmitted (see P2, Formal Agreements).

H. Evaluate the instrumentation, data collection, data handling, coding, and analysis of the program evaluation to determine how carefully and effectively these steps were implemented.

I. Expect that the metaevaluation itself will be subject to rebuttal and evaluation, and maintain a record of all metaevaluation steps, information, and analyses.

❖ COMMON ERRORS

A. Deferring a decision about metaevaluation until the program evaluation is well under way or even completed

B. Failing to record the full range of information needed to judge the program evaluation against each standard pertinent to its conduct

C. Conducting only an internal metaevaluation when conflict of interest or other considerations clearly establish the need for an external metaevaluation

D. Assuming that every program evaluation study requires a formal metaevaluation study

E. Allowing a poorly performed or politically motivated metaevaluation to destroy a fundamentally sound program evaluation

F. Assigning internal metaevaluation responsibility to a junior staff member

Illustrative Case—Description

As part of an organization's efforts to improve its training courses, it required that a "follow-up" evaluation be completed for each course. The term *follow-up* denotes an evaluation of training in terms of the post-training job performance of course graduates. This process provides a check on course development and yields evidence of the contributions that employees who attend training courses subsequently make to their companies.

The study was sponsored by the Training Advisory Board (TAB), a committee formed as part of a consortium of 20 companies in the telecommunication industry. The TAB assigned projects to approximately 170 course designers across the 20 companies. At the end of its first four years, the TAB had produced 95 completed courses and over 50 more in various stages of development. Each course was supposed to have been designed and documented according to a set of standards prepared by the TAB, one of which was the requirement that a follow-up evaluation be conducted. The policy of requiring a follow-up evaluation was not enforced, and, when performed, follow-up evaluations were usually conducted by the course designers, who had little or no experience in evaluation work.

Recently, the TAB had been criticized for the cost and quality of its products. The board commissioned a task force to investigate the extent to which, and the manner in which, courses were being evaluated and to recommend ways of improving the process. The five-person task force consisted of two evaluation specialists, one instructional technologist, and two experienced training managers.

The task force addressed the following four questions: (a) What proportion of courses had been evaluated? (b) How did the evaluation reports compare with "quality" standards? (c) What factors accounted for observed deficiencies? (d) What remedial actions should be taken?

The data collection plan involved obtaining all the available follow-up evaluation reports, devising a checklist for rating these reports, and interviewing project managers about follow-up evaluations. The checklist was created by the task force on the basis of a literature review. It covered project goals, procedures, interpretations, and recommendations. The reports were first rated individually by four task force members using a multiple-matrix design, and then consensus ratings were derived through group discussion. Interviews were conducted by telephone. Of 25 project managers, the 12 who had supervised follow-up evaluations were interviewed about (a) problems in planning the follow-up study, collecting and analyzing data, and writing the report, and (b) reactions to the evaluation report and implementation of recommendations. The remaining 13 project managers were interviewed about the reasons that specific courses had not been evaluated.

Two deficiencies were identified. First, only 20 of the 95 published courses had been evaluated in terms of the post-training job performance of course graduates. This deficiency was attributed to the competition among projects for limited personnel resources, the sometimes punishing consequences of evaluation, and the volatility of course content.

The second deficiency consisted of numerous technical faults in the completed evaluations. A 23-item checklist was used in judging the quality of an evaluation; the more items checked, the better the evaluation. The mean number of items checked was 9.13, or 40% of the maximum number. The faults were grouped into nine categories: evaluation goals not stated, sample not representative of the trainee population, poor data return, questionable reliability of data, job performance deficiencies not identified, evaluation findings not compared with preproject analysis of job performance, administration and implementation problems not studied, inappropriate level of detail throughout the report, and recommendations not supported by data. These faults were attributed to lack of knowledge and inadequate standards for preparing evaluation reports.

The following seven actions were recommended to the TAB: (a) Enforce the requirement to evaluate courses as part of the development process;

(b) assign the evaluation to a neutral party when it is practical to do so; (c) hire a full-time evaluation specialist to train, monitor, coach, and evaluate the evaluation efforts of course developers; (d) revise the Training Development Standards to provide better definition of design and report requirements; (e) develop a "how-to" manual on follow-up evaluation; (f) supplement the manual with instruction; and (g) sponsor research on performance measurement.

All but recommendation c were implemented. Over the next three years, 54 follow-up evaluations were completed, compared with 20 for the preceding four years. Quality ratings improved, particularly for those evaluations in which the evaluator used the "how-to" manual and was not employed by the company who designed the course. The evaluator's affiliation proved to be significant. Evaluators who worked for a consortium company that used but did *not develop* the course were five times more likely to recommend major course revisions than designers evaluating their own courses.

Illustrative Case—Analysis

Note that the purpose of the metaevaluation was to reform an evaluation process, not to analyze a specific evaluation project. The intention was to improve future practice, not merely judge past efforts. This future orientation mitigated a lot of the defensiveness that might have sabotaged a metaevaluation aimed at producing a scorecard of "good" projects and "bad" projects.

This study demonstrates the potential of metaevaluation for producing change. A number of remedial actions were taken, and these actions, in turn, produced improvements in the practice of follow-up evaluation.

There were several elements early in the metaevaluation that contributed to the successful outcome. First, the TAB and, in particular, the chairperson expressed strong commitment to act upon the findings. The TAB also had the power to implement the recommendations without anyone else's approval. Second, the TAB required documentation of course development and evaluation activities. This documentation constituted the major source of information for the metaevaluation. Next, the metaevaluation task force members were carefully chosen for their competence and credibility. They represented different companies within the consortium, and different disciplines, and were not associated with any of the projects under investigation. Finally, the metaevaluation looked beyond the immediate goal of identifying what went wrong and sought reasons for what went wrong. This search led to a wider range of recommendations than would have been available had the analysis been limited to the identification of problems.

If the metaevaluation were to be repeated, what aspects of the study could be improved? First, the political pressures on the TAB were never identified. The task force might have endeavored to find out who was putting pressure on the TAB and why. This inquiry might have uncovered additional uses or requirements for evaluation findings. Similarly, the task force might have asked about the local company politics that influenced course development teams and, in particular, the "signals" that management was giving about the evaluation function. This inquiry might have revealed constraints placed on evaluators and course designers, and this knowledge, in turn, might have led to recommendations about evaluation methods appropriate for different constraints.

Supporting Documentation

Schwandt, T. A., & Halpern, E. S. (1988). *Linking auditing and meta-evaluation: Enhancing quality in applied research.* Newbury Park, CA: Sage.

Stufflebeam, D. L. (1974). *Metaevaluation.* Kalamazoo: Western Michigan University, The Evaluation Center.

Worthen, B. R., & Sanders, J. R. (1987). *Educational evaluation: Alternative approaches and practical guidelines.* White Plains, NY: Longman.

A12 Metaevaluation

Appendix:
❖ The Support Groups ❖

Project Staff

Staff members at the Western Michigan University Evaluation Center who wrote drafts of the 1981 and 1994 *Standards*, coordinated its review and field testing, and carried out other daily project activities included the following:

Mary Anne Bunda
Jeri Ridings Nowakowski
Robert Rodosky
James Sanders
Anthony Shinkfield
Daniel L. Stufflebeam
Rosalie Torres

Validation Panel

The Validation Panel was appointed as an oversight committee to monitor the process and outcomes of the 1994 revision of *The Program Evaluation Standards*. The responsibilities of this panel included analyses of assumptions underlying the project, critique and report on the Joint Committee's validation process, assessment of applicability of *The Program Evaluation Standards*, identification of issues and ideas related to the development of the Standards, and a public assessment of *The Program Evaluation Standards*. The members of the Validation Panel who served during the 1991-1994 revision process were as follows:

Chair

R. Bruce Gould, *Brooks Air Force Base*

Members

David Basarab, *Motorola Corporation*
Christine McGuire, *University of Illinois Medical School*
Phil Robinson, *Detroit, Michigan*
LeRoy Walser, *University of Oklahoma*
Alexandra Wigdor, *National Academy of Sciences*

Panel of Writers

Alternative versions of the 1981 statements of standards were written by the following individuals:

Marvin Alkin, *University of California, Los Angeles*
Beverly Anderson, *Northwest Regional Educational Laboratory*
J. Myron Atkin, *University of Illinois at Urbana-Champaign*
Ralph M. Burke, Jr., *Fairfield Public Schools, Connecticut*
Michael Caldwell, *University of Virginia*
Carolyn Callahan, *University of Virginia*
Nancy S. Cole, *University of Pittsburgh*
Nolan Estes, *University of Texas*
John Flanagan, *American Institute for Research in the Behavioral Sciences*
Howard Freeman, *University of California, Los Angeles*
Gene V Glass, *University of Colorado*
J. Thomas Hastings, *University of Illinois at Urbana-Champaign*
Ernest R. House, *University of Illinois at Urbana-Champaign*
Roosevelt Johnson, *Federal City College*
Michael Kean, *School District of Philadelphia, Pennsylvania*
Stephen Klein, *University of California, Los Angeles*
Richard Kunkel, *St. Louis University*
Henry Levin, *Stanford University*
Murray Levine, *State University of New York at Buffalo*
Samuel Livingston, *Educational Testing Service*
George Mayeske, *United States Office of Education*
Jason Millman, *Cornell University*
Laurence Nicholson, *Harris Teachers College*
David Payne, *University of Georgia*
W. James Popham, *University of California, Los Angeles*
Ralph W. Tyler, *Science Research Associates and Director Emeritus, Center for the Advanced Study of the Behavioral Sciences*
James Wardrop, *University of Illinois at Urbana-Champaign*

William Webster, *Dallas, Texas, Independent School District*
Wayne Welch, *University of Minnesota*
Blaine Worthen, *Northwest Regional Educational Laboratory*

Alternative versions of new illustrative cases for the 1994 *Standards* were written by the following persons:

Charles Adkins, *National Parent Teachers Association*
Mark Albanese, *University of Iowa*
Eta Berner, *University of Alabama, School of Medicine, UAB*
Sally Cavanaugh, *York Hospital*
John Dennison, *University of British Columbia*
Kathy A. Douglas, *Consultant*
Molly Engle, *University of Alabama at Birmingham*
Joanne Farley, *Farley and Associates*
Rob Foshay, *The Roach Organization*
Steven Gill, *Formative Evaluation Research Associates*
Ann Gothler, *Consultant*
Jill Harker, *American College Testing*
Eileen Harris, *University of Minnesota*
Diana Lancaster, *LSU School of Dentistry*
Robert Lerch, *Consultant*
John H. Littlefield, *University of Texas Health Science Center—San Antonio*
Tom Maguire, *University of Alberta*
William C. McGaghie, *Northwestern University*
John Ory, *University of Illinois*
Hallie Preskill, *University of St. Thomas*
Marilyn Ray, *Finger Lakes Law and Social Policy Center*
Elaine Romberg, *University of Maryland Dental School*
Arthur Rothman, *University of Toronto*
Mary Sand, *Federal Aviation Administration*
Martin E. Smith, *New England Telephone*
Jon Wergin, *Virginia Commonwealth University*
Howard J. Zeitz, *Consultant*
Elda D. Zounar, *E G and G Rocky Flats, Inc.*

Consultants

Specialized project functions, including planning meetings, drafting materials, editing manuscripts, and chairing small group work sessions for the 1981 *Standards*, were performed by the following individuals:

David Adams, *Western Michigan University*
Gilbert R. Austin, *University of Maryland*
Robert L. Betz, *Western Michigan University*

Henry M. Brickell, *Policy Studies in Education*
Robert Carlson, *University of Vermont*
Robert W. Consalvo, *Heuristics, Inc.*
Homer O. Elseroad, *Education Commission of the States*
Egon G. Guba, *Indiana University*
Philip Hosford, *New Mexico State University*
Robert L. Linn, *University of Illinois at Urbana-Champaign*
George Madaus, *Boston College*
Walter Marks, *Montclair, New Jersey, Public Schools*
William Mays, Jr., *Michigan Elementary and Middle School
    Principal's Association*
Bernard McKenna, *National Education Association*
Diane Reinhard, *University of Oregon*
David Rindskopf, *Northwestern University*
Darrell K. Root, *Lakota, Ohio, Public Schools*
Rodney Roth, *Western Michigan University*
Michael Scriven, *University of San Francisco*

National Review Panel

The first draft of the 1981 *Standards* was critiqued by the following
persons:

Janice M. Baker, *Rhode Island State Department of Education*
Robert F. Boruch, *Northwestern University*
Patricia M. Bradanini, *Solano Community College*
Ron Brandt, *Lincoln, Nebraska, Public Schools*
Joseph Carol, *Leominster, Massachusetts, Public Schools*
Rebecca E. Carroll, *Baltimore, Maryland, City Public Schools*
William E. Coffman, *University of Iowa*
Robert W. Consalvo, *Heuristics, Inc.*
Wendy M. Cullar, *Florida State Department of Education*
Richard D. Eisenhauer, *Norris Elementary, Firth, Nebraska*
John A. Emrick, *Stanford Research Institute*
Finis Engleman, *Executive Secretary Emeritus, American Association
    of School Administrators*
Gerald R. Firth, *University of Georgia*
Marcia Guttentag, *Harvard University*
Kenneth Hansen, *University of Nebraska, Lincoln*
J. Thomas Hastings, *University of Illinois at Urbana-Champaign*
Dale K. Hayes, *University of Nebraska*
Ernest R. House, *University of Illinois at Urbana-Champaign*
Madeline Hunter, *University of California, Los Angeles*
James C. Impara, *Virginia Polytechnic Institute and State University*
Edward F. Iwanicki, *University of Connecticut*
James N. Jacobs, *Cincinnati, Ohio, Public Schools*

David A. Jenness, *Social Science Research Council*
Michael S. Kneale, *Holdrege, Nebraska, Public Schools*
Mary Kay Kosa, *National Education Association, Director for*
  Michigan
Barbara Lasser, *University of California, Los Angeles*
Rose E. Martinez, *Tempe, Arizona, Elementary School District No. 3*
Leslie S. May, *Massachusetts Department of Education*
Alfonso Migliara, Jr., *Westbriar, Virginia, Elementary School*
Melvin R. Novick, *University of Iowa*
Andrew C. Porter, *Michigan State University*
Joseph S. Renzulli, *University of Connecticut*
Patricia Smith, *Worthington, Ohio, City Schools*
Richard E. Snow, *Stanford University*
Jack Stenner, *National Test Service*
Edwin F. Taylor, *Education Development Center*
Nelle H. Taylor, *National Education Association, Director for South*
  Carolina
Charles L. Thomas, *Research Triangle Institute*
Donald Thomas, *Salt Lake City, Utah, Schools*
Carol K. Tittle, *University of North Carolina*
Karen J. Uncapher, *Alfred I. Dupont, Wilmington, Delaware, School*
  District
Beatrice Ward, *Far West Laboratory*

The first draft of the 1994 *Program Evaluation Standards* was critiqued
by the following individuals:

Adela Allen, *University of Arizona*
Christine A. Ameen, *Starr Commonwealth Schools*
Mary Andrews, *Michigan State University*
Emilio Arribas, *The University of Michigan—Flint*
Gary M. Arsham, *American Institutes for Research*
Lorie Baker, *Starr Commonwealth Schools*
Regina S. Birdsell, *Academy Elementary School, Madison, Connecticut*
Lloyd W. Black
William Block
Boyd Boehlje, *National School Boards Association*
Robert Boldt, *Educational Testing Services*
Milo Brekke
Pamela J. Burrus, *Briarwood Elementary School, Olathe, Kansas*
Martha Ann Carey, *National Center for Nursing Research*
Sharon E. Carpinello, *New York State Office of Mental Health*
Mary Anne Casey, *W. K. Kellogg Foundation*
Karen M. Creagh, *Motorola Corporation*
Cory Cummings, *Northern Illinois University*
Susan Deusinger, *Washington University School of Medicine*

Ken E. Dickie, *The D & D Group, Inc.*
Trudy Dunham, *University of Minnesota*
Rita Dunn, *St. John's University*
David Fetterman, *American Institutes for Research*
Anne Fitzpatrick, *CTB Macmillan/McGraw-Hill*
Jody Fitzpatrick, *University of Colorado at Colorado Springs*
Sandra J. Fox, *Office of Indian Education Program*
James L. Fremming
Jennifer C. Greene, *Cornell University*
Ann Grooms, *Educational Services Institute, Inc.*
Ed Halpern, *AT&T Bell Laboratories*
Ronald Hambleton, *University of Massachusetts*
Herbert K. Heger, *University of Texas at El Paso*
Diane Holmes, *Gobles Elementary School, Gobles, Michigan*
Melanie Hwalek, *SPEC Associates*
Jean A. King, *University of Minnesota*
Tara D. Knott, *Evaluation Resources, Inc.*
Sandra A. Lawrence, *Robert Lucas Elementary School, Iowa City, Iowa*
Larry G. Leslie, *The Upjohn Company*
Glynn Ligon, *Evaluation Software Publishing, Inc.*
Yvonna S. Lincoln, *Texas A & M University*
Garrett Mandeville, *University of South Carolina*
Thomas L. McGreal, *University of Illinois*
James E. McLean, *University of Alabama*
Peter F. Merenda, *University of Rhode Island*
Diane L. Morehouse, *QED*
Michael Morris, *University of New Haven, West Haven, Connecticut*
Amaury Nora, *University of Illinois at Chicago*
John J. Norcini, *American Board of Internal Medicine*
Michael Q. Patton, *Union Graduate School*
Emil J. Posavac, *Loyola University*
Jerald L. Reece, *New Mexico State University*
Martha Romero, *Pikes Peak Community College*
Donald A. Rupp, *The Upjohn Company*
Constance C. Schmitz, *University of Minnesota*
Frank W. Schufletowski, *HQ Air Training Command*
Tom Schwandt, *Indiana University*
Margaret M. Scott, *Oklahoma State University*
William R. Shadish, Jr., *Memphis State University*
Kent Sheets, *University of Michigan*
Sharon A. Shrock, *Southern Illinois University*
David L. Silvernail, *University of Southern Maine*
Midge Smith, *University of Maryland*
Richard C. Sonnichsen, *FBI*
John E. Steffens, *University of Oklahoma*
Arthur W. Steller, *Oklahoma City, Oklahoma, Public Schools*

Floraline I. Stevens, *National Science Foundation*
Robert Sweeney
Martha Taylor, *United Way of America*
Yvonne Walker, *Bingham Farms Elementary School, Birmingham, Michigan*
Michael J. Wargo, *GAO*
William F. Weber, *South Redford School District, Redford, Michigan*
Maria D. Whitsett, *Texas Education Agency*
Susan Wisely, *Lilly Endowment, Inc.*
Karen Wolfe, *Xerox Corporation*

International Review Panel

The first draft of the 1994 *Program Evaluation Standards* was critiqued by the following persons:

Benjamin Alvarez, *International Youth Foundation*
Barry Bannister, *Hongkong Polytechnic*
Doug Castledine, *Hongkong Polytechnic*
Rocio Fernandez-Ballesteros, *Universidad Autonoma de Madrid*
Vincent Greaney, *The World Bank*
John Hattie, *University of Western Australia*
Joan M. Kruger
Kathryn MacRury, *University of Toronto*
Nelly McEwen, *Alberta Education*
Fayez M. Mina, *Cairo, Egypt*
David Nevo, *Tel Aviv University*
Ernesto Schiefelbein, *OREALC*
Anthony Shinkfield, *St. Peters College, Australia*
Ernest D. Skakun, *University of Alberta*

Participants in the Field Test

The following individuals and groups applied the semifinal draft of the 1981 *Standards* to various evaluation tasks in field situations and reported their judgments and recommendations:

Richard Amorose, *Columbus, Ohio, Public Schools*
Carol Aslanian, *The College Board*
Jackson J. Barnette, *University of Virginia*
George Brain, *Washington State University*
Alfreda Brown, *CEMREL, Inc.*
Carole Clymer, *New Mexico State University*
John H. Corbin, *Kalamazoo Valley Community College*
Robert E. Endias, *Western Michigan University*
Richard D. Frisbie, *Community Mental Health Board, Lansing, Michigan*

Robert K. Gable, *University of Connecticut*
Edward F. Iwanicki, *University of Connecticut*
Michael H. Kean, *School District of Philadelphia, Pennsylvania*
Sharon S. Koenings, *CEMREL, Inc.*
Barbara Lasser, *Southwest Regional Educational Laboratory*
William P. McDougall, *Washington State University*
Jason Millman, *Cornell University*
Alan Nowakowski, *Bay City, Michigan, Public Schools*
Office of Evaluation Services, *Lansing, Michigan, School District*
Ellice Oliver, *The Wellington County Board of Education, Guelph, Ontario*
Timothy J. Pettibone, *New Mexico State University*
D. C. Phillips, *Stanford Evaluation Consortium*
Ann Porteus, *Stanford Evaluation Consortium*
Jeffrey T. Resnick, *Western Michigan University*
W. Todd Rogers, *University of British Columbia*
James R. Sanders, *Western Michigan University*
Carol Payne Smith, *Western Michigan University*
Gary L. Wegenke, *Lansing, Michigan, School District*
Blaine R. Worthen, *Utah State University*
Elanna Yalow, *Stanford Evaluation Consortium*

The following individuals and groups applied the semi-final draft of the 1994 *Standards* to various evaluation tasks in field situations and reported their judgments and recommendations:

Jodi Bonner, *Texas Department of Mental Health and Mental Retardation*
Ric Brown, *Fresno State University*
Robert D. Brown, *University of Nebraska*
Suzan Hurley Cogswell, *Legislative Office of Educational Oversight*
Julia Gamon, *Iowa State University at Ames*
Phyllis Grummon, *Michigan State University*
Andrew Hayes, *University of North Carolina-Wilmington*
Joan Hendrix, *Simms Industries, Inc.*
Les Horvath, *Connecticut Department of Education*
Marjorie Kuenz, *National Library of Medicine*
Tony Lam
William W. Lee, *ElectroCom Automation, Inc.*
George A. Martin, Jr., *Child and Family Project*
Jack McKillip, *Southern Illinois University*
Donna M. Mertens, *Gallaudet University*
Harrison Nelson
Diana Newman, *University of Albany/SUNY*
Angela Patterson, *Xerox Corporation*
Jane E. Perkins, *New England Telephone*

Suzanne Purves, *Canada Trust*
Renne Ricciardi, *The Tests Group*
Susan Riles, *Portland Public Schools*
Charlene Rivera, *George Washington University*
William D. Schafer, *University of Maryland*
Yesha Sivan, *Harvard University*
Kathleen Sullivan, *Legislative Peer Committee*
Peter Thacker, *Portland Public Schools*
Kathy Thorne, *Louisiana Technological University*
Jean Williams
John Williams, *Virginia Technological University*
Bob Wingenroth, *City of Phoenix*
Nancy Zajano, *Legislative Office of Educational Oversight*

Participants in the National Hearings

The following persons contributed formal testimony in the National Hearings on the 1981 draft standards:

Cordell Affeldt, *Indiana State Teacher's Association*
Gordon M. Ambach, *University of the State of New York*
Fran Aversa, *Syracuse University*
Robert D. Benton, *Iowa State Superintendent of Public Instruction*
Jean Blatchford, *New Jersey Education Association*
Carol Bloomquist, *University of California, Los Angeles*
Mary Elaine Cadigan, *Guam Department of Education*
Julian Carroll, *Governor of Kentucky*
Jim Chrest, *Oregon House of Representatives*
William Connolly, *Florida Department of Education*
Robert Cope, *Kelvin Grove College, Australia*
Linda Crelian, *University of California, Los Angeles*
Joseph Cronin, *Illinois State Superintendent of Public Instruction*
Walter Dick, *The Florida State University*
Patrick Dunne, *University of California, Los Angeles*
Elinor A. Elfner, *Wakulla County School Board, Florida*
Novice Fawcett, *President Emeritus, The Ohio State University*
G. Foster, *The Florida State University*
Ray E. Foster, *Florida Department of Education*
Luisito C. Fullante, *University of California, Los Angeles*
Robert Gable, *University of Connecticut*
Jean Gabler, *Woodhaven, Michigan, School District*
Nancy O. Gentile, *Syracuse University*
J. D. Giddens, *Oklahoma State Department of Education*
J. Wade Gilley, *Office of the Governor of Virginia*
William D. Grant, *Maryland Department of Education*
Ben M. Harris, *University of Texas at Austin*

Ruthann Heintschel, *Ohio Department of Education*
Edward F. Iwanicki, *University of Connecticut*
Randy L. Kimbrough, *Kentucky Department of Instruction*
Michael Kirst, *California State Board of Education*
David Krathwohl, *Syracuse University*
Robert R. Lange, *Colorado State University*
Charles Lotte, *University of California, Los Angeles*
Kenneth C. Madden, *State Superintendent, Delaware*
Robert J. Manley, *National Educational Leadership Services, Inc.*
Billie Frances McClellan, *Palm Beach Atlantic College*
Robert McClure, *National Education Association*
Robert Morgado, *Secretary to the Governor of New York*
Carl D. Novak, *Lincoln, Nebraska, Public Schools*
Janet Pieter, *University of California, Los Angeles*
Tjeerd Plomp, *Toegepaste Onderwijskunde, The Netherlands*
Edward R. Savage, *American Council of Life Insurance*
Lowell Simpson, *National Educational Leadership Services, Inc.*
M. Herman Sims, *Ohio Department of Education*
Carol Payne Smith, *Western Michigan University*
David C. Smith, *University of Florida*
Robert Stake, *University of Illinois at Urbana-Champaign*
Donald J. Steele, *Toledo, Ohio, Public Schools*
Wayne Teague, *Alabama Superintendent of Education*
Ralph G. Vedros, *Florida Department of Education*
Robert A. Withey, *Vermont Commissioner of Education*
Marda Woodbury, *Research Ventures*
Toby Yager, *Syracuse University*

The following persons contributed formal testimony in the National Hearings on the 1994 draft standards:

Cathy Allen, *School Board Member, Illinois*
Gail Barrington, *Gail V. Barrington & Associates*
Terry Berkeley, *Consultant*
Kathleen Bigby, *Consultant*
Pershing Broome, *School Board Member, Illinois*
Carlos Browne, *Jamaica Ministry of Education*
Margot Cameron-Jones, *Heriot-Watt University, Scotland*
Dennis Cheek, *New York State Education Department*
Nella Corryn, *Rochester City School District, New York*
Stacey Daniels, *Kauffman Foundation*
Henrietta Davis, *School Board Member, Illinois*
James DeGracie, *Mesa Public Schools, Arizona*
Mary Diez, *American Association of Colleges for Teacher Education*
Janice Ducote, *Louisiana Department of Education*
Deborah Ford, *School Board Member, Illinois*

Barbara Freedman, *Dawson College*
Craig Gjerde, *University of Iowa*
Alana Gowdy, *Mount Royal College*
Susan Gross, *National Science Foundation*
Joe Hansen, *Colorado Springs Public Schools, Colorado*
Linda Hanson, *Superintendent, Mundelein High School District 120,
    Illinois*
Marthe Hurteau, *Consultant*
Nancy Johnson, *School Board Member, North Dakota*
Ralph Johnson, *School Board Member, Illinois*
Michael Kean, *CTB Macmillan/McGraw-Hill*
Mark LaCelle-Peterson, *Evaluation Assistance Center East, The
    George Washington University*
Margaret LeCompte, *University of Colorado*
David Miller, *University of Florida*
Robert Nearine, *Hartford Public Schools, Connecticut*
Jeff Northfield, *Monash University, Australia*
Claude Oppenheim, *School Administrator, Alberta, Canada*
James Oswald, *Community College of Philadelphia*
Michael Patton, *Union Graduate School*
David Payne, *University of Georgia*
Nancy Pesz, *School Board Member, Illinois*
Janella Rachal, *Louisiana Department of Education*
Charlene Rivera, *Evaluation Assistance Center East, The George
    Washington University*
Bernard Ryder, *School Board Member, Massachusetts*
Dorren Schmitt, *Louisiana Department of Education*
Thomas Shannon, *National School Boards Association*
Martin Sharp, *Pennsylvania State University*
Joy Talsma, *School Board Member, Illinois*
Charles Teddlie, *Louisiana State University*
Jerome Winston, *Consultant*
Kathleen Zaworski-Burke, *School Board Member, Illinois*
Linda Zimmerman, *School Board Member, Illinois*

Western Michigan University Student Assistants

The following persons contributed variously to the conduct of 1981 and 1994 project activities through courses, donated services, and research assistantships:

Kuriakose Athappilly
Meg Blinkiewicz
Craig Cameron
Randy E. Demaline
David J. Eaton

Phil Harrington
Muriel L. Katzenmeyer
Ronald A. Krol
Grant Lorenz
Lorraine A. Marcantonio
Alan Nowakowski
Wayne W. Petroelje
Mary Piontek
Thomas M. Reed
Laurence E. Rudolph
Eileen Stryker
James W. Sutherland
Robert I. Wells
Huilan Yang

Clerical Assistants

Most of the 1981 and 1994 typing and clerical work was performed by the following persons:

Patricia Burness
Diane Hurley
Klazina Johnston
Delores Minshall
Gabriele Norton
Tamalon Overton
Mary Ramlow
Paula Sammons
Pam Sargent
Sue Stafford
Linda Standish
Jenny Strautman
Jean Sullivan
Karen Wentland

❖ Glossary ❖

Terms are defined in this glossary as they are used in this volume, in the context of evaluation. In other contexts, a number of the terms may have broader or different definitions. The reader may also want to refer to Michael Scriven, *Evaluation Thesaurus* (4th ed., Sage, 1991).

Accuracy   The extent to which an evaluation is truthful or valid in what it says about a program, project, or material.

Adversarial/advocacy group   A group of people who enter into cross-examination of counterplans, strategies, or outcomes.

Advocacy teams   Groups of people who are brought together to develop competing strategies for achieving a given set of objectives.

Affective dimension   The psychological concept that refers to a person's feelings, emotions, or degree of acceptance or rejection of some object.

Anonymity (provision for)   Evaluator action to ensure that the identity of subjects cannot be ascertained during the course of a study, in study reports, or in any other way.

Archival search   An examination of existing records, reports, and documents pertaining to the object of the evaluation.

Assessment   The act of determining the standing of an object on some variable of interest, for example, testing students and reporting scores.

Attrition   Loss of subjects from the defined sample during the course of a study.

Audit (of an evaluation)   An independent examination and verification of the quality of an evaluation plan, the adequacy with which it was implemented, the accuracy of results, and the validity of conclusions.

Bias   A consistent alignment with one point of view.

Case study   An intensive, detailed description and analysis of a single project, program, or instructional material in the context of its environment.

Client The individual, group, or organization that hires the evaluator. Clients are also stakeholders.

Code (information) To translate a given set of data or items into a set of quantitative or qualitative symbols.

Coefficient A value expressing the degree to which some characteristic or relation is to be found in specified instances; for example, the coefficient of correlation is a value expressing the degree to which two variables vary concomitantly.

Cognitive ability The psychological concept that refers to such processes as perceiving, knowing, recognizing, conceptualizing, judging, and reasoning.

Comparative experimental studies Studies that assign a program, project, or instructional material to one group of persons and compare their subsequent performance on some structured task with that of another group that was not exposed to the program, project, or instructional material.

Comparison group (in experimentation) A group that provides a basis for contrast with an experimental group (i.e., the group of people participating in the program or project being evaluated). The comparison group is not subjected to the treatment (independent variable), thus creating a means for comparison with the experimental group that does receive the treatment.

Conclusions (of an evaluation) Final judgments and recommendations.

Conditioning Associating a response with a previously unrelated stimulus.

Content analysis The process of identifying and listing—in accordance with a parsimonious classification system—categories of expression contained in a variety of information sources.

Context (of an evaluation) The combination of the factors accompanying the study that may have influenced its results. These factors include the geographic location of the study, its timing, the political and social climate in the region at that time, the other relevant professional activities that were in progress, and any existing pertinent economic conditions.

Contract A written or oral agreement between the evaluator and the client that is enforceable by law. It is a mutual understanding of expectations and responsibilities for both parties.

Control group A group as closely as possible equivalent to an experimental group (exposed to a program, project, or instructional material), and exposed to all the conditions of the investigation except the program, project, or instructional material being studied.

Convergence group A group that is responsible for incorporating the important features of alternative strategies proposed by advocacy teams into a compromise strategy.

Correlation A statistical measure of the degree of relationship between or among variables. It is expressed in the form of an index that may vary from -1.00 to $+1.00$.

Cost effectiveness The extent to which one program, project, or instructional material produces equal or better results than competitors that cost about the same amount of time, effort, and resources; or the extent to which an object produces the same results as competitors but is less costly.

Covariate A variate occurring concomitantly with the variate of primary interest and measured for the purpose of making informed adjustments on the variate of primary interest (e.g., measuring pretest performance of two groups in order to adjust their posttest scores so that they take account of differences between groups that existed prior to the treatment of one of the groups).

Criterion A standard by which something can be judged.

Criterion-referenced tests Tests whose scores are interpreted by referral to well-defined domains of content or behaviors rather than by referral to the performance of some comparable group of people.

Data Material gathered during the course of an evaluation that serves as the basis for information, discussion, and inference.

Data access The extent to which the evaluator will be permitted to obtain data during the course of an evaluation.

Decision rule A rule for choosing between optional interpretations or courses of action given certain evidence (e.g., a rule by which teachers pass or fail students in a course based on their test scores and other performances in the course, a rule by which a government agency ranks project proposals for funding based on their contents and the ratings assigned to them by judges, or a rule by which an evaluator decides that the difference between the test scores of students exposed to different programs is statistically significant).

Delphi technique A method for obtaining group consensus involving the use of a series of mailed questionnaires and controlled feedback to respondents that continues until consensus is reached.

Dependent variable A measure (e.g., a student's performance on a test) that is assumed to vary as a result of some influence (often taken to be the independent variable).

Design (evaluation) A plan for conducting an evaluation (e.g., data collection schedule, report schedules, questions to be addressed, analysis plan, or management plan). Designs may be either preordinate or emergent.

Dissemination The communication of the actions—by written, oral, and/or audiovisual reporting—of evaluators to foster knowledge of the evaluation findings among all right-to-know audiences.

Editorial authority The extent of the evaluator's authority to edit evaluation reports prior to dissemination.

Education The process of developing knowledge, skill, mind, character, and so on.

Emergent design An implementation plan in which the specification of every step depends upon the results of previous steps, sometimes also known as a cascading or rolling design.

Escrow agent A third party who, by agreement, controls certain information, such as the names on tests, submitted by a first party, so that this information is not obtained by the second party.

Evaluation Systematic investigation of the worth or merit of an object (e.g., a program, project, or instructional material).

Evaluation report A presentation of information resulting from evaluative activity.

Evaluator Anyone who engages in evaluative activity.

Executive report An abbreviated report that has been tailored specifically to address the concerns and questions of a person whose function is to administer an educational program or project.

Executive summary   A nontechnical summary statement designed to provide a quick overview of the full-length report on which it is based.

Expectation   Something looked forward to or anticipated.

Experimental design   The plan of an experiment, including selection of subjects, order of administration of the experimental treatment, the kind of treatment, the procedures by which it is administered, and the recording of the data (with special reference to the particular statistical analyses to be performed).

Experimental group   A group of subjects assigned to receive a treatment (independent variable), the effects of which are measured (dependent variable). Often, comparisons are made between these effects and those observed for a comparison or control (nontreatment) group.

Experimental research   Scientific investigation in which an investigator manipulates and controls one or more independent variables to determine their effects on the outcome (dependent) variable.

External evaluator   An evaluator from outside the organization within which the object of the study is housed.

Extrapolate   To infer an unknown from something that is known. (Statistical definition—to estimate the value of a variable outside its observed range.)

Feasibility   The extent to which resources allow an evaluation to be conducted.

Field test   The study of a program, project, or instructional material in settings like those where it is to be used. Field tests may range from preliminary primitive investigations to full-scale summative studies.

Focus group   A group selected for its relevance to an evaluation that is engaged by a trained facilitator in a series of discussions designed for sharing insights, ideas, and observations on a topic of concern.

Formative evaluation   Evaluation designed and used to improve an object, especially when it is still being developed.

Gain scores   The difference between a student's performance on a test and his or her performance on a previous administration of the same or parallel test.

Generalizability   The extent to which information about a program, project, or instructional material collected in one setting can be used to reach a valid judgment about how it will perform in other settings.

Generic rights   Rights that are shared by all members of a group.

Goal   An end that one strives to achieve.

Goal-free evaluation   Evaluation of outcomes in which the evaluator functions without knowledge of the purposes or goals.

Guideline   A procedural suggestion intended to help evaluators and their audiences to meet the requirements of the evaluation standards; strategy to avoid mistakes in applying the standards.

Hardware (data processing)   The physical components, such as a computer and keypunch machine, of a data processing system, as opposed to the instructional (content-related) components.

Illustrative case   An illustration of how a standard might be applied, which includes the description of a certain setting, a situation in which the standard is not met, and a discussion of corrective actions that would result in the standard being met.

Information Numerical and nonnumerical findings, renderings, or presentations— including facts, narratives, graphs, pictures, maps, displays, statistics, and oral reports—that help illuminate issues, answer questions, and increase knowledge and understanding of a program or other object.

Information needs Information requirements of the evaluator, clients, and other pertinent audiences to be met by the evaluation.

Information sources The persons, groups, and documents from which data are obtained.

Informed consent Agreement by the participants in an evaluation of the use of their names and/or confidential information supplied by them in specified ways, for stated purposes, and in light of possible consequences prior to the collection and/or release of this information in evaluation reports.

Instrument An assessment device adopted, adapted, or constructed for the purpose of the evaluation.

Internal evaluator A staff member or unit from the organization within which the object of the study is housed.

Jury trial for projects Project evaluation patterned after jury trials in their procedures for clarifying issues, introducing and assessing evidence, and reaching conclusions. Sometimes known as the Adversary Model of Evaluation.

Learning The acquiring of knowledge, skill, thought processes, character, and so on.

Level of significance The probability that observed or greater differences occurred by chance.

Matching An experimental procedure in which the subjects are so divided, by means other than lottery, that the groups are regarded for the purposes at hand to be of equal merit or ability. (Often, matched groups are created by ensuring that they are the same or nearly so on such variables as sex, age, grade point averages, and past test scores.)

Materials evaluation Evaluations that assess the merit or worth of content-related physical items, including books, curricular guides, films, tapes, and other tangible instructional products.

Mean (arithmetic) A measure of central tendency calculated by dividing the sum of all the values by the number of the values.

Merit The excellence of an object as assessed by its intrinsic qualities or performance.

Metaevaluation Evaluation of an evaluation.

Modus operandi analysis Deducing the cause of effects based upon analysis of events, process, or properties associated with the effects; analogous to procedures used in detective work.

Nonreactive measures Assessments done without the awareness of those being assessed.

Norm A single value, or a distribution of values, constituting the typical performance of a given group.

"No significant difference" A decision that an observed difference between two statistics occurred by chance.

Null hypothesis The hypothesis of no difference or no differential effects.

Objective Something aimed at or striven for, more specific than a goal.

Objectives-referenced test A test whose scores are referenced to the attainment of the objectives the test was designed to measure, rather than to the performance on the test by some comparison group of people.

Object of the evaluation What one is evaluating (e.g., a program, a project, or instructional material). *Program* is used generically to represent program, project, or materials in these Standards to refer to the object of the evaluation.

Operational definition A definition of a term or object achieved by stating the operations or procedures employed to distinguish it from others.

Overview A conceptual/introductory statement that gives essential definitions; provides a general rationale; and presents summarized procedures, common problems, and special difficulties that are applicable.

Parallel forms Multiple forms of a test constructed to be as comparable and interchangeable as possible in their content, length, and procedures of administration and in the scores and test properties (e.g., means, variances, and reliability indices).

Pilot test A brief and simplified preliminary study designed to try out methods to learn whether a proposed project or program seems likely to yield valuable results.

Pitfall A not easily recognized difficulty believed to be associated with a particular standard. These are mistakes that would be made out of ignorance of the import and intent of a standard.

Population All the persons in a particular group.

Posttest A test to determine performance after the administration of a program, project, or instructional material.

Pretest A test to determine performance prior to the administration of a program, project, or instructional material.

Program evaluations Evaluations that assess ongoing activities that provide services. Educational examples include evaluation of a school district's reading program, a state's special education program, a university's continuing education program in a specialized field such as ophthalmology, and a technical skills training course for government, business, or industry.

Project evaluation Evaluations that assess activities that are funded for a defined period of time to perform a specified task. Some examples are a three-day workshop on behavioral objectives, a two-year development effort, or a three-year career education demonstration.

Propriety The extent to which the evaluation has been conducted in a manner that evidences uncompromising adherence to the highest principles and ideals (including professional ethics, civil law, moral code, and contractual agreements).

Purpose Something one intends to do; intention; aim.

Purposes (of an evaluation study) The objectives of an evaluation (e.g., to judge the relative merits of competing textbooks or to monitor and report on how well a project plan is implemented) and the intended use of its reports (e.g., to help teachers choose a textbook or to help a school district carry out a special project).

Qualitative information Facts and claims presented in narrative, not numerical, form.

Quantitative information Facts and claims that are represented by numbers.

Random   Affected by chance.

Random sampling   Drawing a number of items of any sort from a larger group or population so that every individual item has a specified probability to be chosen.

Regression effect   The tendency of examinees scoring above or below the mean of a distribution on a pretest to score closer to the mean on the posttest.

Reinforce   To strengthen a learned way of behaving by some response-contingent external or internal influence.

Reliability   Consistency of readings on an object. (Also, see Generalizability.)

Replicate   To repeat an evaluation with all essentials unchanged.

Report   A presentation of information resulting from evaluative activity.

Sample   A part of a population.

School profile   A description (graphic, numerical, or variable) of the status of a school with respect to a set of concepts or variables.

Secondary data analysis   A reanalysis of data using the same or other appropriate procedures to verify the accuracy of the results of the initial analysis or for answering different questions.

Self-report instrument   A device in which persons make and report judgments about the functioning of their project, program, or instructional material.

Significant difference (statistically)   A decision that an observed difference between two statistics probably did not occur by chance.

Simulation study   A study in which the probable effects of alternative solutions to a problem are identified by using symbolic representations of real activities, situations, or environments.

Sociodrama   Dramatization and role playing used to teach an audience about the findings of an evaluation and to illustrate their potential applications.

Sponsor   The individual, group, or organization that provides the funds for the evaluation.

Stakeholders   Individuals or groups who may affect or be affected by program evaluation.

Standard   A principle commonly agreed to by experts in the conduct and use of evaluation for the measure of the value or quality of an evaluation.

Standardized test   A sample of items or situations with definite directions for administration and scoring most often accompanied by data on reliability and validity and sometimes by normative information.

Statistic   A summary number that is typically used to describe a characteristic of a sample.

Stratified random sample   A grouping achieved by dividing the population to be surveyed into a number of nonoverlapping classes or categories that together include all cases, followed by taking cases at random from within the categories.

Summative evaluation   Evaluation designed to present conclusions about the merit or worth of an object and recommendations about whether it should be retained, altered, or eliminated.

Table of specifications   A two-way grid, sometimes called a test blueprint, that lists major areas of content to be covered by the test as row headings and major kinds of abilities to be developed and tested as column headings.

Test-retest reliability The extent to which two administrations of the same test to the same group of subjects yield consistent results.

Time series study A study in which periodic measurements are obtained prior to, during, and following the introduction of an intervention or treatment in order to reach conclusions about the effect of the intervention.

Triangulation The use of multiple sources and methods to gather similar information.

Unit of analysis The least divisible element on which measures are taken and analyzed.

Utility The extent to which an evaluation produces and disseminates reports that inform relevant audiences and have beneficial impact on their work.

Validity The soundness of the inferences made from the results of a data-gathering process.

Values clarification techniques Procedures used to help groups recognize the different values held in the groups, to discern conflicts among these values, and to consider how these conflicts might be resolved.

Variable A characteristic that can take on different values.

Variate The quantitative measure of a variable.

Word attack skills Means by which a person recognizes and perceives the meaning of words.

Worth The value of an object in relationship to a purpose.

❖ Bibliography ❖

Alkin, M. C. (1990). *Debates on evaluation.* Newbury Park, CA: Sage.

Alkin, M. C., Daillak, R., & White, P. (1979). *Using evaluation: Does evaluation make a difference?* Beverly Hills, CA: Sage.

Alkin, M., & Solomon, L. C. (1983). Conducting benefit cost analysis of program evaluation. In M. Alkin & L. C. Solomon (Eds.), *The costs of evaluation.* Beverly Hills, CA: Sage.

American Counseling Association/Association for Assessment in Counseling. (1991). *Responsibilities of users of standard tests.* Washington, DC: Author.

American Psychological Association. (1966). *Standards for educational and psychological tests and manuals.* Washington, DC: Author.

American Psychological Association. (1985). *Standards for educational and psychological testing.* Washington, DC: Author.

Ball, S. (1975). Audit of evaluation. In S. B. Anderson et al. (Eds.), *Encyclopedia of educational evaluation.* San Francisco: Jossey-Bass.

Bednarz, D. (1985). Quality and quantity in evaluation research: A divergent view. *Evaluation and Program Planning, 8*(4), 289-306.

Bock, R. D. (1989). *Multilevel analysis of educational data.* New York: Academic Press.

Bogdan, R. C., & Biklen, S. K. (1992). *Qualitative research for education* (2nd ed.). Boston: Allyn & Bacon.

Bradburn, N. M., & Sudman, S. (1979). *Improving interview method and questionnaire design.* San Francisco: Jossey-Bass.

Brannen, J. (Ed.). (1992). *Mixing methods: Qualitative and quantitative research.* Brookfield, VT: Avebury.

Brewer, J., & Hunter, A. (1989). *Multimethod research: A synthesis of styles.* Newbury Park, CA: Sage.

Brinkerhoff, R. O., Brethower, D. M., Hluchyj, T., & Nowakowski, J. R. (1983). *Program evaluation: A practitioner's guide for trainers and educators.* Boston: Kluwer-Nijhoff.

Bryk, A. S., & Raudenbush, S. W. (1992). *Hierarchical linear models: Applications and data analysis methods.* Newbury Park, CA: Sage.

Campbell, D. T. (1988). *Methodology and epistemology for social science: Selected papers* (E. S. Overman, Ed.). Chicago: University of Chicago Press.

Campbell, D. T., & Erlebacher, A. (1975). How regression artifacts in quasi-experimental evaluations can mistakenly make compensatory education look harmful. In M. Guttentag & E. L. Struening (Eds.), *Handbook of evaluation research* (Vol. 1). Beverly Hills, CA: Sage.

Chelimsky, E. (1987). What have we learned about the politics of program evaluation? *Evaluation Practice, 8*(1), 5-21.

Clark, W. W., Jr., & Beers, C. D. (1976). *Ethical considerations in the anthropological evaluation of educational programs.* Paper presented at the annual meeting of the American Educational Research Association.

Cleveland, W. S. (1985). *The elements of graphing data.* Monterey, CA: Wadsworth.

Code of fair testing practices for education. (1988). Washington, DC: American Psychological Association, Joint Committee on Testing Practices.

Cook, T. D., & Reichardt, C. S. (Eds.). (1979). *Qualitative and quantitative methods in evaluation research.* Beverly Hills, CA: Sage.

Cousins, J. B., & Earl, L. M. (1992). The case for participatory evaluation. *Educational Evaluation and Policy Analysis, 14*(4), 397-418.

Crabtree, B. F., & Miller, W. L. (1992). *Doing qualitative research.* Newbury Park, CA: Sage.

Cronbach, L. J., Ambron, S. R., Dornbusch, S. M., Hess, R. D., Hornik, R. C., Phillips, D. C., Walker, D. F., & Weiner, S. S. (1980). *Toward reform of program evaluation.* San Francisco: Jossey-Bass.

Delamont, S. (1992). *Fieldwork in educational settings: Methods, pitfalls and perspectives.* Bristol, PA: Falmer.

Ethical standards of psychologists. (1989). Washington, DC: American Psychological Association.

Fetterman, D. M. (1984). *Ethnography in educational evaluation.* Beverly Hills, CA: Sage.

Fetterman, D. M. (1989). *Ethnography: Step by step.* Newbury Park, CA: Sage.

Fielding, N. G., & Lee, R. M. (1991). *Using computers in qualitative research.* Newbury Park, CA: Sage.

Fitz-Gibbon, C. T., & Morris, L. L. (1987a). How to analyze data. In J. L. Herman (Ed.), *Program evaluation kit* (2nd ed.). Newbury Park, CA: Sage.

Fitz-Gibbon, C. T., & Morris, L. L. (1987b). How to design a program evaluation. In J. L. Herman (Ed.), *Program evaluation kit* (2nd ed.). Newbury Park, CA: Sage.

Frankel, B. (1982). On participant observation as a component of evaluation: Strategies, constraints, and issues. *Evaluation and Program Planning, 5*(3), 239-246.

Freed, M. N., Ryan, J. M., & Hess, R. K. (1991). *Handbook of statistical procedures and computer applications to education and the behavioral sciences.* New York: Macmillan.

Goldstein, H. (1987). *Multilevel models in educational and social research.* London: Oxford University Press.

Greene, J. C. (1988a). Communication of results and utilization in participatory program evaluation. *Evaluation and Program Planning, 11,* 341-351.

Greene, J. C. (1988b). Stakeholder participation and utilization in program evaluation. *Evaluation Review, 12*(2), 96-116.

Greene, J. C. (1991, April). *Responding to evaluation's moral challenge.* Paper presented at the annual meeting of the American Educational Research Association, Chicago.

Guba, E. G. (Ed.). (1990). *The paradigm dialog.* Newbury Park, CA: Sage.

Guba, E. G., & Lincoln, Y. S. (1989). *Fourth generation evaluation.* Newbury Park, CA: Sage.

Hambleton, R. K., & Zaal, J. N. (Eds.). (1991). *Advances in educational and psychological testing.* Boston: Kluwer Academic.

Harrison, M. I. (1987). *Diagnosing organizations* (Applied Social Research Methods, 8). Newbury Park, CA: Sage.

Henderson, M. E., Morris, L. L., & Fitz-Gibbon, C. T. (1987). How to measure attitudes. In J. L. Herman (Ed.), *Program evaluation kit* (2nd ed.). Newbury Park, CA: Sage.

Hendricks, M., & Papagiannis, M. (1990). Do's and don'ts for offering effective recommendations. *Evaluation Practice, 11*(2), 121-125.

Herman, J. L., Morris, L. L., & Fitz-Gibbon, C. T. (1987). Evaluator's handbook. In J. L. Herman (Ed.), *Program evaluation kit* (2nd ed.). Newbury Park, CA: Sage.

Hopkins, K. D., & Glass, G. V. (1978). *Basic statistics for the behavioral sciences.* Englewood Cliffs, NJ: Prentice Hall.

House, E. R. (Ed.). (1973). *School evaluation: The politics and process.* Berkeley, CA: McCutchan.

House, E. R., Rivers, W., & Stufflebeam, D. L. (1974, June). An assessment of Michigan's accountability system. *Phi Delta Kappan,* pp. 663-669.

Howe, K., & Eisenhart, M. (1990). Standards for qualitative (and quantitative) research: A prolegomenon. *Educational Researcher, 19*(4), 2-9.

Jaeger, R. M. (1991). *Statistics: A spectator sport.* Newbury Park, CA: Sage.

Joint Committee on Standards for Educational Evaluation. (1981). *Standards for evaluations of educational programs, projects, and materials.* New York: McGraw-Hill.

Joint Committee on Standards for Educational Evaluation. (1988). *The personnel evaluation standards.* Newbury Park, CA: Sage.

King, J. A., Morris, L. L., & Fitz-Gibbon, C. T. (1987). How to assess program implementation. In J. L. Herman (Ed.), *Program evaluation kit* (2nd ed.). Newbury Park, CA: Sage.

Kirk, J., & Miller, M. L. (1986). *Reliability and validity in qualitative research* (Qualitative Research Methods Series, 1). Newbury Park, CA: Sage.

Kleinfeld, J., & McDiarmid, G. W. (1986). Living to tell the tale: Researching politically controversial topics and communicating the findings. *Educational Evaluation and Policy Analysis, 8*(4), 393-401.

LeCompte, M., & Goetz, J. (1982). Problems of reliability and validity in ethnographic research. *Review of Educational Research, 52,* 31-60.

Leninger, M. (Ed.). (1985). *Qualitative research methods in nursing.* Orlando, FL: Grune & Stratton.

Levin, H. M. (1983). *Cost-effectiveness: A primer.* Beverly Hills, CA: Sage.

Lincoln, Y. S., & Guba, E. G. (1986). But is it rigorous? Trustworthiness and authenticity in naturalistic evaluation. *New Directions for Program Evaluation: Naturalistic Evaluation, 30,* 73-84.

Linn, R. L. (Ed.). (1989). *Educational measurement*. New York: Macmillan.

Linn, R. L., Baker, E. L., & Dunbar, S. B. (1991). Complex, performance-based assessment: Expectations and validation criteria. *Educational Researcher, 20*(8), 5-21.

Lipsey, M. W. (1990). *Design sensitivity*. Newbury Park, CA: Sage.

Love, A. J. (1991). *Internal evaluation*. Newbury Park, CA: Sage.

Madaus, G. F., Scriven, M., & Stufflebeam, D. L. (Eds.). (1983). *Evaluation models: Viewpoints on educational and human services evaluation*. Boston: Kluwer-Nijhoff.

Mathison, S. (1991). What do we know about internal evaluation? *Evaluation and Program Planning, 14*(1), 159-165.

Miles, M. B., & Huberman, A. M. (1984). *Qualitative data analysis: A source book of new methods*. Beverly Hills, CA: Sage.

Mitchell, J. (1990). Policy evaluation for policy communities: Confronting the utilization problem. *Evaluation Practice, 11*(2), 109-114.

Monteau, P. (1987). Establishing corporate evaluation policy: Cost versus benefit. In L. S. May, C. A. Moore, & S. J. Zammit (Eds.), *Evaluating business and industry training*. Boston: Kluwer Academic.

Morris, L. L., Fitz-Gibbon, C. T., & Freeman, M. E. (1987). How to communicate evaluation findings. In J. L. Herman (Ed.), *Program evaluation kit* (2nd ed.). Newbury Park, CA: Sage.

Morris, L. L., Fitz-Gibbon, C. T., & Lindheim, E. (1987). How to measure performance and use tests. In J. L. Herman (Ed.), *Program evaluation kit* (2nd ed.). Newbury Park, CA: Sage.

Mowbray, C. T. (1988). Getting the system to respond to evaluation findings. *New Directions for Program Evaluation: Evaluation Utilization, 39*, 47-57.

Murphy, R. T. (1975). Quality control. In S. B. Anderson et al. (Eds.), *Encyclopedia of educational evaluation*. San Francisco: Jossey-Bass.

Nagel, S. S. (1988). Evaluative decisions under conflicting constraints. *Evaluation Practice, 9*(2), 36-39.

Nowakowski, J. (Ed.). (1987, Winter). The client perspective on evaluation [Entire issue]. *New Directions for Program Evaluation, 36*.

Nowakowski, J., Bunda, M. A., Working, R., Bernacki, G., & Harrington, P. (1985). *A handbook of educational variables*. Boston: Kluwer-Nijhoff.

Patton, M. Q. (1986). *Utilization-focused evaluation* (2nd ed.). Beverly Hills, CA: Sage.

Patton, M. Q. (1987). How to use qualitative methods in evaluation. In J. L. Herman (Ed.), *Program evaluation kit* (2nd ed.). Newbury Park, CA: Sage.

Patton, M. Q. (1988). The evaluator's responsibility for utilization. *Evaluation Practice, 9*(2), 5-24.

Patton, M. Q. (1990). *Qualitative evaluation and research methods* (2nd ed.). Newbury Park, CA: Sage.

Pitz, G. F., & McKillip, J. (1984). *Decision analysis for program evaluators*. Beverly Hills, CA: Sage.

Preskill, H. (1991, Spring). The cultural lens: Bringing utilization into focus. *New Directions in Program Evaluation, 49*, 5-13.

Principles for fair student assessment practices for education in Canada. (1993). Edmonton, Alberta, Canada: University of Alberta, Centre for Research in Applied Measurement and Evaluation, Joint Advisory Committee.

Punch, M. (1986). *The politics and ethics of fieldwork* (Qualitative Research Methods Series, 3). Beverly Hills, CA: Sage.

Rodman, H., & Rolodny, R. L. (1964). Organizational strains in the researcher-practitioner relationship. *Human Organization, 23*(2), 171-182.

Sanders, J. R. (1992). *Evaluating school programs.* Newbury Park, CA: Corwin.

Schwandt, T. A. (1989). Recapturing moral discourse in evaluation. *Educational Researcher, 18*(8), 11-16.

Schwandt, T. A., & Halpern, E. S. (1988). *Linking auditing and meta-evaluation: Enhancing quality in applied research.* Newbury Park, CA: Sage.

Scriven, M. (1967). The methodology of evaluation. In R. E. Stake (Ed.), *Perspectives of curriculum evaluation* (American Educational Research Association monograph series on evaluation, No. 1). Chicago: Rand McNally.

Scriven, M. (1976). Evaluation bias and its control. In G. V. Glass (Ed.), *Evaluation studies review annual* (Vol. 1). Beverly Hills, CA: Sage.

Scriven, M. (1991). *Evaluation thesaurus* (4th ed.). Newbury Park, CA: Sage.

Scriven, M. (1993). *Hard-won lessons in program evaluation* (New Directions for Program Evaluation, No. 58). San Francisco: Jossey-Bass.

Shadish, W. R., Jr., Cook, T. D., & Leviton, L. C. (1991). *Foundations of program evaluation: Theories of practice.* Newbury Park, CA: Sage.

Shavelson, R. J., & Webb, N. M. (1991). *Generalizability theory: A primer.* Newbury Park, CA: Sage.

Sludek, F. E., & Stein, E. L. (1981). *Grants budgeting and finance: Getting the most out of your grant dollar.* New York: Plenum.

Smith, M. F. (1988). Evaluation utilization revisited. *New Directions for Program Evaluation: Evaluation Utilization, 39,* 7-19.

Smith, M. F. (1989). *Evaluability assessment: A practical approach.* Boston: Kluwer Academic.

Smith, M. L. (1986). The whole is greater: Combining qualitative and quantitative approaches in evaluation studies. *New Directions for Program Evaluation: Naturalistic Evaluation, 30,* 37-54.

Stake, R. E. (1976). *Evaluating educational programmes: The need and the response.* Paris: Organization for Economic Cooperation and Development.

Stake, R. E. (1982). How sharp should the evaluator's teeth be? *Evaluation News, 3*(3), 79-80.

Stake, R. E. (1986). *Quieting reform.* Urbana: University of Illinois Press.

Stecher, B. M., & Davis, W. A. (1987). How to focus an evaluation. In J. L. Herman (Ed.), *Program evaluation kit* (2nd ed.). Newbury Park, CA: Sage.

Strauss, A. L. (1987). *Qualitative analysis for social scientists.* New York: Cambridge University Press.

Stufflebeam, D. L. (1974). *Metaevaluation.* Kalamazoo: Western Michigan University, The Evaluation Center.

Stufflebeam, D. L., Foley, W. J., Gephart, W. J., Guba, E. G., Hammond, R. L., Merriman, H. O., & Provus, M. M. (1971). *Educational evaluation and decision making.* Itasca, IL: F. E. Peacock.

Sudman, S., & Bradburn, N. M. (1982). *Asking questions.* San Francisco: Jossey-Bass.

Tesch, R. (1990). *Qualitative research: Analysis types and software tools.* New York: Falmer.

Thompson, B. (1992). Misuse of ANCOVA and related "statistical control" procedures. *Reading Psychology, 13*(1), iii-xviii.

Torres, R. T. (1991). Improving the quality of internal evaluation: The evaluator as consultant-mediator. *Evaluation and Program Planning, 14*(1), 189-198.

Ulschak, F. L., & Weiss, R. G. (1976). The interpersonal aspects of evaluation: A transactional analysis model for viewing evaluator-client relationships. *Educational Technology, 16*(11), 18-25.

Weinberger, J., & Michael, J. A. (1977). Federal restrictions on educational research: A status report on the Privacy Act. *Educational Researcher, 6*(2), 5-8; also see *5*(11), 3-8.

Weller, S., & Romney, A. K. (1988). *Systematic data collection* (Qualitative Research Methods, 10). Newbury Park, CA: Sage.

Wiersma, W. (1991). *Research methods in education* (5th ed.). Boston: Allyn & Bacon.

Winberg, A. (1991). Maximizing the contributions of internal evaluation units. *Evaluation and Program Planning, 14*(1), 167-172.

Windle, C., & Neigher, W. (1978). Ethical problems in program evaluation: Advice for tripped evaluators. *Evaluation and Program Planning, 1*(2), 97-107.

Worthen, B. R., & Sanders, J. R. (1987). *Educational evaluation: Alternative approaches and practical guidelines.* White Plains, NY: Longman.

Worthen, B. R., & White, K. R. (1987). *Evaluating educational and social programs: Guidelines for proposal review, on-site evaluation, evaluation contracts, and technical assistance.* Boston: Kluwer Academic.

Yin, R. K. (1991). *Case study research: Design and methods.* Newbury Park, CA: Sage.

❖ Index ❖

THE PROGRAM EVALUATION STANDARDS

Sound evaluations of educational programs, projects, and materials in a variety of settings should have four basic attributes:

- Utility
- Feasibility
- Propriety
- Accuracy

The Program Evaluation Standards, established by sixteen professional education associations, identify evaluation principles that when addressed should result in improved program evaluations containing the above four attributes.

Dr. James R. Sanders, Chair
The Joint Committee on Standards
  for Educational Evaluation
The Evaluation Center
Western Michigan University
Kalamazoo, Michigan 49008-5178
616-387-5895

Sage Publications, Inc.
2455 Teller Road
Thousand Oaks, CA 91320
805-499-0721

JCSEE PR-1994
Approved by the American
National Standards Institute
as an American National
Standard. Approval date:
March 15, 1994.

This tearout is not copyrighted material. Reproduction and dissemination are encouraged.

Utility

The utility standards are intended to ensure that an evaluation will serve the information needs of intended users.

U1   Stakeholder Identification   Persons involved in or affected by the evaluation should be identified, so that their needs can be addressed.

U2   Evaluator Credibility   The persons conducting the evaluation should be both trustworthy and competent to perform the evaluation, so that the evaluation findings achieve maximum credibility and acceptance.

U3   Information Scope and Selection   Information collected should be broadly selected to address pertinent questions about the program and be responsive to the needs and interests of clients and other specified stakeholders.

U4   Values Identification   The perspectives, procedures, and rationale used to interpret the findings should be carefully described, so that the bases for value judgments are clear.

U5   Report Clarity   Evaluation reports should clearly describe the program being evaluated, including its context, and the purposes, procedures, and findings of the evaluation, so that essential information is provided and easily understood.

U6   Report Timeliness and Dissemination   Significant interim findings and evaluation reports should be disseminated to intended users, so that they can be used in a timely fashion.

U7   Evaluation Impact   Evaluations should be planned, conducted, and reported in ways that encourage follow-through by stakeholders, so that the likelihood that the evaluation will be used is increased.

Feasibility

The feasibility standards are intended to ensure that an evaluation will be realistic, prudent, diplomatic, and frugal.

F1   Practical Procedures   The evaluation procedures should be practical, to keep disruption to a minimum while needed information is obtained.

F2   Political Viability   The evaluation should be planned and conducted with anticipation of the different positions of various interest groups, so that their cooperation may be obtained, and so that possible attempts by any of these groups to curtail evaluation operations or to bias or misapply the results can be averted or counteracted.

F3   Cost Effectiveness   The evaluation should be efficient and produce information of sufficient value, so that the resources expended can be justified.

Propriety

The propriety standards are intended to ensure that an evaluation will be conducted legally, ethically, and with due regard for the welfare of those involved in the evaluation, as well as those affected by its results.

P1 **Service Orientation** Evaluations should be designed to assist organizations to address and effectively serve the needs of the full range of targeted participants.

P2 **Formal Agreements** Obligations of the formal parties to an evaluation (what is to be done, how, by whom, when) should be agreed to in writing, so that these parties are obligated to adhere to all conditions of the agreement or formally to renegotiate it.

P3 **Rights of Human Subjects** Evaluations should be designed and conducted to respect and protect the rights and welfare of human subjects.

P4 **Human Interactions** Evaluators should respect human dignity and worth in their interactions with other persons associated with an evaluation, so that participants are not threatened or harmed.

P5 **Complete and Fair Assessment** The evaluation should be complete and fair in its examination and recording of strengths and weaknesses of the program being evaluated, so that strengths can be built upon and problem areas addressed.

P6 **Disclosure of Findings** The formal parties to an evaluation should ensure that the full set of evaluation findings along with pertinent limitations are made accessible to the persons affected by the evaluation, and any others with expressed legal rights to receive the results.

P7 **Conflict of Interest** Conflict of interest should be dealt with openly and honestly, so that it does not compromise the evaluation processes and results.

P8 **Fiscal Responsibility** The evaluator's allocation and expenditure of resources should reflect sound accountability procedures and otherwise be prudent and ethically responsible, so that expenditures are accounted for and appropriate.

Accuracy

The accuracy standards are intended to ensure that an evaluation will reveal and convey technically adequate information about the features that determine worth of merit of the program being evaluated.

A1 **Program Documentation** The program being evaluated should be described and documented clearly and accurately, so that the program is clearly identified.

A2 **Context Analysis** The context in which the program exists should be examined in enough detail, so that its likely influences on the program can be identified.

A3 **Described Purposes and Procedures** The purposes and procedures of the evaluation should be monitored and described in enough detail, so that they can be identified and assessed.

A4 **Defensible Information Sources** The sources of information used in a program evaluation should be described in enough detail, so that the adequacy of the information can be assessed.

A5 **Valid Information** The information gathering procedures should be chosen or developed and then implemented so that they will assure that the interpretation arrived at is valid for the intended use.

A6 **Reliable Information** The information gathering procedures should be chosen or developed and then implemented so that they will assure that the information obtained is sufficiently reliable for the intended use.

A7 **Systematic Information** The information collected, processed, and reported in an evaluation should be systematically reviewed and any errors found should be corrected.

A8 **Analysis of Quantitative Information** Quantitative information in an evaluation should be appropriately and systematically analyzed so that evaluation questions are effectively answered.

A9 **Analysis of Qualitative Information** Qualitative information in an evaluation should be appropriately and systematically analyzed so that evaluation questions are effectively answered.

A10 **Justified Conclusions** The conclusions reached in an evaluation should be explicitly justified, so that stakeholders can assess them.

A11 **Impartial Reporting** Reporting procedures should guard against distortion caused by personal feelings and biases of any party to the evaluation, so that evaluation reports fairly reflect the evaluation findings.

A12 **Metaevaluation** The evaluation itself should be formatively and summatively evaluated against these and other pertinent standards, so that its conduct is appropriately guided and, on completion, stakeholders can closely examine its strengths and weaknesses.

Guidelines and illustrative cases to assist evaluation participants in meeting each of these standards are provided in *The Program Evaluation Standards* (Sage, 1994). The illustrative cases are based in a variety of educational settings that include schools, universities, medical and health care fields, the military, business and industry, the government, and law.